PEOPLE OF THE
PLAINS AND MOUNTAINS

Everett Dick

PEOPLE OF THE PLAINS AND MOUNTAINS

ESSAYS IN THE HISTORY OF THE WEST DEDICATED TO EVERETT DICK

Edited by Ray Allen Billington

With the Assistance of Vern Carner

Contributions in American History, Number 25

GREENWOOD PRESS
Westport, Connecticut • London, England

Library of Congress Cataloging in Publication Data

Main entry under title:

People of the plains and mountains.

(Contributions in American History, no. 25)
Includes bibliographical references.
CONTENTS: Hicks, J. D. Everett Dick: teacher, scholar, churchman--Clark, T. D. Social and cultural continuity in American frontiering.--Mattes, M. J. New horizons on the Old Oregon Trail. [etc.]

1. Frontier and pioneer life--The West--Addresses, essays, lectures. 2. The West--History--Addresses, essays, lectures. 3. Dick, Everett Newfon, 1898-
I. Dick, Everett Newfon, 1898-   II. Billington, Ray Allen, 1903-   ed.
F596.P46   917.8'03   72-784
ISBN 0-8371-6358-7

Copyright © 1973 by Greenwood Press, Inc.

All rights reserved. No portion of this book may be reproduced, by any process or technique, without the express written consent of the author and publisher.

Library of Congress Catalog Card Number: 72-784
ISBN: 0-8371-6358-7

First published in 1973

Greenwood Press, Inc., Publishing Division
51 Riverside Avenue, Westport, Connecticut 06880

Manufactured in the United States of America

CONTENTS

Introduction — vii

1 Everett Dick: Teacher, Scholar, Churchman — 3
  John D. Hicks

2 Social and Cultural Continuity in American Frontiering — 21
  Thomas D. Clark

3 New Horizons on the Old Oregon Trail — 45
  Merrill J. Mattes

4 Pioneer Life on the Plains and in the Mines: A Comparison — 63
  W. Turrentine Jackson

5 Frontier Violence: Another Look — 86
  W. Eugene Hollon

6 The Town Marshal and the Police — 101
  Philip D. Jordan

CONTENTS

7 Indian Policy Reform and American Protestantism, 1880—1900 ... *120*
  Francis Paul Prucha, S.J.

8 Corporation Farming in California ... *146*
  Paul Wallace Gates

9 The Taming of the West: Military Archives as a Source for the Social History of the Trans-Mississippi Region to 1900 ... *175*
  James B. Rhoads

Appendix: The Writings of Everett Dick ... *204*

Index ... *215*

INTRODUCTION

When Everett Dick's former students determined to honor their mentor with a volume of essays, they came face-to-face with a seemingly insurmountable problem. Professor Dick had trained hundreds of undergraduates during his years at Union College in Lincoln, Nebraska, a small Seventh-day Adventist college, but none were graduate students normally called upon to contribute to such a tribute. Who among them could serve as editor; where could authors worthy of the subject be found?

Their answer was a sensible one. Everett Dick, they knew, had won the respect and affection of dozens of the most prominent historians of the American West. His own books, particularly *The Sod-House Frontier,* ranked among the most significant contributions of his generation. He was universally admired for his unwillingness to sacrifice religious principles for personal gain; this had led him to choose to remain at a Seventh-day Adventist college, where he could practice and propagate his faith, rather than to teach in more prestigious institutions. Everett Dick's students decided to ask some of the many historians who knew and admired their teacher to contribute to a book in his honor.

The rest proved easy. I certainly could not refuse to edit such a volume and accepted the assignment gladly. Others felt as I did. Of the dozen eminent historians of the West invited to contribute, only two refused—one because of illness, the other because of unbreakable commitments. All others responded with enthusiasm, despite the pressing burdens common among scholars of their stature. They did so because they felt that Everett Dick's many contributions to historical knowledge were worthy of any sacrifice.

A deadline of May 1, 1972, was established for submission of the essays, a date necessary to allow publication by July 10, 1973, when Everett Dick would celebrate his seventy-fifth birthday. On April 28, 1972, the last essay arrived by special delivery mail! That nine busy scholars, all with numerous publishing commitments and several with pressing classroom duties, should complete their assignments on time must be viewed as a modern miracle. No better evidence could possibly exist of the high esteem in which Everett Dick is held by his professional colleagues.

All contributors were asked to deal with an aspect of the social or economic history of the trans-Mississippi West, the area in which Everett Dick has made his most significant contributions, but no other guidelines were established. Each author was expected to develop a theme mirroring his current research interest. The result is a collection of excellent studies that reveal the individualism of their authors, but display a surprising degree of unity.

The essays begin with a biographical sketch of Everett Dick's life, prepared by his former teacher at the University of Nebraska, the late John D. Hicks. This is a revealing document, notable for showing both the deep affection that John Hicks felt for his pupil, and aspects of Everett Dick's academic career that have been unknown even to his close friends in the historical world. John Hicks has painted a moving portrait of a gifted young historian struggling to write while burdened with financial problems and excessive instructional duties inevitable in a small

Introduction

denominational college. He has also described Everett Dick's impressive contributions to his church, not only in writing books and articles that rival in volume his historical publications, but also in conceiving and creating, almost singlehandedly, the Medical Cadet Corps that allowed Adventists to serve their country during World War II and later conflicts without betraying their selective pacifism.

The historical essays that follow this biographical sketch fall naturally into a sequential pattern. Thomas D. Clark, of Indiana University, explores a problem as old as the frontier itself: the degree of continuity in the frontier process. He advances evidence showing that social customs and cultural institutions were transplanted from one frontier to the next, often by migrating families that gave the West such colorful names as Daniel Boone, Milton Sublette, and William Henry Russell.

The pioneers studied by Professor Clark followed a number of trails, but none better known than the one described by Merrill J. Mattes, of the National Park Service. That highway—the Oregon Trail—would appear to be (in his words) "a threadbare subject for scholarly investigation, a road that has been traveled and retraveled to boredom." But Mattes, building on the vast knowledge gained while gathering material for his recent book, *The Great Platte River Road,* shows that a great deal more is to be learned from the source materials if scholars ask the right questions. A re-examination of the materials, Mattes explains, could tell us much about the cultural life of the overland emigrants, their attitude toward Indians and minorities, their treatment of women, and the extent of organization and control they would accept.

Professor W. Turrentine Jackson, of the University of California at Davis, uses modern comparative techniques to re-examine the settlement process. He compares the evolution and cultural development of the agricultural and mining frontiers in the Far West by drawing on a vast knowledge of mining camps and borrowing information on farm settlements from Everett Dick's *The Sod-House Frontier.* His essay adds significantly to our understanding of the frontier process and reaches conclusions that no follower of Frederick Jackson Turner can ignore.

The next two articles take a searching look at violence on the American frontier. The first, by Professor W. Eugene Hollon, Ohio Regents Professor of History at the University of Toledo, explores the treatment of minority groups in the West. His colorful narrative and thoughtful conclusions are startlingly pertinent to modern times. The second, by Professor Emeritus Philip D. Jordan, of the University of Minnesota, traces the evolution of the law-enforcement official from the marshalmen of Elizabethan days through the marshals of the Far West to the police officers of today. His is no stifling legal treatise, but an action-packed narrative of some of the frontier's most glamorous characters.

If the outlaw was an enemy to the frontiersman, so was the Indian—with tragic results. Professor Francis Paul Prucha, S.J., of Marquette University, takes a fresh look at the connection between evangelical Protestantism and Indian policy during the last two decades of the nineteenth century. He demonstrates that the churchmen's concern with individual salvation helped shape the Dawes Severalty Act and other measures designed to shatter tribal organization and force the red men to enter American society as individuals. His conclusions not only make governmental policy far more understandable, but help explain the present Indian protest movements.

Professor Emeritus Paul Wallace Gates, of Cornell University, contributes a discussion of land and agricultural policy, subjects in which Everett Dick is particularly interested. Gates' essay outlines the history of two of California's giant landholding corporations, showing how deficiencies in the land laws contributed to their growth, and discusses the threat they present, even today, to the small farmer.

The volume concludes with a bibliographical essay by James Berton Rhoads, Archivist of the United States, who was a student of Professor Dick at both Union College and the University of California at Berkeley. Rhoads first planned to prepare

Introduction

a survey of sources for western social history in the National Archives, but preliminary investigation showed this to be a project far too large to handle. Instead, he has described the social history materials in the military archives section. His findings exhibit the considerable resources that await the would-be investigator.

Dr. Rhoads' contribution is followed by a bibliography of Everett Dick's writings, which was supplied by his wife. This compilation provides interesting reading for those of us who have known him only as an eminent historian as it shows the great number of his publications on religious topics.

Those of us concerned with this volume share a sense of indebtedness to a good friend and fine historian who has done far more than his share in pushing back the borders of knowledge. If this book shows our esteem and affection even in a small way, we will not have labored in vain. We join with his many former students in wishing him bountiful happiness in the years that lie beyond his seventy-fifth birthday—years that we hope will bring forth even more publications, historical and religious, to enrich and ennoble the world.

Ray Allen Billington
The Huntington Library

June 1972

PEOPLE OF THE
PLAINS AND MOUNTAINS

CHAPTER 1

EVERETT DICK:

Teacher, Scholar, Churchman

John D. Hicks

That the late John D. Hicks should prepare this warm biographical sketch of his good friend and former student is singularly appropriate. John Hicks was teaching at the University of Nebraska when Dick began his graduate career in the summer of 1924. The friendship formed in the classroom that summer ripened over the years as Everett Dick rose to fame as a historian and John Hicks became a professor at the University of Wisconsin and then Morrison Professor of American History at the University of California at Berkeley.

Professor Hicks retired from his distinguished teaching career in 1957, after training forty-five doctoral students, producing ten books and numerous articles, and teaching more than twenty-five thousand undergraduates. Of all who passed through his classes, none won his respect and affection more than Everett Dick. This tribute is his last essay; John Hicks died on February 5, 1972.*

Everett Dick was a product of the American frontier about which he wrote so well. His parents, Grandville Gentry Dick

---

*The principal source for this sketch was a thirty-three page manuscript, "A Brief Account of my Life Experiences written for my Children," prepared by Everett Dick and kindly loaned to me by Mrs. Dick. This was supplemented by correspondence with Everett Dick and others.

and Hannah Frances Smalley, were both Kentucky-born. His father's Scotch-Irish ancestors had settled in the hill country of Kentucky, and his mother's family had migrated from New England to the blue grass region. Both the Dicks and the Smalleys, as Everett later noted, had the characteristic marks of the early West upon them, and when troubled times came, they, like so many others, followed the westward movement to the Missouri-Kansas frontier.

Everett was born on July 10, 1898, near the town of Ozawkie, Kansas, some twenty miles north of Topeka. He was the youngest of four children, all boys. His middle name, Newfon, had no family origin but honored a clergyman whom his parents admired; in his later life Everett dropped it more often than not. Neither Everett's father nor his mother had more of a formal education than was available in the country schools of the times, with one notable exception. Everett's father earned a diploma in classes given by an itinerant penmanship expert, a feat that so impressed Everett that he, in his turn, also learned the art.

Dick's parents made several additional moves, but in 1908 settled on a large farm near La Harpe, Kansas, where his father specialized in raising Herefords. Here Everett acquired his easy familiarity with farm life and farm problems. It was here, too, that he first discovered his interest in history. The family who had occupied the farm house into which the Dicks had moved left behind some books, including readers with stirring stories of such battles as Hastings, Crecy, and Bannockburn, which Everett "devoured." He also found and absorbed John Bunyan's *Pilgrims Progress,* Washington Irving's *Life of Washington,* and a biography of Jesse James that he read on the sly. The schools that Everett attended supplied him with further historical reading, such as James Redpath's *History of the United States,* Thomas Babington Macaulay's *Lays of Ancient Rome,* and some of the George Henty books of historical fiction that so many boys of his time found fascinating.

After his elementary schooling Everett spent one year at the Union College Academy, where his older brother, Ernest, was a college senior. He continued his high school work at Oswego

Academy, a boarding school maintained by the Kansas Conference of Seventh-day Adventists. He was a senior when World War I broke out and, despite his Adventist upbringing, promptly joined the United States Marines.

After basic training at Parris Island, South Carolina, his unit spent nearly a year at Quantico, Virginia, and Indian Head, Maryland, learning to handle guns and testing a variety of ordnance. Everett's unit, its training completed, was at the League Island Navy Yard ready to embark for the front when the armistice intervened.

While Everett's military experience was short and included no combat duty, it made a deep impression on him. He was still a "buck private in the rear rank" when he left the service, but he had attained a sharpshooter's medal for proficiency with a rifle, and he later used to good advantage the indoctrination in military conduct that his training had involved.

Everett returned to Oswego Academy to continue his studies, graduating in May 1919. At the end of the summer he entered Union College, an institution toward which he was drawn naturally by denominational and family ties. Indeed, his parents, who had in 1890 accepted Adventist doctrines and joined the Adventist church in Ozawkie, had contributed from their slender financial resources to the early beginnings of the college, and Everett's first letters, composed when he was only about five years old, were to his brother, Arthur, who was then at Union.

World War I veterans had no GI benefits, and the sixty-dollar severance pay Everett received when he left the marines, together with all that he had saved from his pay checks, disappeared during his first year. He was obliged to drop out for a time to earn more money. He first took a job as a railway mail clerk; then, after adventuring through California and Texas, he landed a position in the fall of 1921 as a schoolteacher on the Burt Ranch, ninety miles east of Helena, Montana. Here he roomed and boarded at the ranch house, heard stories of an earlier frontier from an old-timer, fraternized with cowboys and sheepherders, and explored the adjacent territory on a horse named Whiteman. When he later began to write about the frontier,

Everett had much more to draw on than the records he found in libraries.

Everett returned to Union College in 1922 and that year met Opal Wheeler, whose home was in Kansas not far from his own. Everett's special interest in history had already asserted itself, and Opal was taking a commercial course, "with heavy emphasis on English." Nevertheless, they found they had much in common. They were engaged before the year was out and were married on August 15, 1923.

Everett had accepted a teaching position in Castle, Montana and there the young couple started housekeeping in a one-room log cabin. That winter Everett considered teaching penmanship as a career, for the typewriter had not yet entirely superseded the skilled penman, and he had demonstrated in a correspondence course his exceptional skill in the craft. He and Opal once agreed that he would teach her penmanship and she would teach him typewriting, but one lesson convinced the partners of the futility of this enterprise, and a wise counselor eventually persuaded Everett that history afforded cultural values that penmanship did not.

Actually, the Dicks were not long in learning that they could operate best as a team. As time went on, Opal not only earned money as a teacher and practitioner of typing, but she also became her husband's constant helper, as copyeditor, typist, proofreader, collector of material, maker of bibliographies and indexes, and adviser in all aspects of historical composition.

Despite his prolonged absences from college, Everett, by earning a substantial number of correspondence credits, was able to obtain his bachelor's degree at Union in 1924, and that summer he registered for graduate work at the University of Nebraska. It was there I first met him. I was a devoted follower of Frederick Jackson Turner and, like Everett in Montana, had two years of schoolteaching in Wyoming behind me. We immediately saw eye to eye. Dick took my course in the History of the West, which I had patterned after Frederic Logan Paxson's lectures on that subject at Wisconsin, and in which Turner's *The Frontier in American History,* only recently published and at

Everett Dick

the time the Bible of western historians, was required reading. Among the names of my Nebraska students, Everett Dick stands out. He was a candidate for the Master's degree, took my seminar on frontier history, and emerged with a thesis so superior to the run-of-the-mill dissertation that I at once encouraged him to work toward a doctorate at Wisconsin with my major professor and chief mentor, Frederic L. Paxson. When Dick's thesis, "The Long Drive," was published by the Kansas State Historical Society, I was inordinately proud.[1] Dick showed then a willingness to do painstaking research and an unusually smooth descriptive and narrative historical style.

By that time Dick knew that he wanted to be a historian, but he lacked the means to go on immediately with his graduate work and accepted instead a position as teacher of history and dean of boys at Oak Park Academy, an Adventist boarding school in Nevada, Iowa. There, according to one of his students, he "opened the window to higher education for many of us Iowans who had been satisfied to think of a high school diploma as the end." In some of them, too, he "laid the habits and foundations of research" through his "interminable term paper assignments." Even then he always carried copious notes to class, but, as another student recalls, he was at his best "when he would forget his notes and just talk. . . .Carried away by the subject, we'll say the camp meetings out on the frontier, he would sing for us some of those early revival hymns. He wasn't exactly a Caruso, but we enjoyed those little impromptu solos."[2]

But Dick was interested also in his own educational progress; he knew that he needed further graduate work and a Ph.D. to qualify for the kind of teaching he wanted to do. He thought seriously of going to the universities of Iowa or Kansas, where he might have avoided out-of-state tuition fees, but his wife, knowing that his heart was set on Wisconsin, insisted that he go there. She made use of her varied talents to balance the family budget, and during his second year Dick received a scholarship and the remission of all fees.

His major interest was the American frontier, so Dick naturally chose Frederic Logan Paxson as his major professor.

Paxson promptly vetoed his plans for taking a maximum number of courses and expanding "The Long Drive" into a dissertation. He permitted Dick, however, to choose for his new subject the Millerite Movement, evidence that Paxson had faith in the historical integrity of his student, because he would never have permitted his advisee to write on a subject in which he might have a strong personal bias. Paxson also made Dick understand that he must seek out the sources, wherever they might be. "You can't sit down in one place and cover your subject," he said. "You must go where your sources are. If you don't you will have some flat places. You must go to the Library of Congress or wherever your leads demand."

In October 1929, oblivious of the panic and the oncoming depression, Dick started out. Before he returned he had gone as far east as Portland, Maine, and had visited more than twenty-five libraries. This trip was an example from which Dick was to profit for the rest of his life. Most of the books he wrote later could never have been written had he not been willing, whatever the difficulties might be, to seek out the sources, wherever they were.

He completed his dissertation, "The Adventist Crisis, 1831–1844," and received his Ph.D. in the spring of 1930. To his great satisfaction he was invited to teach at Union College the following fall as a temporary replacement for a history teacher who was on leave. As it turned out, the instructor never returned, and Dick stayed on for more than forty years. He was to serve his alma mater, not only as teacher of history and chairman of the history department, but also as head of its bureau of recommendations, chairman of its summer session, and academic dean. "Always inventive," as one of his admirers pointed out, he was the one to whom his colleagues turned when they wanted to "put together a college curriculum or a new course to meet the practical needs of the community or the students and get it approved by the college administrative committees." Not without reason, he was sometimes called "Mr. Union College."[3]

The normal teaching load at Union was sixteen to eighteen

hours a week, and in Dick's case included such varied subjects as world history, world politics, modern European history, and American government, even an education class in a crisis and some courses in agriculture. But it was for his history of the American frontier that his students remembered him best. He made the westward movement come alive, partly because he was able to identify his parents and himself with pioneering, to describe from experience the primitive life that the pioneers had endured, and to emphasize the deep community interest that they had developed. His natural "wit and homespun charm" helped him maintain an air of "casualness and informality" in his classes—if necessary he could sing a song or recite a poem to drive home a point. In the words of one who was there:

He would lead his students across America with the ever-moving westward frontier, showing glimpses of every-day kinds of common-man stuff, chuckling as he went. We learned and felt the sweat and eagerness and tenacity of the pioneers and glimpsed the challenge and the grit as well as the glory of America. . . .Not only could he look from the position of the pioneer but he also knew the scene from the student's point of view and could bring about a kind of reconciliation with one's past and a renewal of faith and excitement in the country's future.

According to another, "No one could attend his lectures without wanting to know more of the past. After his classes history changed for me; it was no longer the memorization of facts and dates but an appreciation and interest in people and events of the past."[4]

However effective his reproduction of the past, Dick was at his best in introducing his students to sound research methods. "Not only did he teach us the techniques of research, but also how to think critically, evaluate materials, and to verify facts by going back to source materials in order to authenticate them. Also, since he was a writer, he had us rewrite the topics on which we wrote until in his judgment, they were worth reading." On one occasion he "told me that what I had written was merely a catalogue of facts, that it was uninteresting, lacked life, color, and movement and that he wanted me to rewrite it. He wanted the day-by-day experiences these people had to be real and become alive."[5]

Dick's contacts with his students went far beyond the mere business of education. He took an interest in their personal lives and helped them plan their futures. They "sought his counsel in vocational guidance, advanced education plans, and marriage choice." He regularly took a carload of his students with him to attend the meetings of the Mississippi Valley Historical Association. His interest in his students continued beyond graduation; he sent them Christmas cards adorned with his decorative handwriting; encouraged them to work for advanced degrees, voiced his regrets when they abandoned history for another profession. "It was his personal, fatherly interest that saved me from being a college dropout," writes one successful editor. "He most insistently urged me to finish my undergraduate work and take an advanced degree. . . .I count Dr. Dick as the person who has had the greatest single influence and inspiration on my life."[6]

Dick arrived at Union College along with the great depression, when salary cuts were the order of the day, a new one, it seemed, with each new Dick baby. Three children were born during those years—Donald David in 1932, Lorle Ann in 1934, and Arthur Lynn in 1937. But despite the hard times Dick's loyalty to the college and the cause of education never faltered. As one of his colleagues put it: "We all endured together, and with intersympathy, the severities—and character building lessons—of the drouth and depression years. . . .It was no time, and no place for sissies."[7]

In 1931, despite the inability of the college to help pay his expenses, Dick attended the meetings of the American Historical Association in St. Paul. During the trip he heard of the projects of other historians, and he returned to Union determined to make a contribution of his own. Since he had no money for travel, he looked for a project that he could do in Lincoln, and began to collect notes for a study of the social history of Nebraska.

Dick had every excuse not to write: He was on a twelve-month schedule, with a heavy teaching load during the nine months of the academic year, the directorship of the summer session for another nine weeks, and responsibility for recruiting students during the rest of the summer. But with the approval of his president, he not only devoted his vacations to research, but interspersed his travels as recruiter with stops at libraries along the way, for he realized that, whatever the treasures of the Nebraska State Historical Society in Lincoln might be, his study must not be limited to a single state. Heroic efforts allowed him to spend some time in Topeka, Bismarck, and Pierre as he enlarged his study to include Kansas and the Dakotas.

Dick's research was so rewarding that he soon discovered that the material he was collecting would make two books rather than one. The first, he decided, would deal with the era of pre-settlement, when the explorers, fur traders, and trappers held sway. Since this theme had already been exploited to some extent, he chose to concentrate for the time being on the second, a volume on the farmer's frontier, a subject that previous writers had largely ignored. He would concentrate on the four-state area—Kansas, Nebraska, and the two Dakotas. As he began to write, he met one of the problems that confront so many young instructors: he was constantly bothered by students when at college, and tempted by the first two Dick babies when at home. The Dick family at this time, along with other faculty members, was quartered in an old dormitory, and down in the basement Dick found "a dusty old room with a dirt floor, heated only by the big main steam pipes going through it." There, "with a blanket around my feet and lap" *The Sod-House Frontier* began to take form.[8]

By the spring of 1936 the manuscript was finished, and in August 1937, *The Sod-House Frontier: A Social History of the Northern Plains from the Creation of Kansas and Nebraska to the Admission of the Dakotas* was published by D. Appleton-Century. The well-known critic Dorothy Canfield Fisher hailed it with praise, and the autumn book review number of the *New York Times* gave it an entire front page. For Everett and Opal Dick this was the thrill of a lifetime. They soon became accustomed to favorable reviews, however, for the book was so well received that eventually it was rated by a group of eminent historians as one of the fifteen "Preferred Works in American History, 1936—1950."[9]

Sinclair Lewis is said to have remarked that writers got most of their inspiration from "the application of the seat of the pants to the seat of a chair." Everett Dick had that kind of inspiration, but he also had much more. He had rare narrative and descriptive powers, a gift for organization that enabled him to handle immense detail with easy skill, and a healthy preference for short, Anglo-Saxon words. Moreover, he had the tradition of the frontier in his background. As an English professor who knows him well points out: "It seems fortunate that a man writing about the early emergence and triumphs of a people should have his sociological roots deep in the cultural heritage of the folk almost as if he had lived with them, been one of them, and known first-hand their common hardships and frustrations. Everett thus writes naturally in the idiom of the people and unconsciously transmits true feeling for their day-by-day temper, problems, and exigencies."[10]

Compulsive writers of the Dick variety are always a book ahead of themselves in their planning. Dick knew that when he had finished with the farmers' frontier he must also do the frontier that had preceded it, but to achieve unity for that theme he would have to extend his research to include the entire Northwestern United States to the Rocky Mountains. The Social Science Research Council gave him a grant of $500 that would enable him to take six months off from his teaching duties to travel, and his college granted him the first sabbatical leave it had ever given. He bought a half-finished trailer, had it completed at minimum cost in the college carpenter shop, hitched it to his second-hand car, and with his family set out in July 1938 to explore the Northwest. They visited libraries and historical places in Colorado, Wyoming, Utah, Idaho, Montana, South Dakota, North Dakota, Minnesota, Wisconsin, and Iowa.

By the middle of October Dick was ready to write. To obtain a maximum amount of freedom he settled with his family on the old Kansas farm where his father still lived, and there in a secluded room he turned his notes and knowledge into another book, *Vanguards of the Frontier,* published by D. Appleton-Century in 1941, and published again later by the Tudor Press as *The Story of the Frontier.* *Vanguards* was less immediately successful than *The Sod-House Frontier,* but it was well received by the academic world and enhanced the scholarly reputation of its writer. After the Tudor edition went out of print, Dick permitted the University of Nebraska Press to bring out *Vanguards* as a paperback, and in this form it sold more copies than any of Dick's other books.

Dick's next book, *The Dixie Frontier,* was made possible by a $5,000 grant from the Rockefeller Foundation. His college granted him a year's leave of absence, and in the summer of 1944, the family set out on another research tour. Dick had learned at the University of Wisconsin that many documents relating to the southern frontier were in northern libraries, so he took off through the Old Northwest, visiting Springfield and Chicago, Illinois; Madison, Wisconsin; Lansing, Ann Arbor, and Detroit, Michigan; and Columbus, Ohio. After that he circled the South: Washington, D.C.; Charlottesville, Virginia; Knoxville, Tennessee; Lexington, Frankfort, and Louisville, Kentucky; Montgomery, Alabama; Jackson, Mississippi; Monroe, Louisiana; and Little Rock, Arkansas. At Montgomery, Alabama, in an old newspaper office Dick found the entire file of the *Montgomery Republican,* 125 years of it, a priceless treasure for his purposes. And at Monroe, Louisiana, when he asked for frontier material, he was amused and delighted when the lady librarian offered him a copy of his own book, *The Sod-House Frontier.*

The following spring the Dick family ended their journey, again in Kansas, this time in a vacant farm house two miles from the family home, and here, while the children roamed the woods, Dick wrote most of *The Dixie Frontier.* Alfred A. Knopf published the book, somewhat belatedly, in 1948. It was a good book, but it covered a well-known field, and sales did not equal those of its predecessors.

While Dick was teaching in the 1946 summer session of the

University of Wisconsin, he received a grant from the Wisconsin State Historical Society and the University of Wisconsin to write a social history of the Old Northwest. Again he made the rounds with the trailer and the family, but this time the manuscript he produced was not published, mainly because the field was preempted by other writers before Dick's work was available. As a byproduct of his research, however, he had collected numerous interesting stories of frontier experiences. From these he selected a number that dealt with the middlewestern frontier, and the University of Nebraska Press brought them out in 1963 under the title, *Tales of the Frontier.*

As Frederick Jackson Turner many times pointed out, the call of free land had acted as a magnet to draw the American pioneers across the continent. It was almost inevitable that Dick would eventually exploit this theme. While he was visiting professor at the University of Missouri in the summer of 1948, the Newberry Foundation offered him a grant to write a social history of the public lands, and for a year he worked steadily on the project before other duties ended progress. Not until some years later did he finish the manuscript, *The Lure of the Land,* which the University of Nebraska Press published in 1970.

Dick's many other writings reflect his devotion to his religion and his college. In a series of articles written for a Seventh-day Adventist paper, *The Youth's Instructor,* he recounted inspirational moments from the lives of such church leaders as James White, William Miller, and John Nevins Andrews, which later appeared in book form under the title *Founders of the Message* (1938). To help celebrate the first half-century of the life of his college, he collaborated with David D. Rees to produce a volume entitled *Union College, Fifty Years of Service* (1941); and to celebrate its seventy-fifth anniversary he wrote another, more complete study, *Union, College of the Golden Cords* (1967). Both books profited from his experience as a writer of social history. They were not the usual dull, dreary compilations of presidential addresses and registrars' data, but the living record of dedicated men and women like himself who put foundations under what often seemed impossible dreams. Both of these

Everett Dick

books were printed, bound, and published by facilities at Union College. Union College printers also made available a little volume Dick wrote for junior and senior high school students, *Life in the West Before the Sod-House Frontier* (1947).

Dick was conscious, too, of his obligations to his profession. He attended professional meetings, accepted professional assignments—he was a member of the executive committee of the Mississippi Valley Historical Association for one term and for twenty-five years was chairman of the Organization of American Historians' Historic Sites Committee. He contributed to such enterprises as the *Dictionary of American Biography* and the *Dictionary of American History*, wrote for the historical journals—his article on "Water, a Frontier Problem," won the James L. Sellers award for the best article published in *Nebraska History* during the year 1968—and he was one of the founders of the Western History Association.

While Dick's achievements as teacher and writer seem adequate in themselves to account for the activities of a lifetime, he has still a third and equally important contribution to his credit. He was the prime mover in the creation of the Seventh-day Adventists Medical Cadet Corps and eventually, with the rank of Colonel conferred on him by his denominational chief, its commanding officer.[11]

As early as 1933 Dick foresaw the prospect of a second world war and discussed with his colleagues at Union College the means whereby Adventist boys might avoid the pitfalls that had trapped some of their predecessors during World War I. The Adventist stand on war differed from that of other pacifist sects. Members of the denomination objected to bearing arms and taking life, but were willing to serve their country as noncombatants. Sometimes, however, Adventist youths who were inducted into the army had trouble obtaining noncombatant assignments or found their assigned duties incompatible with their Seventh-day scruples.

It seemed obvious to Dick and some of his colleagues that the place for Adventist draftees in case another war broke out would be with the medical service, for they would "have no objection to doing works of mercy on Saturday or any other day of the week." Accordingly they conceived of a training corps, comparable to the ROTC, that would prepare students for assignment to medical rather than combat units. Hoping for official church endorsement of the plan, Dick wrote his president, M. L. Andreasen, who was attending the fall meeting of the Council of the Seventh-day Adventists General Conference, suggesting that the Missionary Volunteer Department of the denomination initiate such a program. When Andreasen failed to get affirmative action from the Council, he created a Union College committee with Dick at its head to see what could be done locally. Dick had no trouble interesting the State Adjutant General's office in his proposal, and also won the help of Major Emil H. Burgher, a regular army officer who was in charge of training medical units of the Nebraska National Guard. It was thus that the SDA Medical Cadet Corps was born. Practically all male students at Union College were eager to participate in the program, which for the second semester replaced the normal physical education course.

Beginning in January 1934, Dick put the trainees through the prescribed manual for army drill, and, with castoff Nebraska National Guard equipment, taught them such field duties as might be required of them—the use of the litter, transportation of the wounded, camp sanitation, and the like. The men also learned much about military etiquette, which made life far easier for those destined to be inducted into service. In the summer of 1939, with the shadows of war close at hand, Dick asked and received permission to hold a summer camp for non-students (the first such camp ever held), attended by fifty boys.

By the outbreak of World War II four other Adventist colleges, following the Union College example, had inaugurated medical training for students, and the church had given its blessing to what was now called officially the Medical Cadet Corps. In the fall of 1940 Dick was placed in charge of the program in the Middle West and a little later became General Conference training officer for the country as a whole, an assignment that took him away from his normal college duties for the next two years. Eventually the plan devised at Union College spread to nearly all the Adventist colleges and led to statewide camps in Iowa and Minnesota, of which Dick and his staff took charge. At the personal invitation of General George Marshall, Dick and two other Medical Cadet Corps leaders attended a civilian orientation course at the Command and General Staff School at Fort Leavenworth, graduating as members of a class of about fifteen the day before Pearl Harbor. Since the army was the only branch of the service to use drafted men before World War II, the hope of the MCC leaders was to place the men they had trained in the Army Medical Department, and with the full cooperation of the Surgeon General's Office, this generally was done.

After World War II the church permitted the MCC training to lapse. At Union College, however, Dick, who became academic dean in 1944, kept it alive, and when the Korean War broke out in 1950 he was placed in charge of a reactivated program, first in the United States, then throughout the world. During and following the Korean War, MCC activities were extended to annual National Officers' Training Camps, designed to train officers for the schools, and to offer training to boys who were not in school and did not otherwise have access to the program. Dick interviewed the Surgeon General of the United States Army for his suggestions on a suitable course combining the latest training procedures, and the Surgeon General, Major General George Armstrong, was so pleased with the program that was worked out that each year thereafter he or his representative personally inspected and evaluated the work done at the national camp at Grand Loedge, Michigan—Camp Desmond T. Doss.

At the invitation of the Canadian church leaders, Dick took charge of a training camp at Oshawa, Ontario, to provide officers needed for the establishment of the MCC in Canadian Adventist schools. He went to Puerto Rico and Hawaii in 1952 and 1953 to hold similar training camps. While in Hawaii, Dick received an order from the SDA General Conference "to go to the Far East, visit our boys in uniform, and hold a Medical

Cadet Corps training camp for young Korean Adventists." With the permission of General Maxwell Taylor, he complied, and was accorded a cordial reception. In Korea, Dick and his party found SDA boys among the troops as company aid men, armed only with their convictions, their litters, and their first-aid equipment. When casualties occurred, the noncombatants gave the injured men first aid, transported them to the battalion aid station about two miles in the rear, then to a temporary hospital. Among the supporting medical personnel of three hundred in each of the three infantry divisions that Dick visited, about one-tenth were Adventists. General Taylor ordered SDA men from as far away as 140 miles to "go to church" with Dick in Seoul. Here he met 126 SDA men who were doing their assignments "calmly, earnestly, loyally," "conscientious cooperators" rather than conscientious objectors. He also held a camp at Seoul, and visited the Korean army units elsewhere in which Korean Adventist boys were in training.[12]

Under church orders Dick also set up an MCC program at the SDA Missionary College in Japan, and went from there to other parts of Eastern Asia: Taiwan, Hong Kong, the Philippines, Singapore, and Thailand. In each he started an MCC training program. In Lebanon, on his way back to the United States, he gave instructions that resulted in the establishment of an MCC camp shortly after he left. His inability to spend more than a minimum amount of time in each country worried him, but when he returned on inspection tours in 1955 and 1957 he found his program still in operation, and in many instances going well. A representative from Brazil, sent to Camp Doss in 1951, returned to start the training in that country, where it received government recognition, and in 1956 Dick held the first MCC camp in Mexico, about 100 miles south of Mexico City.

Dick's service as commanding officer of the MCC lasted until July 1958, when he returned to his research professorship—at Union College. By that time about 8,000 Adventist youths in the United States and unnumbered thousands in other lands had

Everett Dick

gone through MCC training. According to one of his MCC collaborators, Dick

> could be as stern as the typical marine that he was and was very demanding in military discipline. At the same time he was as kind and fatherly when advising a young fellow of how to get along in the military as anybody could be. He had an instinctive understanding of the fine line between hardnosed discipline and kindly guidance and used whichever attitude was necessary to achieve his goal. He had an outstanding reputation among the military men in the highest branches of the service. Men in the medical department, generals, and colonels knew his work, knew his name, and were very favorably impressed with the entire denomination as a result of these contacts.[13]

Dick's services to his profession, to his college, to his denomination, and to his country did not go unappreciated. When his college designated him a research professor in 1946, it meant that, unlike other Union College faculty members, he would have his summers for research and writing and would be free to accept such outside grants as might come his way. In August 1967, Andrews University, Berrien Springs, Michigan, honored him with an LL.D., and in a laudatory citation paid tribute to his remarkable contributions to scholarship and his church. The following year, during a camp meeting held on the campus of Enterprise Academy, Enterprise, Kansas, Adventist leaders dedicated a program to him. In 1969 Union College named a library reading room after him.

Everett Dick has never officially retired, but he teaches only one or two classes now, and enjoys greater freedom to write. He has a back log of unexploited notes, some accumulated during the spring quarter that he taught at Denver University in 1966, some as the result of a grant by the Woods Foundation for a book on the social history of Nebraska, some for a similar project on Kansas, centering about his father's family, some on the frontier woman gathered under a research grant from the Huntington Library in 1969. In addition he hopes to fill out the autobiographic sketch he did for his children, and to write a full-length history of the Medical Cadet Corps, to which he contributed so much. Once when asked by the librarian of Union College: "Where would you like to retire?" he replied: "Where there is a library. This is my life."[14]

NOTES

1. Kansas State Historical Society *Collections* 17 (1926—1928), 27—97.
2. Janet Jacobs to Everett Dick, June 4, 1968. This is a typed version of a "This Is Your Life" ceremony held in Dick's honor at Enterprise, Kansas, June 6, 1968.
3. Jacobs to John D. Hicks, June 2, 1971; "Presentation of Dick Portrait," a typescript from a tape recording of proceedings in the College View Seventh Day Adventist Church, October 19, 1970.
4. Jacobs to Hicks, June 2, 1971; Verlie Ward to Hicks, June 12, 1971.
5. Louis W. Pettis to Hicks, May 23, 1971; L. G. Barker to Hicks, May 25, 1971.
6. Jacobs to Hicks, June 2, 1971; Fred B. Moore to Hicks, June 28, 1971; Pettis to Hicks, May 23, 1971; Lowell Litten to Hicks, June 4, 1971.
7. T. A. Little, in "This Is Your Life" typescript, p. 4.
8. Dick, "Life Experiences," p. 15.
9. *Mississippi Valley Historical Review,* 39 (September 1952), 289—302.
10. Little to Hicks, June 27, 1971.
11. Everett Dick, "Medical Cadet Corps," an eleven-page unpublished manuscript. This brief account covers the subject with sparing detail.
12. Ibid., p. 6; Everett Dick, "We Meet in Korea," *The Youth's Instructor,* September 1, 1933, pp. 13, 20, 22.
13. W. A. Howe to Hicks, June 17, 1971.
14. "This Is Your Life" typescript, p. 5.

CHAPTER 2

SOCIAL AND CULTURAL CONTINUITY IN AMERICAN FRONTIERING

Thomas D. Clark

> *Tom Clark and Everett Dick have been close friends for a generation, drawn together by their mutual interest in the history of the common folk of the West and South. Both have benefited greatly from their association. Dick leaned heavily on Clark for advice when touring the southern states in 1944 gathering material for* The Dixie Frontier, *while Clark's extensive writings have been enriched by the products of Dick's careful researches. Today Tom Clark ranks among the leaders of the historical profession, with such books as* Frontier America *(1959) and* The Emerging South *(1961) demonstrating his excellence in fields of history dear to Everett Dick. For many years, Clark was professor of history at the University of Kentucky; since his "retirement" in 1968 he has divided his time between a Distinguished Service Professorship at Indiana University and the secretaryship of the Organization of American Historians, a society that he once served as president. In this essay he draws on a wealth of evidence to show that continuity no less than environment played a determinative role in the process of frontiering.*

Frontiering, Americans have long believed, generally served as a centrifugal force that fragmentized social units; compact communities in the East were disjointed as men advanced westward on three or four levels of society, leaving at various times and settling in widely scattered homes.[1] Such a generalization ignores the fact that in the pioneering pattern there was a distinct continuity that gave a warm human dimension to the eventual occupation of the continent, for however, whenever, and wherever people moved, a direct blood relationship persisted between one wave of emigrants and the next. Between the eighteenth and mid-nineteenth centuries, when mobility was at its highest, only a handful of states fed the principal migratory streams that flowed over the Appalachians, across the Mississippi, and out along the trails to the far western plains, valleys, and mountains. Virginia, Maryland, North Carolina, and western Pennsylvania fed pioneers into the Kentucky and Tennessee settlements. Kentucky joined Virginia, Pennsylvania, and New England in stocking Ohio; and Kentucky, Virginia, and Tennessee fed the westward moving population stream into pioneer Indiana and Illinois.[2]

More than half of Missouri's population in 1850 had been born in Tennessee, Kentucky, North Carolina, Virginia, and Indiana. The same was true of the populations of Indiana, Illinois, and Iowa. As settlement spread to the Pacific Coast this pattern prevailed. It was no accident that in July 1968 almost two hundred descendants of the Boone family gathered in reunion at Tacoma, Washington. There was even more glamour in the fact that Boone kith and kin had come from all parts of the Pacific slope. Their heritage was a rich chapter of American pioneering.

The Pioneering Tradition

Boone kinsmen were proud of their ancestors' accomplishments on the trails between Bucks County, Pennsylvania, and the Yadkin settlements in North Carolina, and between the Yadkin and the upper Tennessee, and across the Cumberland Gap to Kentucky. The earliest Kentuckians to adventure into the new western or trans-Appalachian settlements were trail-breakers, and many of these durable frontiersmen—men like Daniel Boone, Simon Kenton, Benjamin Logan, William Whitley, and the McAfee brothers—planted their names indelibly upon the advancing frontier.[3]

The old hunter Daniel Boone and his sons moved from Kentucky to Indiana in 1795, and in 1799, to the new lands of Missouri. Once again the Boones organized a pioneering party. Most of the family paddled a huge tulip poplar canoe loaded with household goods down the Ohio and up the Mississippi, while Daniel, the older boys, and the slaves drove the livestock overland just as they had on their way to Boonesborough in 1775 and 1776. Already he and his people had paid heavy tribute to pioneer history by establishing their names in Pennsylvania, North Carolina, and Kentucky. Now they were to add further luster to frontier adventures all across the western part of the continent.[4]

Other names of famous old woodsmen and Indian fighters tied the Rocky Mountain West inseparably to the Appalachian frontier. The Sublette brothers—Andrew W., Milton, William, Solomon, and Pinckney—associated themselves with the fur trade and mountain adventures as intimately as their grandfather, William Whitley, had done in the Kentucky backwoods. That stout old pioneer had followed the Valley and Wilderness trails from Augusta County, Virginia, to the headwaters of Skagg's Branch in Kentucky.

At heart Whitley was an Indian fighter. He had helped stalk Cherokee along the Wilderness Trail, and had accompanied John Bowman and, later, George Rogers Clark on their expeditions against marauding Shawnee in the Miami Valley beyond the Ohio. On October 5, 1813, he was part of Richard M. Johnson's "Forlorn Hope" in the Battle of the Thames and was said to have killed Chief Tecumseh. He lost his own life in that battle and was buried beside the Thames.[5]

Colonel Whitley's grandsons carried on their family pioneering tradition on the Rocky Mountain frontier in Indian relations and fur trading. They made the name Sublette even better known in the Mountain West than their swashbuckling grandfather had along the Ohio.

Like William Whitely and his grandsons, Colonel William Russell and his grandson William Henry Russell were to play active parts in pioneering. Colonel Russell was born in Culpeper County, Virginia, and moved onto the Tennessee and Kentucky frontiers in the 1770s. He was with Daniel Boone in the disastrous defeat in the saddle of Cumberland Gap in 1774, and later fought Shawnee beyond the Ohio with Charles Scott and James Wilkinson. His real moments of glory, however, were in the battles of Tippecanoe and Fallen Timbers. He later commanded the Northwestern army on the Indiana, Illinois, and Missouri frontiers.[6] His grandson, William Henry ("Owl") Russell, retraced his grandfather's steps to Missouri to fight in the Black Hawk War and to serve as United States Marshall. In 1846 he was elected captain of a wagon train of California emigrants. In California he joined Fremont's California Battalion with the rank of major; later Fremont appointed Russell Secretary of State for California.[7]

Another Kentuckian frontier name was added to the list of western immigrants when James Robert Estill of Madison County, Kentucky, followed the Boones to Howard County, Missouri. He was the grandson of Captain James Estill, who had commanded frontiersmen in the bloody Indian fight of Estill's Defeat which became a heroic chapter in local frontier history.

No less typical was the Carson family, which settled on Tate's Creek in Madison County, Kentucky, not too far down the Kentucky River from Boonesborough. The histories of the Carsons and Boones were intertwined both geographically and historically; family tradition even held that they had been associated back in Scotland and Ireland. The Carsons moved from Pennsylvania to the Yadkin Valley of North Carolina in the early 1750s. Lindsey Carson was born on the Yadkin.

In 1793 Lindsey Carson crossed the Cumberland Gap to settle once again near the Boones. It was here that Christopher was born on December 24, 1809. Soon thereafter his father moved

Social and Cultural Continuity

the family to Howard County, Missouri, where it is said young Kit took lessons in marksmanship from Daniel Boone himself.[8]

The names of interlinking pioneer families could be multiplied endlessly. The folk-pattern of the new territories was woven so solidly of the same human warp and woof that it is now impossible to identify all the strands. Wherever fresh lands became available and were temporarily free from old political entanglements, boundary confusions, and legal problems in general, frontiersmen appeared, attracted by fertile soils, and driven to move from one frontier to the next by an imponderable wanderlust. "Good" land on the frontier was a highly relative term.

As new lands were opened in the Old Northwest Territory by Indian treaties or legislative and congressional acts there was a corresponding in-rush of settlers. In Indiana the Ohio River counties and the southern hills were quickly populated by small farmers. All of them transported in their cultural baggage the kindred folk tastes, personal likes, and modest behavior of semi-literate and primitive people.

The remarkably harmonious social and folk pattern that prevailed among frontiersmen in the Ohio Valley after 1790 had, by 1820, colored the whole human approach to the frontier and was to be carried on westward. One of the most dramatic tides of emigration was that which flowed into Missouri from older neighboring states in the Ohio Valley following the War of 1812. In 1810 Missouri is estimated to have had a population of 19,783; the total had grown to 25,845 in 1814 and to 66,586 by 1820.[9] In the decade 1820–1830, the emigration flow increased the Missouri population to the staggering total of 140,455, largely from Kentucky and North Carolina. Later, in 1824–1825, these states further swelled the stream of emigrants, and between 1821 and 1829 sent enough of their sons westward to stock seven new counties. The *Missouri Republican* of November 18, 1828, reported that a man had counted two hundred wagons loaded with Kentucky and Virginia families moving along the road between Louisville and St. Louis.[10]

As significant as the human souls drifting westward in the pack and wagon trains were the cultural and spiritual traditions which they carried with them. In their baggage were faded notebooks that contained recipes for concocting all sorts of folk-remedies, dyes, soap, lard oil, whiskey, bread, and almost every other household material. In their memories they transported enough knowledge of folk-medicines, folklore, and simple human institutions to fill a scholarly volume. Above all they possessed the great frontier asset of inurement to hardship, disappointment, grief, and misfortune. Three generations of pioneering life had bred into them a willingness to accept whatever fate decreed with minimum emotional resistance. Either they brought with them simple theological beliefs or they had receptive minds which were stimulated by the missionaries and preachers who followed them into the wilderness.[11]

The Spiritual Tradition

Moving among the ranks of pioneers emigrating from Virginia, Pennsylvania, and eastern Tennessee were numbers of rough and unruly individuals. Some were squatters who fled before legal land claimants, and some were fugitives from the law. Most of them, to some degree, fled the refinements of older communities. No reliable statistical sources sustain this fact, and contemporary personal observations have to be accepted with highly discriminatory judgment. Many a frontier rowdy was branded a near-criminal when actually he was little more than a crude animalistic greenhorn who never in his life had come into intimate association with a single truly refining influence. There were the rowdies of Crab Orchard, so described by the sober Bishop Francis Asbury, or the denizens of "Rogues Harbour" bemoaned by the self-righteous Peter Cartwright, or John Mason Peck's "barbarians" who squatted in outlying settlements of the Missouri bottoms.[12] A raffish element was as common to the pioneering experience as the raising of stick and mud chimneys, and its progress across the frontier accepted no geographical bounds.

Persistent though they were, frontier ruffians were either in a decided minority or too poorly led to make their weight felt, for the vast majority of pioneers preferred God to lawlessness. During the great religious awakening in mid-eighteenth century in the colonial backwoods, frontiersmen in droves turned to an involved calvinistic predestinarian-fundamentalist religious view of life.[13] Elijah and Lewis Craig, in 1780 and 1781, led the two separatist Baptist congregations from Fauquier and Spotsylvania Counties in Virginia over the Wilderness Road to establish numerous congregations of that faith. Lay Baptist ministers shepherded other flocks and gathered the faithful about them to be indoctrinated through literal-minded preaching. David Rice, a more sophisticated Calvinist, brought to the Kentucky frontier the seeds of Presbyterianism, and Bishop Francis Asbury repeatedly crossed the Appalachians to tincture a Methodist doctrine of brotherly love with a stern authoritarianism. About Bardstown, Kentucky, Anglo-Catholics from Maryland established a powerful beachhead for their faith.

Even immigrants affiliated with no organized church brought to the western country Bibles from which they extracted their own notions of man's relationships with God, and from which they developed simplistic theological concepts which could be adapted to their conditions of time and place. Many of the moral concepts of an older and more refined society could not be maintained under conditions of a brutally demanding way of life—Sabbatarianism, for instance, was all but ignored where families were heavily taxed physically to perform the labors of pioneering—yet there was on the frontier a willingness to accept the more puritanical aspects of formally organized religion preached at camp meetings or by circuit-riding missionaries.[14]

In 1800 the Mud River revival, which occurred in Peter Cartwright's "Rogues Harbour" in Logan County, Kentucky, and which was led by the furious James McReady and William and John Magee, opened a new era in frontier religious activity. In 1801 the "Great Revival" at Cane Ridge in Bourbon County, Kentucky, helped establish the camp meeting and revivalism as frontier phenomena.[15] Following these explosions of religious emotionalism, Baptists, Methodists, Campbellites, and Stoneites sought to organize churches, to seek out human souls wherever they lodged in the backwoods flow of population, and to establish a moral atmosphere grounded in fundamentalism. John Finley, Allen Wiley, Bishop William McKendree, Timothy Flint, John Mason Peck, and literally hundreds of unnamed lay Baptist preachers and destitute Methodist circuit riders tilled the spiritual garden of the western settlements between 1800 and 1850.

Frequently in the journals of the earlier emigrants, and later in those of "Forty-Niners," there were notations of Sabbatarianism and the names of ministers who accompanied the wagon trains westward. In 1841 the Reverend Joseph Williams of Napoleon, Indiana, followed the Overland Trail and recorded his experiences in a delightful pamphlet. In 1846 the Reverend Joseph Adamson Cornwall moved his family from Georgia by way of Kentucky and Missouri to Arkansas, and then to Oregon. The Reverend James Dunleavy traveled with the Russell party in 1846, and six years later the Reverend Jesse Moreland of Tennessee led a party up the Platte to Oregon. How many other emigrant patriarchs were ministers is unknown, but they must have been numerous.[16]

Methodist circuit riders who broke spiritual trails into Ohio, Indiana, Illinois, and Missouri were tireless emissaries of a rapidly maturing western civilization. The highly compartmentalized system of circuits and conferences was well designed to appeal to a highly restless mobile society. Less well organized Baptist sects, with their predominantly lay preachers, enabled frontiersmen to feel emotionally comfortable because they were as mobile as the society itself, there was little or no dogma, no central administrative authority, and no restrictive creed to limit the organization of as many sects as there were personal interpretations of the Scriptures. Congregations and preachers of this faith were flexible enough to permit physical and emotional compromises with most of the social and moral realities of the backwoods settlement. Finally, the Baptist doctrine of an uneducated and unpaid ministry fitted well the penuriousness of most frontiersmen.

Although the impact of religion on the American frontier cannot be exactly measured, a strong inference can be drawn that frontiersmen carried across the continent a strong, if not militant, Protestantism, which influenced personal behavior and attitudes, bore upon the organization of schools, shaped political beliefs, and governed general conditions of community organization and society. The church houses and bush arbors of the annual camp meetings became focal centers of interest and excitement in backwoods settlements.[17] No doubt John Mason Peck spoke for ministers of every shade of religious doctrine and spiritual belief when he observed:

These States have been unparalleled in their growth, both in increase of population and property, and in the advance of intellectual and moral improvement. Such an extent of forest as never before was cleared—such a vast field of prairie was never before subdued and cultivated by hand of man, in the same short period of time.[18]

How many souls had actually been garnered was another matter, but the spread of religion across the frontier was as much a yeoman act as clearing the forest and responding to the beckoning land.

The Art of Pioneering

After 1830, and the great migration to Missouri, very little startlingly original or fundamental was introduced into the basic art of pioneering. This does not ignore the enormously important experiences of crossing the plains and western mountain ranges to reach the Pacific slope in the years from 1840 to 1855, and of making adaptations to the semiarid West in the basic ways of life. So long as families ventured into virgin country they were called upon to adjust to new conditions when they moved from one soil, topographical situation, or climatic region to another. Not always were the traditional raw materials for pioneering at hand, and it was necessary for emigrants to make radical substitutions. Wood, water, and grass, for instance, were often in short supply beyond the hundredth meridian or almost totally lacking. It is not hard to imagine the consternation of pioneers on the plains who found themselves without firewood and had to use buffalo chips and sage stems for cooking.[19]

Elisha Douglas Perkins described eloquently his emotions upon spotting the cedar trees at Cedar Grove just above Ash Hollow in western Nebraska after a monotonous bout with the Kansas-Nebraska plains. "About 10 arrived at a pretty place known as Cedar Grove where we laid in a supply of firewood. Here is a grove of cedar trees entirely isolated. Not another green thing to be seen but the grass of the Prairie & we were much refreshed by their shade. Trees are a perfect luxury to our Prairie sick eyes."[20] Three years earlier Edwin Bryant wrote, "At present, the water stands in stagnant pools. A few cottonwoods are scattered along the stream. The dead limbs of these, with 'buffalo chips,' compose our fuel."[21]

Despite the dramatic challenges of each new tier of opening country, the basic patterns and human approaches in pioneering were acquired back in central Pennsylvania, the Valley of Virginia, and along the headwaters of those seminal streams of eastern Tennessee. The procession of settlers who struggled through Cumberland Gap or drifted downstream in flatboats and rafts from Pittsburgh contained people already schooled in the art of pioneering.

Much earlier, backwoodsmen had learned to cut timbers and erect pole cabins, to hew and fit logs and rugged square beams to form more elaborate dog-trot houses, and to use wood to the best advantage for all other domestic needs. Surviving pioneer housing across the American frontier, except for the plains area where the dugout and sod houses were popular, reflects a remarkable similarity to those sturdy old buildings which still stand in Valley Virginia, in the Watagua settlements in eastern Tennessee, and along the Wilderness Road in Kentucky.[22]

Frontiersmen learned harsh lessons of primitive defense during the border raids of the French and Indian War and subsequently in Dunmore's War. They erected blockhouses and puncheon forts to withstand the hit-and-run raids of enraged Indians. It was in this same era that the term "station" came into popular use. Along the frontier the temporary and semi-military defensive structure was as much a landmark of pioneering as the pole cabin. In later decades, and in places where wood was unavailable, men devised portable fortresses in the circular wagon corrals. On May 12, 1846, Edwin Bryant wrote,

At one O'clock, P.M., we reached a small grove, (composed of a few oaks, cottonwood, maple, and hickory trees, on the banks of a small branch,) head of Blue Creek, [Kansas] where we encamped for the day. The wagons, in forming the encampment, were what is called *corraled,* an anglicized Spanish word, the significance of which, in our use of the term, is, that they were formed in a circle; constituting a wall of defense in the event of an attack from the Indians, and a compound for confinement of the cattle and horses, whenever necessary or desirable.[23]

What Edwin Bryant described was an adaptation of the old commons or "closes" of Harrod's Town and Boonesborough, or any of the other stations on the trans-Appalachian frontier.

The same degree of cooperative enterprise that marked eastern pioneering was apparent in the overland migrations and subsequent settlement in Oregon and California; each emigrant band and wagon train constituted, of necessity, a community enterprise in which everybody assumed responsibility. It would not be too farfetched to look upon the group movement of settlers in wagon trains as a sustained "common working" akin to log-rollings, cabin raisings, quiltings, cornshuckings, and barn dances. There were literally thousands of incidents in which this aspect of pioneering was put to the acid test.[24] Men cooperated, although not always willingly or peaceably, because human preservation demanded it. Emigrant diaries, journals, and reminiscences are filled with descriptions of the enormous common effort and generous sharing that the rigors of the folk-movement demanded.

In a more somber manner pioneering involved human emotions and fortitude. Strung out from Augusta County, Virginia, to Portland, Oregon, is a row of almost obliterated monuments, mute testaments to the perils of migrating. Roadside graves mark not only the end of the trail for the individual buried there, but are monuments to the stoicism so necessary to endure the rigors of pioneering. Between Cumberland Gap and Harrodsburg and Boonesborough are the graves of many individuals who failed to last out the journey. Parents lowered the bodies of children, "uncoffined and almost unshrouded," into bare raw earth graves, put in crude and ungraven rock markers, and passed on. This was the human price of pioneering. The dream was bright, but the price was high, and it required courage and stoicism to endure it. Frontier physical demands were impartial; they favored no group of pioneers, nor did they soften their harsh exactions at any place or time.

The Dietary Tradition

No part of the cultural pattern was more firmly ingrained in human life than dietary tastes and habits. On the early valley frontier of Pennsylvania, Virginia, and the Carolinas, backwoodsmen adjusted to the resources of the land on which they settled. They depended upon the woods for part of their meat supply, and some fruits, vegetables, and herbs. From corn and wheat patches, wooded ranges, and gardens, they gathered most of their staples. Corn was the most readily available bread source. It was a versatile grain, yielding tender green edible ears at an early stage of growth, coarser "gritted" bread, meal, grits, and mush when matured and it was both edible and portable in parched form. Hunters and emigrants alike depended upon meal and parched grains to sustain them on long woodland journeys. The Appalachian pioneers frequently mentioned use of corn in some form, and when they were without it their hunger approached an obsession. It was the first crop planted on new lands, and the first harvested. Virginia officially recognized its importance in one of its early land acts known as the "corn patch and cabin" law which assured prior claim to any settler who cleared a patch and built a cabin.

Wheat at first was not a staple grain, partly because pioneers were unable to spin grinding mill stones fast enough to prevent "gumming" of the burrs. In time, however, wheat bread became popular and the milling process was greatly improved with the application of water power. Both corn and wheat supplied breadstuffs, as well as furnishing early home distillers with necessary ingredients for the making of whiskey.

Western settlers had a taste for wild meats, but the steadily diminishing supply forced them to look elsewhere for a dietary staple. They found it in cured pork. All across the wooded frontier the hog was a popular farm animal, because it was highly adaptable to backwoods forest ranges with their abundance of mast, roots, and succulent plants and because it could be driven long distances and usually arrived at its destination much heavier than it had been at the start. Too, pork could be butchered and cured under the most primitive conditions. Cured meats, with some care, could be stored or transported with a minimum amount of spoilage. The lard kettle and press, sausage mill, and smokehouse remain the most common artifacts of pioneering.

The cow and sheep rivaled the hog as basic pioneer farm animals. Like the hog, both were reasonably good drovers, and both supplied basic human needs. The cow yielded milk, butter, meat, leather, and tallow. Bulls and steers were dependable draft animals on the road and before the plow. Sheep supplied wool, meat, and skins, although large numbers of frontiersmen had little taste for mutton. Woolen fibre comprised the woof for traditional "linsey-woolsey," for jeans, and even for some Osnaburgs. The spinning wheel, cards, loom, and dye pots for processing wool were as symbolic of pioneering as were the axe and rifle. Many a pioneer woman fetched westward with her "drafts" for the manufacture of woven coverlets, cloth patterns, and even common jeans.

Closely guarded in settler baggage, whether struggling over the pack trail through Cumberland Gap or crawling up the Platte in covered wagons, were pouches of precious garden and fruit seeds and onion buttons. Pioneers relished turnips and greens, cabbage, radishes, beans, pumpkin, squash, and melons. Seeds of these vegetables were among the most precious things carried by settlers. Modern plant breeders would be horrified to know how far from parent stock pioneers planted seeds of their favorite vegetables and plants. Some stock journeyed from Virginia to Kentucky, and from Kentucky across Indiana, Illinois, to Missouri, and on to the Pacific Coast. The only selection or plant improvement practiced was choice of better specimens from which to extract seeds. Tastes, and even dietary habits, were shaped by available staple vegetables.

"Emigration," as one scholar has noted, "was usually undertaken in the autumn, because of the prevailing fine weather. Such provisions as corn, smoked pork, beans, peas, rice, flour, cheese, and fruit were taken on the journey. The livestock had to be carefully tethered or it would start back home." Once on the selected tract of land,

a site for the house was chosen near a good spring, and over the spring in time would be built a small house in order to prevent pollution of the water, and also to afford a place to keep milk, butter, and meat. . . .The settler built a crude log cabin. For the vast majority, apparently at first and for a long time, meat and corn were not only the principal, but almost the sole articles of diet in Tennessee.[25]

These cultural traits were carried another step westward by the emigrant trains that left Missouri for Oregon and California in the early forties. It almost seemed that pioneers had only stopped to rest a generation before assembling at Independence and St. Joseph to push up the Platte. It is difficult to find a precise inventory of the foods favored by these later travelers, but it is certain they were traditional ones. Edwin Bryant gave some notion of what they ate when he described his last meal in civilization as consisting of fried bacon, eggs, fresh butter, corn bread and biscuits. On May 22, 1849, Elisha D. Perkins at St. Joseph, Missouri, noted in his diary: "Wagons go out of this place and come back loaded with ham, flour, pilot bread,

Beans, Sheet iron stoves, extra axeltrees & wheels, medicines, Tools of all kinds & personal clothing of all descriptions."[26] Margaret Haun said her family wagons were heavily loaded with flour ground in their own mill, home cured bacon, barrels of home distilled alcohol, other dried and salted meats, crabapple and blackberry jelly, and other groceries.[27]

The Pioneering Institutions

Just as emigrants tried desperately to transport so much of "home" with them in their baggage and personal tastes, so they clung steadfastly to institutional patterns. Three basic institutions, newspapers, schools, and local government, were of primary importance. Of these, none did more to bridge the continental gap between Philadelphia and Portland, Oregon, than the frontier print shop and rural newspaper.

Newspapers

The *Kentucke Gazette,* founded in Lexington, Kentucky, in 1787, was a seminal frontier paper.[28] It is impossible to assess fully its influence across the spreading American frontier, through printers trained in its shop, or the impact it had on western newspaper organization. In a remarkably short time after the *Gazette* began, other journals made their appearance in Cincinnati and Louisville. In Cincinnati on November 9, 1793, William Maxwell added a new cubit to western cultural beginnings by bringing the *Centinel of the Northwest Territory* from the press.[29] In time Cincinnati became an important printing and journalistic center, and like Lexington it sent on to new frontiers editors, printers, and booksellers.

Two of the most fascinating pioneer printers to come from Kentucky shops were Elihu Stout and Joseph Charless. Stout had worked with John, James, and Fielding Bradford on the *Kentucky Journal,* and the Frankfort *Guardian of Freedom.* In Frankfort he purchased type and a press and shipped them by river to Vincennes. There he published first the Indiana *Gazette* in 1804, and then the more influential *Vincennes Sun.* The impact of Stout seems to have been almost as great as that of John Bradford, who had founded the *Kentucke Gazette* because within three decades Indiana had more than a score of newspapers.[30]

An Irishman, Joseph Charless, worked his way in printshops from Philadelphia to the Missouri backwoods to make frontier newspaper history. In Kentucky Charless was a partner of Francis Peniston in the publication of the *Western American* and the *Louisville Gazette*. Later he was associated with Samuel Vail briefly in editing the *Farmer's Library*, and was one of the projectors of the *Missouri Correspondent* and *Illinois Gazette*. The latter paper was never published, but in 1808 Charless began publication of the influential *Missouri Gazette*. Later he and his son Edward became significant chroniclers of the great migrations.[31]

The first half of the nineteenth century saw newspapers multiply almost as rapidly as new western settlements. In Missouri Joseph Charless' meager newspaper beginnings soon expanded into a galaxy of journals. Of these none was more colorful and imaginative than the *St. Louis Reveille,* edited by J. M. Field and John S. Robb between 1844 and 1850. This sprightly paper was less concerned with politics than with life in the West. Its reporters were especially diligent in gathering news about the great emigrations, and incidents of transcontinental trail travel. One of its reporters, George Law Curry, prepared graphic descriptions of the organization and departure of the Keyes-Boggs-Russell-Bryant party on May 6, 1846. Curry was so entranced with the adventure that he joined Edwin Bryant's company of mule-riders to cross the country to California. Beyond South Pass Curry chose to go to Oregon and turned northward to Fort Hall. In subsequent years he played an important political role in the new territory. He was clerk of the Territorial Council, served in the territorial legislature, and was Territorial Governor for a brief time. It was, however, as editor of the *Oregon Spectator* and of the *Oregon Free Press* that he exerted his greatest and most lasting influence.[32]

Schools

Closely paralleling the rise of the press as a frontier institution was the development of the frontier school. Educational patterns on the frontier west of the Appalachians varied almost as much as personalities of the people. Variations, however, were in degree rather than in fundamental philosophy or basic practice. It is indeed doubtful that many frontiersmen stopped to define the purposes of rudimentary education. Those who gave the matter serious thought simply repeated the generalities of preachers, politicians, and itinerant school teachers. Either abjectly illiterate or barely able to pass the test of signing names and reading a few words, frontiersmen were not of the sort to contribute to the philosophy of education. Yet schools were a primary concern of nearly all.

Many pilgrims straggling along the road westward brought texts in arithmatic, geometry, spelling, and English. These were teacher's handbooks, copied and brought over the mountains by ambitious "professors."[33] Whenever the migrants paused to establish a new settlement, some kind of school was usually founded almost as soon as the first cabins were raised. At Harrod's Fort in Kentucky in 1775, Mary Coomes instructed children in a fireside dame school. Off to the side of the fort in Lexington John McKinney taught children and battled wildcats. Advertising columns of the *Kentucke Gazette* and the *Centinel of the Northwest* carried from the start notices from prospective schoolmasters who wanted to organize private academies. These early schools emphasized the "three R's" and the most elementary of the classics, and depended almost entirely upon voluntary subscriptions for support. Frontiersmen were stubbornly reluctant to levy and pay taxes for establishment of schools. They reasoned that every man should assume responsibility for educating his children; too they expected to follow the landed frontier on west and did not wish to invest in institutions they would leave behind. Educational provisions made in the Northwest ordinances of 1785 and 1787 were so disappointingly inadequate that little genuine headway was made in the actual development of a public school system until after 1840.

To the religiously inclined, educational objectives on the frontier were moral and spiritual; to schoolmasters they were basic and classical; and to the materially inclined education was a tool of business. Some saw education as a pragmatic tool by which the resources of the West could be exploited, roads could be built, stream channels improved, and commerce established. To accomplish these ends the country needed engineers, surveyors, lawyers, doctors, and teachers. Other early leaders reasoned that education was necessary in order to prepare the mass of male voters to stave off all forms of oppressive political tyranny.

Preachers and churches organized schools and colleges to serve the narrower objectives of denominational faiths. Presbyterians especially extended John Witherspoon's log college concept into the emerging settlement areas. By 1850 all of the western states had their share of small church colleges. The roll call was fairly extensive and included Transylvania, Centre, Hanover, Ohio University, Wabash, Illinois College, DePauw, Knox, and Jonesborough colleges. It was not until 1809 that Ohio assumed the lead in establishing a public college when it chartered Miami University, and nine years later Indiana legislators chartered Indiana Seminary, later Indiana University. Both of these institutions were essentially land-grant colleges designed to carry out the objectives of the Northwest ordinances.

Lower on the educational ladder the land-grant public school idea was a failure. Few truly public schools were organized and supported; instead, semi-public semi-religious patterns prevailed all across the frontier. Itinerant teachers were drawn from the ministry, the law, and even from the farms. Nevertheless, the country school was an institutional part of the westward movement. The advent of the steamboat, and the country newspaper, and the rising crescendo of the Jacksonian political dialogue gave new point to education as expressed in terms of commerce and political partisanism. Too, the increased demand for professional services in the field of engineering, law, and medicine had an important impact on development of public attitudes toward education. Perhaps after 1820 the Jeffersonian ideals of educating the common man to assume his place in a republican

Social and Cultural Continuity

intellectual "aristocracy" had some slight bearing on the growth of schools. It is not without significance that the great trails to the Far West were opened to the flood of emigration at the moment when crusaders had begun to make headway in their drive to establish public education. Whether or not the overland trains contained schoolteachers, the significance of education was borne westward in the minds of settlers, and schools were quickly established in rising Far West and Northwest settlements.

Local Government

As the population expanded on to spreading western frontiers there was immediate need for organized government at the local level. To the average settler the county had greater practical significance than any other political or social institution. It was the depository for his land deed. Its clerks registered his various claims, recorded many of his vital statistics, kept track of his law suits, and collected his taxes. Sheriffs kept civil order, and judges and probate officials looked after estates and fiscal affairs. It is little wonder that the courthouse was the first public building raised in an aspiring county seat, or that in time it became the village center.[34]

The organization of the western country into states after 1787 was a mere formality. The constitutional formula was repeated with remarkably little innovation or inclusion of regional philosophical points of view or fundamental expressions of experiences. It was through the county, however, with its direct services to individuals, that the clearest grass-roots responses were made to many fundamental political issues. It was within this local framework of government that Jeffersonians and Jacksonians were most comfortable in the management of public affairs and in the control of the state itself. County politicians made the earthy approaches which a rural backwoods people found least in conflict with their social, cultural, and economic status. Most important, the county was more readily transported and transplanted than any other political unit of government. It adjusted to the constant movement of population into new country with surprising resilience and was highly expressive of the permanence of settlement made by the influx of emigrants.

Conclusion

There was intense human motion in the West during the two decades between 1835 and 1855. Many forces bore upon the social, political, and economic activities of this period: the expansion of American interest in the Pacific area; the concentration of a large, land-hungry population on the outer edges of Missouri, Illinois, and the eastern fringe of Iowa that was confronted with a long journey between wooded frontiers; the annexation of Texas and the Mexican War, along with an intensification of nationalism and a sense of manifest destiny; the rumbling sectional conflict and the impact of slavery; and the gold rush. All of these were catalytic forces.

During the later ante-bellum decades, technological advances—such as improvement of steamboat travel and transportation, development of railroads, and an advance in the profession of applied engineering—all bore upon the surge westward. Improvements and expansion of the art of printing and newspaper distribution also played a significant role in this era. Population statistics reflect the restlessness of Americans after 1820, especially the census report for 1860.

In the outward flow of emigrants were many individuals who in time stood out from the crowd. The roll of these is extensive, but it contained such names as Israel Boone, Lillburn Boggs, Francis Preston Blair, "Kit" Carson, James Ohio Pattie, "Bill" Williams, John C. Edwards, Silas Bent, William Becknell, Henry Dodge, Ewing Young, Charles Bent, Lewis Fields Linn, Joseph Lane, Stephen Watts Kearny, Duff Green, A.W. Donniphan, Peter H. Burnett, Ben Holladay, David R. Atchison, George Law Curry, William Martin, and James W. Nesmith. There were many others, of course; all of them took away elements of younger and more aggressive potential leadership from their parent communities.

It was, however, the nameless settler, with his simple tools and courageous family, who gave the westward movement such a vital human dimension. It was he who hacked away the heavy forest to open corn and wheat fields; who drove a "start" of livestock literally thousands of miles over rugged trails; and who transplanted religious denominations and country churches, schools, courthouses, and villages to the West. He transported in his heart precious memories of "home" and planted them in the new land in the nostalgic names he gave villages, communities, and counties. A pleasant vista, the turn of a hill, the chatter of a lively stream, a burst of spring, all stirred memories of the Richmonds, Frankforts, Lexingtons, Lancasters, Nashvilles, Raleighs, Cincinnatis, Fayettevilles, and Shelbyvilles left behind. In Indiana, for instance, 42 out of 92 county names were the same as those in Kentucky and Ohio; out of 102 counties in Missouri 50 bore Kentucky, Tennessee, and Indiana names. Kansas repeated 15 out of 69 names, and a majority of Oregon's nongeographical county names duplicated those of Kentucky and Indiana.[35]

At the time of J.W. Nesmith's death (an 1843 emigrant) Harvey W. Scott reflected in an *Oregonian* editorial on June 21, 1885, "The same class of adventurous spirits who laid the foundations of our state can be traced in unbroken succession to the handful of hardy men who built the log fort at Boonesborough; and, in reading the history of one, we may perceive that of the other." Later he wrote, "What was called pioneer life in our older states was rapidly passing away and becoming only a memory when Oregon was settled, but the movement to Oregon continued and prolonged it—on a small scale it is true, but it still was the same here in spirit and method as it had been in Indiana, Illinois and Missouri and other states."[36] Scott was only partially right in concluding the pioneer spirit had disappeared in Oregon. So long as there was open land and a cloak of geographical and cultural isolation, "the pioneering spirit and method of Kentucky, Indiana, Illinois, and Missouri" remained a live force in the organization of American life.

NOTES

1. For examples, see John Mason Peck, *A Guide for Emigrants, Containing Sketches of Illinois, Missouri and Adjacent Parts* (Boston, 1831), pp. 114-20. Peck, *A New Guide for Emigrants to the West, Containing Sketches of Ohio,*

Indiana, Illinois, Missouri, Michigan with the Territories of Wisconsin and Arkansas (Boston, 1836), pp. 102–12. Robert Baird (Bache), *View of the Mississippi Valley, or the Emigrant's and Traveler's Guide to the West* (Philadelphia, 1834), pp. 196–206. Roscoe C. Buley, *The Old Northwest Pioneer Period 1815-1840,* 2 vols. (Bloomington, 1951), I, 25–34.

2. United States *Sixth, Seventh* and *Eighth Census Reports,* especially the *Eighth Census,* IV, Tables II and plates li and lxi, pp. 562, 862; and Buley, *The Old Northwest Pioneer Period,* I, pp. 19–29.

3. For histories of these men, see Richard H. Collins, *History of Kentucky,* 2 vols. (Covington, 1876), II, pp. 442–43, 482–86, 760–61; Charles G. Talbert, "William Whitley 1749–1813," *The Filson Club History Quarterly,* XXV (April, July, October 1951), 101–21, 210–16, 300–16; John Bakeless, *Master of the Wilderness, Daniel Boone* (New York, 1939); Charles G. Talbert, *Benjamin, Logan, Kentucky Frontiersman* (Lexington, 1962); Edna Kenton, *Simon Kenton: His Life and Period, 1755-1836* (Garden City, 1930).

4. See Bakeless, *Master of the Wilderness,* pp. 358–66; H. Addington Bruce, *Daniel Boone and the Wilderness Road* (New York, 1929), pp. 87–89; and W. S. Bryan, "Daniel Boone," *Missouri Historical Review* III (January, April 1909), 89–98, 198–205.

5. Collins, *History of Kentucky,* Leland Winfield Meyers, *Life and Times of Richard M. Johnson of Kentucky* (New York, 1932), pp. 128–30.

6. Collins *History of Kentucky,* II, 226, 282, 695-96. Anna Russell des Cognets, *William Russell and His Descendants* (Lexington, 1884).

7. Douglas S. Watson, "The Great Express Extra of the California Star of April 1, 1848," *Quarterly of the California Historical Society,* XI (June 1932), 129–133; George Tay, "Pio Pico's Correspondence with the Mexican Government 1846–1848," ibid., XIII (June 1934), 133–34; George Walcott Ames, Jr., "A Doctor Comes to California, The Diary of John S. Griffin, Assistant Surgeon with Kearney's Dragoons 1846–1847," ibid., XXII (March 1943), 41–42.

8. M. Morgan Estergreen, *Kit Carson: A Portrait in Courage* (Norman, 1962), pp. 3, 16–17.

9. Hattie M. Anderson, "Missouri, 1814–1828: Peopling a Frontier State," *Missouri Historical Review,* XXXI (January 1937), 150–81.

10. Quoted by Hattie M. Anderson, ibid., p. 173.

11. See Timothy Flint, *Recollections of the Last Ten Years, Passed in Occasional Residences and Journeyings in the Valley of the Mississippi* (Boston, 1826), pp. 110–16; Rufus Babcock, ed., *Forty Years of Pioneer Life, Memoir of John Mason Peck D.D., Edited from his Journals and Correspondence* (Carbondale, Ill., 1965), pp. 100–02; Robert Carlton (Baynard Rush Hall), *The New Purchase or, Seven and a Half Years in the Far West* (Princeton, 1916), pp. 119–23, 170–74.

12. W. P. Strickland, ed., *Autobiography of Peter Cartwright the Backwoods Preacher* (New York, 1856), pp. 24–25; Gov. Thomas Ford, *A History of Illinois from Its Commencement as a State in 1818 to 1847* (Chicago, 1854), pp.

232–37; Boggess, *The Settlement of Illinois 1778-1830* (Chicago, 1908), pp. 50–51, 132–33, 139–41.

13. See William Warren Sweet, *Revivalism In America* (Nashville, 1944), pp. 112–39; Madison Evans, *Biographical Sketches of the Pioneer Preachers of Indiana* (Philadelphia, 1862), pp. 11–28, 29–41.

14. See Elizabeth K. Nottingham, *Methodism and the Indiana Proving Ground* (New York, 1941), pp. 18–32; William Warren Sweet, *Circuit-Rider Days Along the Ohio, Being the Journals of the Ohio Conference from its Organization in 1812 to 1826* (New York, 1923), pp. 43–62.

15. See Strickland, *Peter Cartwright*, pp. 29–33; John F. Wright, *Sketches of Life and Labors of James Quinn* (Cincinnati, 1851), pp. 112–14.

16. See Dale Morgan, ed., *Diaries and Letters of the California-Oregon Trail*, 2 vols. (Georgetown, Calif., 1963), pp. 238, 404; Harvey W. Scott, comp., *History of the Oregon Country by Harvey W. Scott Forty Years Editor of the Morning Oregonian*. 6 vols. (Cambridge, 1924), III, 235.

17. See Sweet, *Circuit-Rider Days Along the Ohio,* pp. 35–36; Sweet, *Revivalism in America,* pp. 112–39; Babcock, *Peck,* pp. 200–03.

18. Babcock, *Peck,* XXVI.

19. See Edwin Bryant, *What I Saw in California Being the Journal of a Tour* (New York, 1848), p. 80; Dale Morgan, ed., *Overland in 1846* (Journal of William E. Taylor), I, 125, 131, (Journal of George McKinstry), p. 213.

20. Thomas D. Clark, ed., *Gold Rush Diary, Being the Journal of Elisha Douglas Perkins on the Overland Trail in the Spring and Summer of 1849* (Lexington, 1967), p. 42.

21. Bryant, *What I Saw in California,* p. 85.

22. See Bernice Calmes Caudill, *Pioneers of Eastern Kentucky, Their Feuds and Settlements* (Cincinnati, 1969), pp. 14, 17; J. Winston Coleman, ed., *A Pictorial History of Kentucky* (Lexington, 1971), pp. 167, 182, 184; Hartley and Jean Alley, *Southern Indiana* (Bloomington, 1965), pp. 8, 31, 71; Wayne E. Keifer, *Rush County Indiana. A Study in Rural Settlement and Geography* (Bloomington, 1969), pp. 60, 111; *Oregon Native Son, 1900-1901,* II (June 1900), 72; *The Oregon Trail, The Missouri River to the Pacific Ocean* (Federal Writers Project) (New York, 1939), pp. 69, 180.

23. Bryant, *What I Saw in California,* p. 33.

24. Excellent examples of neighborliness and cooperation on the trails were revealed at the various fording places of rivers and streams and the steep inclines and declines of mountain passes. Nowhere was this fact more clearly demonstrated than the crossing of the Sierra Nevada Range above Truckee Lake. See Clark, *Perkins,* pp. 131–133.

25. Anderson, "Peopling a Frontier State," p. 172.

26. Clark, *Gold Rush Diary,* p. 6.

27. Kate Horn Dewey, Recollections of Catherine Margaret Haun, a Woman's Trip Across the Plains in 1849, original typescript.

28. Douglas C. McMurtrie, "Notes on Printing in Kentucky in the Eighteenth

Century, with Special Reference to the Work of Thomas Parvin, First Journeyman Printer in Kentucky," *The Filson Club History Quarterly,* X (October 1936), 261−280; William Henry Perrin, *The Pioneer Press of Kentucky* (Louisville, 1888), pp. 8−14.

29. W. H. Venable, *Beginnings of Literary Culture in the Ohio Valley, Historical and Biographical Sketches* (Cincinnati, 1891), pp. 36−43; Douglas C. McMurtrie, "Antecedent Experience in Kentucky of Williams Maxwell, Ohio's First Printer," *The Filson Club History Quarterly,* V (July 1931), 153−57.

30. George S. Cottman, "The Early Newspapers of Indiana," *The Indiana Magazine of History,* II (September 1906), 107−21; Douglas C. McMurtrie, "The Early Career of Joseph Charless, The First Printer in Missouri," *Missouri Historical Review,* XXVI (July 1932), 342−53.

31. McMurtrie, "The Early Career of Joseph Charless, The First Printer in Missouri," pp. 342−53; Mary Verhoeff, "Louisville's First Newspaper—the Farmer's Library," *Filson Club History Quarterly,* XXI (October 1947), 275−300; Minnie Organ, "History of the County Press of Missouri," *Missouri Historical Review,* IV (January 1910), 110−33.

32. George H. Himes, "History of the Press of Oregon, 1839−1850," *Quarterly of the Oregon Historical Society,* III (March to December 1902), 327−370; Harvey W. Scott, *History of the Oregon Country,* 6 vols. (Cambridge, 1924), I, 24, 309; V, 22−223.

33. The University of Kentucky Rare Books Collection has several copies of manuscript arithmatics and geometries.

34. See Pooley, *The Settlement of Illinois,* pp. 375−96, 440−60; Schroeder, "Spread of Settlement in Howard County, Missouri," pp. 1−37. Clearer evidence of the significance of the county in the westward movement lies in the literally hundreds of county histories, which in fact are pioneer chronicles.

35. The comparative county listings are taken from *A Statistical Abstract Supplement County and City Data Book 1956* (Washington, 1957).

36. Harvey W. Scott, *History of the Oregon Country,* quoting the *Morning Oregonian,* I, 243−244, 241.

CHAPTER 3

NEW HORIZONS ON THE OLD OREGON TRAIL

Merrill J. Mattes

The friendship between Merrill Mattes and Everett Dick began in 1946 when both were named to the Committee on Historic Sites of the Mississippi Valley Historical Association. Dick later became chairman, and Mattes secretary of that important committee. Their friendship ripened in the sixteen years after 1950 when Dick was teaching at Lincoln, Nebraska, and Mattes was serving as Regional Historian of the National Park Service in nearby Omaha. From that post Merrill Mattes advanced to become Chief of History and Historical Architecture in the Park Service's San Francisco regional office, and more recently Chief of the Office of Historic Preservation with headquarters at Denver. Despite his many duties, he has found time to write four excellent books and some sixty articles, most of them on the history of the West. His latest volume, <u>The Great Platte River Road</u> (1969), inspired the stimulating essay that he has contributed to this book, an essay picturing the rich returns still awaiting investigators who take a fresh look at the overland migrations of the mid-nineteenth century.

The story of the overland migrations that peopled the Pacific Coast in the mid-nineteenth century is one of the best publicized—and under-exploited—phases of American frontier social history. Such a statement may well shock even the most sophisticated students of the nation's westward expansion, for most would hold that the Old Oregon Trail is a threadbare subject for scholarly investigation, a road that has been traveled and retraveled to boredom.[1] That it does so only demonstrates the degree to which scholars and lay readers alike become victims of concept stereotypes which choke off scholarly inquiry. "The Old Oregon Trail" itself is just such a harmful stereotype.

There is much still to be learned about the westward trails and the people who used them. A start was made in *The Great Platte River Road,* which was the first attempt to assemble all available source material on the mid-nineteenth century overland migrations and to interpret that material comprehensively.[2] That work, made possible by a Nebraska centennial research grant, gave an indication of the insights that could be gained from a more massive research effort.

Although the Oregon, California, and related trails have been examined and recorded in much detail, many unsolved problems remain, such as the location of various cut-offs, campgrounds, and river crossings. The following examples of new geographical interpretations resulting from a massive and analytical use of sources are to be found in *The Great Platte River Road:* 1) Contrary to a widespread impression, there were not just the two crossings of the South Platte mentioned by most writers, but several such crossings, resulting in several alternative routes to Ash Hollow on the North Platte that have never been mentioned, much less mapped. 2) The fact that there were not one but two major routes from Nebraska City to Fort Kearny on the Platte was published for the first time. 3) Most surprising was the discovery of another fact about which all previous histories were silent—that there was a major overland travel route north from St. Joseph to Council Bluffs up the east side of the Missouri River, with a whole chain of optional crossings of the Missouri. Despite the obliteration of trail evidence by agriculture and construction projects, more fruitful work remains to be done in this department, with exciting implications for the enrichment of roadside interpretation as well as regional history textbooks.

While there has never been any mystery about the identity of the primary emigrant jumping-off places along the Missouri River—the Kansas City, St. Joseph, and Council Bluffs-Omaha vicinities—there had been no previous effort, based upon factual contemporary evidence, to identify *all* such places and evaluate their relative importance, by statistical method, from one year to the next, during the twenty-five year primary migration period, 1841-1866. In the Nebraska Centennial Project, which resulted in *The Great Platte River Road,* a fair start was made on this, with documented new conclusions. Among these were the primacy of St. Joseph in the peak years of California Gold Rush, the primacy of the Council Bluffs-Omaha area in later years, and the rather impressive extent to which now-obscure Weston in Missouri, Fort Leavenworth in Kansas, and Nebraska City and Plattsmouth in Nebraska figured in family migrations as well as in overland freighting. A new focus on localities clarified the relative importance and chronology of Independence and Westport in the Kansas City complex, and the existence of three primary crossings and trail convergences in the Council Bluffs-Omaha area. All of these new findings are necessarily tentative and much more remains to be done from more extensive examination of sources and topographic evidence. This intensive method was used with equally interesting result in analysis of the divergent approaches to Fort Kearny, as well as the relative use of both sides of the main Platte and its two Forks. Not unreasonably, one might expect some day the development of graphs and flow charts that would reveal, even more clearly than at present, the relative use of all overland trail variants, trunkline and branches, in time sequence.

No terminology is more stereotyped or confusing than that linked to overland route identification. There *was* an Oregon Trail and also a Mormon Trail, but from the usage of these terms today one is led to believe that the Oregon Trail was the main trail to all points westward the south side of the Platte, while the Mormon Trail was the primary route on the north side of the Platte. The fact is that there were major trails on both sides of the Platte River, from Fort Kearny to beyond the Forks, but it is grossly misleading to identify these as *the* Oregon Trail and *the* Mormon Trail. The Oregon Trail was an appropriate term only during the 1840s, when Oregon was the destination of most travelers. From 1849 on this was primarily the California Trail or, to use the contemporary term, the California Road, with feeder lines from Independence, St. Joseph, and old Fort Kearny. To be sure, throughout the Gold Rush period there were some who went to Oregon instead, but if it is true that about 90 percent of those bound for the west coast during the overall period went to California, why call their main route the Oregon Trail?

Similarly, the Mormons followed the north side of the Platte, shunning the "gentiles" on the south side, from 1847 onward. But in contemporary literature there is little reference to a Mormon Trail as such. Instead, the route on the north bank was commonly called the Council Bluffs Road, to differentiate it from the Independence-St. Joseph-Nebraska City road complex south of the Platte, which became the main California road. Contrary to the prevalent impression, except during the pioneering year 1847, the road on the north side was not actually dominated by Mormons. California- and even Oregon- bound emigrants thronged over this road in the early 1850s by the tens of thousands, and later it was the primary route to Montana gold fields. Mormon historians and publicists are highly articulate, and the Mormon saga has rightly captivated the public imagination. But it is a mistake to ignore the vast and preponderant number of non-Mormons who followed the north bank, or to ignore the fact, which emerges from the dispassionate examination of hundreds of contemporary journals, that during the migrations themselves this was *not* "the Mormon Trail." It was "the Council Bluffs Road."

Awareness of the way this confused and distorted terminology obscured the subject led me to develop the concept of a "Great

Platte River Road." This concept emphasizes the essential homogeneity of the Platte River Valley as a primary central route overland during a period of several decades, with parallel lanes on either side of the river heading west, and with several well-defined tributary trails from the Missouri River to the east. The name for the Platte route changed frequently, but it was always the same basic route.

Closely related to the matter of routes, and far less clear than the identity of home-town origins or jumping-off places, is the identity of ultimate destinations. The *Great Platte River Road* discovered some new information about origins and initial routes, but begged the question of destinations by simply suspending the plot in midair, at Fort Laramie. A serious graphical study of just where people ended their continental journey has never been done. If in California, just where in California? What proportion from one year to the next went to California, Oregon, Utah, or Montana? What number came by boat around the Horn, or by Mexico, or the Isthmus of Panama rather than overland? How many, having reached their destination, became disillusioned and returned? How many Oregonians subsequently changed their minds and went south to California, or vice versa? Obviously, research in many sources other than overland accounts themselves will be necessary to answer these questions, but the answers will be important; they will do much to illuminate early state and local history in the Far West.

This writer, in *The Great Platte River Road,* rashly attempted to firm up travel figures or floating population figures for each of the twenty-five years involved (those related to travel up the main Platte, via Fort Kearny, regardless of subsequent destination). These figures represent the best possible estimates based on all data available, including internal evidence of the journals, scattered reports of the official head counts at Forts Kearny and Laramie, and general impressions from circumstances which varied from one travel season to the next. Except for the Oregon migrations of the middle 1840s and the peak California Gold Rush years, 1849–1852, there is little published evidence as to the seasonal trail populations; this information gap is conspicuous in regard to the period 1853—1866, making guesswork unavoidable in calculations for those years. The overall twenty-five year figure, 350,000, was made intentionally conservative to avoid exaggeration. Ezra Meeker, an 1852 participant, guessed a gross figure of 500,000 for that approximate period, apparently being more generous as to the Colorado and Montana phases.[3] Establishing whether either of these figures is reasonably accurate is another ideal project for some ambitious researcher. Even then the task cannot be completed until someone determines the number of Pacific Coast arrivals by boat and attempts to correlate both overland and oversea migration figures with the earlier California and Oregon populations. In addition, some kind of a hypothesis would have to be made about birth rates en route as well as in established settlements of the Far West.

Evaluation of a statistical method I used in *The Great Platte River Road* might also be a fruitful line of inquiry. Overland journals offer occasional evidence of contemporary numbers, either arithmetical or impressionistic; they also suggest, in turn, the proportionate number in a given year who kept such records. Witness the phenomenon of one journal of record to every 150 travelers in 1849 versus one to every 500 or so in the 1860s. How can one account for this discrepancy? Is it valid to assume some correlation between the activities of the relatively few known journalists and those of the much larger number of unknown non-journalists? For example, I developed a rising and declining curve on the density of covered wagon traffic passing Fort Kearny in 1849, based upon the arrival dates of the journal-keepers. Although in this case, other evidence, such as reports or entries in the Fort Kearny register, reinforced the statistical conclusion, the method could be applied to other areas of inquiry, and subjected to more rigid controls. If this correlative method is valid, the data, perhaps subjected to computer analysis, could confirm or modify all kinds of stereotyped generalizations, such as mortality statistics. Another application would be compiled profile descriptions of certain geographic or cultural features or trailside events, serving to place in perspective events that tended to become distorted by the passage of time, just as the eyewitness account of a crime today becomes distorted after it is verbally relayed through successive versions. This method was used in the *The Great Platte River Road* to convey emigrant impressions of notable landmarks, such as Chimney Rock and Ash Hollow, and experiences of encountering buffalo herds and traversing major river crossings.

There are numerous examples of distortion through unthinking repetition, or prejudiced thinking, or the simple romantic urge to embellish a good story. A fair example would be the prevalence of two conflicting concepts about the occurrence of Indian attacks on wagon trains. The more traditional view, reflected in literature and entertainment, is that Indian attacks were commonplace. When some scholars pointed out that Indian attacks were not all that common, the converse notion of a peaceful Way West, with Indians lending local color only, gained currency. One familiar with the documentable facts would be particularly wary of such generalizations. Some wagon trains were attacked, in some places more than others, and in some years more than others. Other wagon trains went through without ever seeing an Indian. Most wagon trains did encounter trailside Indians who, while not hostile, were a nuisance as thieves and beggars. Again, the truth will not be known until all the evidence has been examined. It will be a salubrious influence if historians can catalog all known instances of Indian friendship, or at least peaceableness, as well as instances of Indian hostility, and put things, racially, in proportion.

Another fascinating subject that has been little researched is the number of blacks who went West. There were black emigrants, just as there were black Indian-fighters, cowboys, and homesteaders. While I have not encountered an overland journal written by a known black, some white journals, as well as contemporary newspapers of that period do give some idea of how many blacks there were in border towns, along the trails, and at the mines.

The romantic approach to the social history of the frontier West must yield to scientific studies based upon careful objective analysis of maximum, rather than random, data. Such an approach applied to the sociology of the overland migrations, as well as their geography and nomenclature, will result in the emergence of whole new scholarly vistas. When new light is thrown on what actually happened, the migration story is enriched, the infinite variety of human nature gains a new time perspective, and a paradox becomes apparent. There was no lack of bona fide romance as well as bona fide tragedy, comedy, monotony, excitement, misery, and glory in the composite phenomenon of the overland experience. Documentable realities of the Western American frontier have an epic quality, without need for fictional adornment.

The imposing array of overland journals, reports and reminiscences identified in *The Great Platte River Road* bibliography is not merely a body of source materials to be combed for data.[4] It is also a branch of American folk literature that has not been sufficiently recognized for its eye-witness freshness, its revelation of contemporary customs, attitudes, and events, and its rich store of insights into the human psyche, particularly under strange conditions, and under abnormal stress.[5]

These sources vary greatly in literacy, style, length, and intrinsic values, both literary and historic. Admittedly, some are so sparse, so stingy with information, that they constitute little more than trip logs, but even these cold-blooded mileage-counters occasionally betray a flash of humanity, in noting accidents, births, or deaths. Some reflect limited schooling, random spelling, confused expression and poor penmanship, making interpretation difficult. Others are self-consciously literate and expansive, making it difficult sometimes to distinguish between fact and fancy. However, most journalists show good powers of observation and some degree of awareness of being caught up in one of the great adventures of mankind. A careful reading and re-reading of these honest testaments will result in the emergence of fresh facts not only concerning the physical elements of the journey but concerning contemporary customs, beliefs, methods, practices and techniques. Close examination of these journals also reveals attitudes, prejudices, and psychological factors of keen interest to a generation bent on reevaluating the human equation.

We are not concerned here primarily with physical equipment, traveling and camping gear, provisions, cargo, and dress, except to note in passing that a host of misconceptions must be modified when the full range of trail literature is systematically explored. The preponderant evidence is, for example, that the large boat-shaped Conestoga-type wagon of song and story was used by freighting outfits but rarely by emigrant groups. The famed prairie schooner, in fact, was relatively short, flat-bottomed, and purely functional. There is much more to be learned about the relative numbers and merits of oxen, mules, and horses used to draw the wagons, and about the design and frequent trailside modification of wagonbeds, bows, wheels, harness, and accessories. Similarly there is much to learn about personal equipment, primarily firearms, axes, knives, and other weapons, as well as wagon and trenching tools. Of even greater interest than pots, pans, utensils, stoves, and the preciousness of matches is the question of food—provisions brought from the border towns, as well as buffalo and other items foraged en route. A composite picture of these physical components has begun to emerge, but any one of them could be pursued much more exhaustively.

More research could also be done on the wagon trains themselves. One of the most fascinating aspects of the ephemeral wagon train culture was the more or less spontaneous process of "getting organized." Sometimes sizable contingents from back home were fully regimented to begin with, complete with a hierarchy of officers, roster of members, voting qualifications, company insignia, and even uniforms. Sometimes individual outfits would rally around a selected or self-chosen leader at one of the border towns. Sometimes rugged independent types who disdained organization to start with would hurriedly organize or would attach themselves to other outfits, when they received rumors of the first Indian scare.

The size of the organized trains or companies varied from two to more than one hundred, but hard experience taught the covered wagon travelers that there was an optimum number of wagons—each representing a small family group or a bachelor group—that could be managed effectively, both from the standpoint of effective communication by shouting or bugle calls, and from the standpoint of just what constituted psychologically a viable human community. One wagon alone was a microcosm too confined for comfort; too many wagons became a traveling metropolis with attendant evils of traffic congestion, general bedlam, and what might be called overnight urban sprawl. Research to date suggests that the optimum number of wagon units would range from as few as six to not more than twenty, with ten or twelve as the golden mean.

While some trains organized and later disorganized with no formality whatever, the general rule seemed to be that organization was formalized in some manner, often with a sworn and sealed document, sometimes described as a constitution, complete with by-laws. Such incorporations were more apt to obtain with groups homogenized by origin. In any event, a more thorough systematic study of wagon train organization promises to be among the more fruitful fields of study, and would add a new chapter in the history of the American democratic process.

Equally engaging would be a more intensive study of the evolving and shifting patterns of cross-country travel, including departure dates, daily mileage averages and maximums, and lapsed time between jumping-off places and ultimate destinations, as well as travel time between various intermediate key points, such as Fort Kearny, Fort Laramie, and Salt Lake City. Investigators should reconstruct a profile of experiences in daily travel, with the incidence of single, parallel and multiple lanes, by-passes, traffic bottlenecks, and hourly schedules for starts, rest stops, and camp stops. Incidental to this is the intriguing matter of wagon train corrals, the various types of such formations, the frequency of their occurrence, and their comparative utility. Finally, there is a whole new expanding horizon on the

New Horizons on the Old Oregon Trail

subject of emigrant camping practices and procedures under conditions which became gradually tougher on the slow progression from plains to mountain and desert. This includes such matters as cooking facilities and methods, sleeping arrangements, guard duty, reveille, and campfire entertainment. Some scholarly inquiry has begun on these subjects, and many assumptions about them have been made by fiction writers, but the Nebraska Centennial Project was able to turn up voluminous data and project their scope and depth for more thorough treatment.

While items of equipment and the minutiae of trailside routine would intrigue some, others might find more relevant to modern studies the social science of the covered wagon migrations. These would include aspects of the psychology of the individual emigrant, as well as "covered wagon sociology," or what might be considered the patterns of emigrant group behavior.

Although Oregon fever, gold fever, wanderlust, escape from the law, patriotism, economic recession, and unemployment are frequently cited among the motives which propelled people on their epic ordeal, no one has ever systematically consulted the emigrant journals on this subject. Sometimes journalists are specific about this, sometimes silent, and of course the avowed motives may not always be the basic ones. Nevertheless, there is sufficient source material on this subject for a major study.

The search for motives leads one to curiosity about a larger question, which might be called emigrant character. Granted that emigrants collectively had a mixture of motives and represented a wide diversity of character types, a study of the voluminous written record suggests that some character traits predominated. Whether or not a cross-section of the journalists accurately represents a cross-section of emigrants as a whole, the journalists' writings frequently reveal the character of fellow travelers. While a profile of the composite emigrant may be of dubious worth, recognition of the elements that appear in the makeup of the successful emigrant, the one who made it to his goal, may help to illuminate traits and attitudes that might be helpful today if America is to survive new challenges.

Some aspects of the traveler's character are already known. First, no one tackled "the elephant" (the California Argonauts' term for hazards of the Trail) if he was perfectly content with his lot back home. So there were elements of discontent on the one hand, and unquenchable optimism on the other. Complacency was not an emigrant hallmark; an inner drive to change one's life condition was always present. What emerges as the real key to emigrant character, however, was the discovery of inner reservoirs of courage when "the elephant" went on a rampage and misfortune befell. A succession of trail hazards, hardships, and heartaches forged the character of our emigrant ancestors. Those who emerged from this crucible—and this included all who did not die en route and all who did not constitute the despised "turnarounds"—were a decided majority, on the order of 80 per cent or more, and it was their character that laid the foundations of the American West.

It is scarcely possible to psychoanalyze people who have been dead for a century, but one clue to the high survival rate may be discerned. This was the fundamentalist religious outlook of the mid-nineteenth century, an undergirding faith in God and His ultimate goodness, that kept one from sinking in the Slough of Despond. A large percentage of covered wagon travelers affirmed their religious bent, not in the form of theological niceties, but in a rock-ribbed conviction that their glorious travel plan was part of their divine destiny.

A concomitant trait was an ingrained respect for authority and a stern Anglo-Saxon sense of justice. The grueling hardships of the Trail placed a strain on authoritarian relationships in the wagon trains, giving rise to a succession of reorganizations. Although few of the original organizations survived intact all the way to the Willamette or the Sacramento, and many disintegrated altogether, the principle of social cohesion was there.

A more vivid manifestation of the penchant for a manageable society was the emigrant reaction to trailside crime. One of the findings of the Nebraska Centennial Project, though with admittedly tentative conclusions, was the nature and extent of criminal behavior in wagon train society. Generally speaking, while rowdiness and misbehavior characterized some of the border settlements where emigrants congregated, there is surprisingly little evidence of petty crimes among the emigrant population. On the other hand, there is abundant evidence of mayhem and homicide. Crimes of passion or psychopathic violence which abound in frontier fiction are seldom encountered in Trail literature. Instead crimes of record were much more often attributable to what might be called wagon fever, quarrels resulting from too-close or too-long associations under often severe conditions that stretched nerves taut. This little-known aspect of the migration deserves deeper study. Whatever the cause, and no matter how extenuating the circumstances, few of the crimes went unacquitted. When a murder took place, the murderer was usually placed on trial by a quickly impaneled jury of his peers. More often than not he was found guilty, with no chance of appeal, and executed on the spot, usually by hanging from a tree if handy, or from two elevated wagon tongues tied together, if on the treeless plains.

The emigrant character was severely tested by other, sometimes melodramatic, adversities—cattle stampedes, buffalo stampedes or blockades, occasional devastating storms, crossings of rivers at flood stage, and the painful necessity of making logistical adjustments, such as shooting wornout draft animals, drastically reducing wagon overloads by jettisoning precious cargo, and, if necessary, abandoning wagons and resorting of pack trains.

The accident rate of the Great Migration was appalling, with hundreds of fatalities recorded. The principal causes were careless handling of firearms, drownings, getting run over by wagon wheels or kicked by animals. Of course, the major cause of trailside deaths was disease, everything from measles and mumps to appendicitis, dysentery and pneumonia; the worst killer was the Asiatic cholera or bubonic plague, which was particularly devastating in the peak migration years 1849-1852. Material on this subject is abundant, and much enriched by the surprisingly large number of emigrant physicians and Army post surgeons who kept journals. Much more study and correlation of data is needed about the health, public hygiene, illness, and mortality factors of the migrations.

Equally interesting to social historians as well as anthropologists are the trailside burial customs, a subject about which the trail literature is eloquent. When deaths occurred in the early stages of the migration, funerals were apt to be formally traditional. Services were respectful, other activities were suspended, coffins were buried at the orthodox depth, and graves were suitably marked. Under increasingly severe trail conditions and the pressure of time as the trains crawled westward, the traditional last rites were discarded in favor of hurried burials with little or no ceremony, and token grave-digging that resulted in burials so shallow as to attract ravenous wolves and coyotes. Markers too became expendable. This, coupled with the propensity of modern man to change the landscape, has consigned all but a few emigrant graves to oblivion. Nevertheless, there is an abundant record of just who died when and where that has never been tabulated.

Adversities multiplied on the way west, sometimes culminating in the extremities of exposure, starvation and—at least in the case of the Donner party—cannibalism. While the incidents of hardship are a matter of commonplace record, clear evidence of the psychological reactions of those who suffered and endured requires more searching and appraisal. Journals show the reactions of some; for the most part, however, the reactions of the travelers can be ascertained only by inference. While trail-traumas or the emigrant psyche may seem questionable areas of inquiry for fact-oriented historians, and more suitable for treatment by imaginative novelists, sensitive social historians can make a contribution here by systematizing and interpreting such data as do exist.

It is worth noting that overland trail literature yields much more evidence of the female psyche than the male. Whether or not women are constitutionally "more emotional" than men, women journalists frequently gave vent to their feelings on all kinds of matters, not only those of major concern such as life, death and destiny, but also day-to-day matters, such as their relations with other people, particularly those who rubbed them the wrong way, like despotic wagon bosses or the authors of inaccurate guide-books. They also expressed themselves strongly on the curiosities of the Plains—the pungent buffalo chips, the stringy buffalo meat, the fearsome phenomenon of the panting, bellowing, earth-shaking buffalo herds on the move, and hunters who would wastefully exterminate these creatures. In contrast, masculine writers were usually inhibited by the prevailing code of stoicism.

Since the women who kept journals reveal so much of the inward soul as well as the objective world, it is a pity there were not more of them. The Centennial Project identified approximately sixty women out of some 750 journal writers. This leaves us with a tentative ratio of one female for every twelve male recorders, or only one female recorder for every 60,000 emigrants. This is clearly not a fair cross-section, but it must be accepted until more trail diaries emerge.

The female journalists were for the most part superior observers and recorders, and many had literary talent. The unpublished journals of Helen Carpenter, Ada Millington, and Martha Missouri Moore, and the published journals of Rebecca Ketcham, Lucy Cooke, Amelia Knight, Lavinia Porter, Lodisa Frizzell, and Margaret Frink,[6] although enjoying no fame whatsoever, are among the prime documents of the overland migrations. Except for samplings of their riches in *In The Wake of the Prairie Schooner* and *The Great Platte River Road* they await study and recognition. A more thorough study of this literature will enable us to construct a much better data profile of the women during the migration. Now we have only a fair impression of certain fascinating facets—the ratio of women to men, pre-marital moral standards, marriages, births, fashions, and the problem of white women in Indian territory.

We do know, for instance, that while nationally the ratio of women to men was approximately one to one, on the Oregon-California Trail in 1849, according to available evidence, the ratio was one woman to every fifty men. In later stages of the California fever women evidently appeared in higher percentages, presumably because they were tired of staying at home while the menfolk were having high adventure. In the Oregon phase of the 1840s and Montana phase of the 1860s family groups predominated, with women and children in more normal proportion. In 1847 the Mormons left all women and children at home; thereafter Mormon women dominated the trail scene in a polygamous society. These and other sociological phenomena of family and non-family groupings under abnormal frontier conditions are depths which have never been adequately plumbed.

True romance on the Oregon-California Trail is difficult to document. Instances of undying devotion to the girl back home are ascertainable, as well as marriages en route. There are also certified cases of honor violated and adultery, or dishonor discovered, but these are a rarity, again at least as far as the record has been studied. From all available evidence the high moral standards that prevailed, at least ostensibly, in mid-nineteenth century settled America also prevailed on the old Oregon–California Trail. Chastity before marriage and fidelity after marriage were the norms. Violations were either infrequent or unrecorded. Women once won were taken for granted as household (or covered wagon) adjuncts.

Much research remains to be done on courtship customs and trailside fashions. While we can only surmise as to the former, two salient facts emerge as to the latter. First, women often started their epic journey in garb totally unsuited to trail conditions, with finery, long trailing skirts, layers of undergarments, and high shoes. Second, trail conditions dictated drastic changes, with resultant modifications—elimination of non-essentials, comfortable shoes, skirts deliberately shortened, and later the adoption of bloomers, or simplified pantaloons. When the question became one of survival in a hostile environment love might languish but the species had to adapt physically or expire. Modesty, if not virtue, ceased to be a moral absolute during the California Gold Rush.

There is much yet to be gained from further study of the Westward trails, if scholars will accept the challenge and explore the subject I have mentioned only briefly here.

NOTES

Treatments of the subject in recent historical writing include

1. W. J. Ghent, *The Road to Oregon* (New York, 1929); George R. Stewart, *The California Trail* (New York, 1962); Archer Butler Hulbert, *The Forty-Niners* (Boston, 1931); Irene D. Paden, *In The Wake of the Prairie Schooner* (New York, 1944); and Dale L. Morgan, ed., *The Overland Diary of James A. Prichard from Kentucky to California in 1849* (Denver, 1959). There are also a large number of editions of overland journals. Among superior examples of published journals are the following: G. W. Read and R. Gaines, eds., *Gold Rush: The Journals, Drawings, and other Papers of J. Goldsborough Bruff,* 2 vols. (New York, 1944); Thomas D. Clark, ed., *Gold Rush Diary: The Journal of Elisha Douglass Perkins, 1849* (Lexington, 1967); and R. W. and M. L. Settle, eds., *Overland Days to Montana in 1865: The Diary of Sarah Raymond and The Journal of Dr. Waid Howard* (Glendale, 1971).

2. Merrill J. Mattes, *The Great Platte River Road: The Covered Wagon Mainline via Fort Kearny to Fort Laramie* (Lincoln, 1969).

3. Ezra Meeker and Howard R. Driggs, *Covered Wagon Centennial and Ox-Team Days* (New York, 1931), pp. 49–50.

4. Mattes, *Great Platte River Road,* pp. 523–71.

5. Some of the well-known journals and government reports include Francis Parkman, *The Oregon Trail* (New York, 1946); John C. Fremont, *Report of the Exploring Expedition to the Rocky Mountains* (Washington, D.C., 1945); Howard Stansbury, *Exploration and Survey of the Great Salt Lake of Utah* (Philadelphia, 1852); Richard F. Burton, *The City of the Saints* (New York, 1862); John Minto, "Reminiscences," *Oregon Historical Quarterly,* II (June 1901), 119–67; Joel Palmer, *Journal of Travels to the Rocky Mountains* (Cincinnati, 1847); Edwin Bryant, *What I Saw in California* (New York, 1849); Isaac J. Wistar, *Autobiography, 1827-1905 (New York, 1937); William Clayton, Journal* (Salt Lake City, 1921).

6. Helen Carpenter, "A Trip Across the Plains," 1856 ms. in the Huntington Library, San Marino, California; Ada Millington, "Journal Kept While Crossing the Plains," photostat of 1862 ms. at Bancroft Library, Berkeley, California; Martha Missouri Moore, Journal of 1859, *typescript,* Missouri Historical Society, St. Louis; Rebecca Ketcham, "From Ithaca to Clatsop Plains, 1853," *Oregon Historical Quarterly,* LXII (September 1961), 237–87; (December 1961),

337–402; Lucy R. Cooke, *Crossing the Plains* (Modesto, Calif., 1923); Amelia S. Knight, *Transactions, Oregon Pioneer Association* (1928), 38–53; Lavinia Porter, *By Ox Team to California* (Oakland, 1910); Lodisa Frizzell, *Across the Plains to California* (New York, 1915); Margaret A. Frink, *Journal of a Party of California Gold Seekers* (Oakland, 1897).

CHAPTER 4

PIONEER LIFE ON THE PLAINS AND IN THE MINES:

A Comparison

W. Turrentine Jackson

W. Turrentine Jackson, for many years professor of history at the University of California at Davis, has long been in the vanguard of historians seeking meaning for the present by studying the frontier past. In his several books, and notably in The Enterprising Scot: Investors in the American West after 1873 *(1968), he has applied his extensive knowledge of economic theory to the problem of investment in underdeveloped areas, a subject as timely today as in the nineteenth century. Currently he is investigating British and Scottish investment in the mines of Australia. "Turpie" Jackson and Everett Dick have been fellow committee-members and good friends for many years. In the pages that follow Professor Jackson uses* The Sod-House Frontier *as the basis for a comparative study of social development in mining and farming communities. The result is an essay that broadens our knowledge of the frontier process and provides entertaining reading.*

With the publication of *The Sod-House Frontier* in 1937, Everett Dick provided his fellow-historians with not only a delightfully informative chronicle of life on the Great Plains but with the basic information necessary for delineating the distinctive characteristics of any new, rapidly developing, unstable region. This he accomplished partly by devising the techniques useful in analyzing developing societies, partly by amassing an impressive quantity of data that illuminated virtually every aspect of the form of pioneer life he was studying. *The Sod-House Frontier,* in other words, describes frontier living in elaborate detail from any number of vantage points. How typical of the frontier process in other regions was the area on which Everett Dick focused his attention—the agricultural frontier of the Great Plains? This question may be partially answered by comparing life on the plains with life in the mining camps of the Far West, beginning with a comparative survey of the westward migration in each case, continuing with the settlement and exploitation of economic resources, and concluding with the emergence of social and economic institutions that blended into the national society.

Certainly the migration patterns differed more in degree than in kind. Most settlers seeking new homes on the Plains journeyed by riverboat to the Missouri towns, and from there overland by wagon, carrying their meager belongings with them. Comparatively speaking, their slow journey covered only a short distance. The rush of the miners to California, however, was characterized by speed, confusion, and diversity of method and routes traveled. A decade later, in the rush of the Fifty-Niners to the Comstock Lode, many of those same men hurried eastward across the Sierra Nevada on horseback or on foot to reach the promising Washoe mines. Simultaneously, would-be prospectors hurried up the tributaries of the Missouri in wagons, pushing wheel-carts, riding horseback, or on foot, all heading for the central Rockies with a single purpose in mind, "Pike's Peak or Bust." Scarcely had they arrived before some men organized or joined pack trains to push northward to the newer discoveries along the Snake River tributaries in Idaho or across the Divide into Montana.

Having reached their destinations, farmers and miners alike had one goal—to take possession of the land. The first arrivals

Pioneer Life on the Plains and in the Mines

in the Plains filed pre-emption claims to their acreage. Once the land surveyor had done his work, those arriving after 1862 could file for a homestead or purchase acreage from the government. Miners, on the other hand, were squatters on the public domain and therefore had to ignore the laws that prohibited granting fee simple title to mineral lands. They organized mining districts establishing the rules whereby their claims could be guaranteed and their rights protected by community agreement. Both in purpose and in methods, the countless mining districts scattered throughout the Far West were similar to the Claims Clubs of the Plains where pre-emptors had organized to assure the right to purchase claims for the minimum price once they had been surveyed and placed on the market. When the frontiersman, be he farmer or miner, was in possession of his land he knew that two requirements, work and improvement, were essential to maintain his claim.

Indian titles to the lands of Kansas, Nebraska, and the Dakotas usually had been cleared before the farmers attempted to break the sod. In contrast, the impatient miners too often violated the rights of Indians by overrunning their most cherished and sacred domains, in the foothills of the California Sierra, along the Clearwater Fork of the Snake River, in the Black Hills of South Dakota. The movement of large numbers of people into western areas for farming and mining had devastating effects on the Indian cultures in their paths. Most widely known are the bloody encounters between whites and Indians in the latter nineteenth century; far more serious was the impact on traditional Indian economies and life styles.

Decimation of buffalo herds meant more than the reduction of the basic source of housing, food, and clothing. The buffalo hunt was the focal point of many ceremonials, including ritual observance of the transition from youth to manhood, and when the animals were no longer readily available great damage was done to both the individual and society. Stripping the forests for mining timbers and for fuel to raise and process ore destroyed many sources of pine nuts for the Indians. For people living off the land, the increased numbers of human beings per square mile meant that subsistence became more difficult. Even where there was no actual contact between whites and Indians, the oxen, cattle, sheep, or pigs of the settlers consumed grasses and seeds, or acorns from the oaks on the hillsides of California, thus depleting the food supply. In the Plains area Indians were placed on reservations, and the federal government provided subsistence to replace what had been destroyed. In other regions, notably the Great Basin, Indians adapted themselves to the developing farming and cattle enterprises by becoming day laborers and moving with the harvests, much as they had done in earlier times. While for some the adjustment was relatively easy, too often the contact of cultures brought on disorganization, disintegration, disease, and death. Most probably felt much as the Sioux doctor, Charles Eastman (Ohiyesa), when he moved from Canada into the United States and contacted white men for the first time in the 1880s: "I felt as if I were dead and traveling to the Spirit Land; for now all my old ideas were to give place to new ones, and my life was to be entirely different from that of the past."[1]

The movement of population westward occurred more swiftly than either Indians or Easterners could really comprehend. Scarcely had the land been broken in Kansas and Nebraska before town site speculators were at work selecting feasible locations for potential supply towns or county seats, optimistically drawing plans, and erecting a single building, usually a hotel, for display purposes. Just as rapidly, every western mining district had its supply town where food, clothing, and entertainment could be obtained. If the mines showed promise, other single-purpose centers for milling or smelting sprang up. One certain way for a town to achieve permanence was to become a political capital. Once county government replaced or assimilated the mining districts, every community fought bitterly to be named county seat. As economic fortunes waxed or waned when the district's mines were in bonanza or borrasca, so did the possibility of holding the county government. Even territorial capitals followed the miners when a more promising district developed, as in the classic case of Montana, whose capital was first Bannock, then Virginia City, and finally Helena.

Nature frowned on the pioneer whether he was plowing the field, working a mineral claim, or residing in town. Out on the Plains

> in the spring, floods menaced the cabin or dugout built too close to the stream; in summer, drought and hot winds withered the promising crop, and insects everywhere took a terrible toll of the scanty cultivated acres, in the autumn, the prairie fires swept furiously across the plains, jumping creeks and sweeping everything before them, destroying crops, fuel, food for man and beast, homes, and even whole towns; in the winter came the dreaded blizzards and unbearable sub-zero temperature.[2]

The miner's life was equally strenuous and uncertain. A placer miner working the streams of California in spring and summer often stood in near freezing water while the sun scorched the exposed portions of his body. The spontaneous growth of many camps also meant inadequate housing against the harsher elements of the mountain climates at higher elevations. The typical mining camp or town burned to the ground twice, if not thrice. Nature made life arduous, but miners magnified its hazards by destroying the natural fabric of the land.

During the pioneer period, the Plains farmer cherished his holdings; he often overextended himself by plowing more land than he could adequately cultivate, or breaking the natural sod in arid areas that never should have been put to the plow, but he was not a willful exploiter of the natural environment. Inadvertently he made the possibility of floods greater and crop production lower in marginal areas that, once abandoned, became dustbowls. Miners, on the other hand, perhaps more than any other frontier group, destroyed the natural environment. A modern writer has identified "five relentless horsemen of every mining apocalypse: greed, waste, hardship, breakdown, and environmental butchery."[3] Miners cut timber to shore up their mines and to generate steam for hoists and other apparatus until entire hillsides were denuded. They diverted streams from their beds to wash the river gravels. They impounded water with dams, releasing it in torrents and under pressure in hydraulic operations that washed down mountain sides and left barren fields of rock and debris. They polluted the streams with wastes from their mills, and the air with smoke from their smelters. Everything was used for the immediate need with no thought for the future.

In seeking shelter as new arrivals in a strange environment, both farmer and miner were compelled to utilize the resources that nature had provided. The Plains pioneer sought a hill or a ravine in the otherwise flat terrain and burrowed a dugout in its side. The family lived in the wagon box while the farmer used the running gear to haul the poles, brush, and grass—if he was fortunate enough to scrounge them—needed to improve the roof or extend the entry. Soon the family graduated to the sod house built of three-foot bricks cut with a spade from the ground covering. The major task was constructing the roof, which had to be braced and framed with logs and covered with branches capable of holding the sod, and both were in limited supply. These structures provided minimal light and air for ventilation, and their roofs dripped mud in wet weather, but they were cool in summer and warm in winter. Furniture and household equipment was crude and sparse, usually including stove, bed, cupboard, table, and chairs.

Housekeeping for the women was arduous beyond belief, but they persevered in spite of a lonely, monotonous, and discouraging life, the drabness of their homes, the lack of companionship of other adult women, and demanding children. They remained behind in an isolated sod house for days or weeks, while the husband went to the mill or to town to market the crop, deal with business matters, or secure sustenance for the family. However, the woman's position on the Plains was legally, educationally, and socially more advanced than it was in the East.

The housing and family life associated with the Plains frontier was duplicated, with variations, on the mining frontier. Miners in every district left records of "coyote hole" habitations seized from animals or burrowed by the occupants, of brush lean-tos, and of temporary tent-homes of canvas, blankets, and clothing. Miners repeatedly used sod or mud to chink the holes and construct the roofs of their first brush homes. On both frontiers, residents strove to build frame houses as a symbol of stability, although initially many of these structures might have been aptly described as "shanties." At times the ill-fitting boards were lined on the inside with newspapers or tar paper by the enterprising farmer's wife; the remains of many mining ghost towns reveal that the miners, or their wives, did likewise.

Women were not uncommon on the mining frontier. The first to come were chiefly entertainers or prostitutes, who congregated in the camps and were recognized as sex symbols, but as the various claims were consolidated and a labor force was employed to work both mines and processing plants, the camps became permanent and an ever-increasing number of workers were married men. Their wives, like those on the Plains, had manifold duties and because here, too, women were scarce, they enjoyed greater political participation and opportunity to encourage cultural institutions than their eastern counterparts.

The Plains farmer used the materials at hand for fuel—buffalo chips, hay, or corn when the prices were low. In most instances, fuel was not as great a problem in the mining districts because forests were nearby. The limited water supply was always a problem on the Plains and a great deal of time, expense, and ingenuity was consumed in digging deep wells to tap underground sources and constructing windmills to pump the supply to the surface. An adequate water supply was just as essential to the miner as the farmer, for every known method of obtaining precious metal was dependent, directly or indirectly, upon water. Miners normally tapped a flowing stream at the highest possible elevation, then constructed elaborate and lengthy ditches to convey the water to the site where it was needed, usually a quartz deposit or a processing mill. Many quickly learned that economic success could be achieved as easily by organizing a ditch company to control and deliver water as by working a mining claim.

A proven and accessible water supply was as essential for the survival of the farming community or mining camp as it was for individual farmers or miners. In the Plains a pump was operated by a windmill to keep the public tank full for thirsty stock. Springs or lakes were tapped for the water supply in the mining camp. Sometimes elaborate pumping equipment was required to increase the pressure created by gravity to carry water across a ridge or up a mountainside into town. The community water tank for fire protection had highest priority, followed by the needs of mills and other business establishments, while a pipe line system serving residents was a luxury.

Because subsistence on the newly and rapidly developing frontiers was precarious, diets were usually limited, monotonous, unappetizing, and often unhealthful. The prospector survived on staples of flour, bacon, beans, and coffee, with rare additions of sugar or dried fruit. On both frontiers men hunted to provide a meat supply. Buffalo, deer, elk, turkeys, raccoons, and prairie chickens were available on the Plains. In the mining country deer and an occasional bear were killed; the butchering of a cow driven into any camp was a major event. If a surplus of meat existed, men on both frontiers preserved it by drying or jerking.

Clothing was also a problem. Overcoats and boots for the farmer's family often came from Army surplus. Trousers were made of duck, jeans, and denim; women wore calico sunbonnets and dresses of homespun linsey-woolsey. Children and adults went barefoot as much of the year as the weather permitted. This same simplicity and informality of dress pervaded the mining camp. Over-size, ill-fitting boots—purchased that way to allow for shrinkage when wet, as they were most of the time—woolen underwear and trousers, a flannel shirt, and a beaten, slouch hat most often made up the working outfit of the miner.

Travel was inevitably a hardship on any frontier. In the initial stages of settlement there were no roads for the Plains farmer and he had to break his own wagon trail to the nearest town or mill, frequently seventy to a hundred miles distant, or to the railhead when shipping grain. Rivers had to be forded because there were no bridges or ferries. In contrast, the maintenance of transportation and communication was early recognized as essential to the survival of the mining camp. Stagecoaches brought not only potential residents, but businessmen, entertainers, capitalists, and mining experts. They also brought in the express, including mail from relatives and friends, business and legal documents, and carried away the precious gold and silver consigned to the care of the express company. Necessary goods, ordered by the town's merchants, were delivered by wagon freighters. Any disruption of the service meant a supply shortage, inflationary prices, and in time, panic. Events in Denver in 1864 when the Indians cut the supply lines on the Plains and in Idaho City during the "bread riots" in the winter of 1864–1865 indicated clearly what could happen when transportation was disrupted. Stage stations on routes between the outlying mining camps and major towns, where food and sometimes lodging could be obtained, served as centers of frontier hospitality, and occasionally ranching operations and other towns developed around them. Their counterparts on the sod house frontier were known as road ranches.

The coming of the railroad revolutionized life on all western frontiers. On the Plains it hastened settlement by bringing in large numbers of immigrants and promoting the sale of lands granted the builders by the government to encourage construction. New town sites were promoted along the right-of-way and once-flourishing communities died as a result of being by-passed by the rails. Railroad services became essential to competitive marketing, and the charge for delivering and storing grain largely determined the economic well-being of the farmer and his family. The miner needed the railroad as much as the farmer. He used it to import mining equipment and consumer goods and to export ore to the market as cheaply as possible. Larger quantities and lower grades of ore could be transported to distant mills and smelters by railroad, loads that would have been uneconomical to move by pack train or wagon. Smelting and milling operations could be located away from the mines, where the terrain was more adaptable or transportation and communication better. In short, the railroad brought the pioneering stage of the mining industry to a close, as the formerly isolated community moved into the mainstream of national economic and industrial growth.

The towns that grew up on both the mining and farming frontiers were much alike. Plains farmers taking their crops to market were likely to drive their wagons down Main Street passing along a double row of business establishments including one or more hotels, a saloon, a general merchandise store, a newspaper office, a drug store dispensing medicines, a magazine and cigar vender, a blacksmith shop, a harness-maker's establishment, and a livery stable. The miner going to the town closest to his claim for supplies or a Sunday's entertainment would encounter the same establishments, plus a larger number of saloons, dance halls, and a theater, possibly dignified by the title "Opera House." In the mining camp, the assay office, express company, stage and telegraph headquarters were also present to serve the special needs of the industry; the land office, the loan and mortgage broker, and the grain and coal dealers were their counterparts in the Plains communities.

Once farmer or miner left the homestead or the claim where all workingmen were equal, he found in the town a society more structured, based on professional status, income, or the necessity for and scarcity of the services one performed. Frontiersmen, as a group, were always in debt. With interest rates running from 4 percent to 6 percent a month in Nebraska in 1857, men with money to lend were at the pinnacle in the structure of society. In the mining camp the need was less for cash and more for goods; the prospector saw the bank not as a source of loans but as a place to sell his gold or silver, make deposits, or serve as a forwarding agent to deliver accumulated wealth to a member of his family or a creditor. In the mining town's initial years, merchants often performed the services of bankers. At the general store the prospector secured his needed supplies, often on credit, a practice that proved to be an annoyance, even a disaster, for many merchants. To compete with his rivals on Main Street, the businessman had to extend credit; if he misjudged the integrity of too many of his customers, he was likely to end in bankruptcy. Just as bankers in the Plains ran a land mortgage business, when professional bankers became established in the mining districts they served as real estate agents or as assayers.

Though newspaper editors were ever-present on all frontiers, they were most numerous, in proportion to population, in the mining areas. Few confined their time solely to the business of running a newspaper. They were expected to be the town boosters, and their offices were the scene of convivial gatherings for promoters and politicians. Few settlers and prospectors could afford a newspaper subscription, so payment often came in kind rather than in cash. All residents sought the goodwill of the editor because he determined the contents of the "Local Items," usually appearing on page three, column one, where coming events, openings or anniversaries of business establishments, and personal comments were noted in a sympathetic or a jocular way. If a mining camp declined, the type and press were placed in a flatbed wagon, hauled to the nearest prosperous or promising camp, and launched again. Wherever he was, the newspaper editor was spokesman for his community.

Pioneer doctors, few in number and ill-trained, were called upon to deal with epidemics or cholera, smallpox, typhoid fever, and diphtheria. On the Great Plains they were forced to travel long distances at all hours of the day and night. Problems of distance, irregular transportation, uncertain supply of medicines and information meant that they often had to rely upon herbs and home-tested remedies to minister to the needs of their patients. In the mining camp where, more often than elsewhere, the local doctor was called upon to repair the damage caused by accidents; amputations of hands, feet, and limbs were regular assignments. Hospitals were nonexistent, so the doctor's office served for surgery. When a contagious disease broke out, a temporary isolation house was designated and someone, usually one of the town's prostitutes, volunteered to minister to the ill and dying. Pioneers always thought the fees charged by doctors and dentists were too high, although excessive charges for medical service would be more justified in the mining camps than elsewhere because the community usually did not last long enough for the doctor to have an established practice and predictable income.

Lawyers were more numerous and more versatile in frontier areas than members of any other profession. In the Plains they also worked as carpenters, editors, mill-operators, town promoters, storekeepers, and school teachers. The early years were ususally lean ones and lawyers learned to work hard. Litigation developed over fights and thievery, but the bulk of the business had to do with land claims, disputes over boundaries, or the legality of a title. Into the far western mining camp lawyers swarmed, intent upon profiting from litigation over disputed mining claims. The procedures in organizing a mining district, in describing and recording the location of claims, were haphazard to say the least. The discoverer of every new bonanza could expect to confront the lawyers of his various neighbors who would dispute the claim in hopes of being bought off. Many mining camp lawyers made a speciality of this type of blackmail; several became United States Senators.

Frontiersmen everywhere attempted to establish institutions they had found serviceable or had cherished in the settled communities from which they had come. If children were present, schooling was considered essential as the key that might open the door to opportunity. Farm families raised money to hire a teacher, and the first schools were usually taught in a farmhouse. The pupils brought what books they had from home. The teacher's life was far from pleasant. He or she boarded in the homes of pupils, staying longest with the family having the greatest number of children. Teachers were expected to serve as procurement officers for supplies and as janitors. Their private lives were a matter of public interest and they were often criticized for lack of discipline or inadequate preparation. The school term was a short one and varied with the need for assistance in planting and harvesting.

Education in the mining camps was much the same. As long as the mining camp was composed of a transient, male population, little thought was given to schooling, but once miners with families arrived, agitation began to raise funds to construct and maintain a school. The building replaced, or at least competed with, the saloon and dance hall as a center of community activity. The problems of the school system were the same everywhere: inadequate financing, low salaries, overcrowded classrooms, inadequate equipment and books.

The church was of primary importance as a frontier social institution. The major denominations were represented among the Plains settlers, but few had congregations large enough to build a permanent church. Responsibility for the religious well-being of the flock rested with an overworked and underpaid itinerant preacher who learned that the most important thing was to arrive on time. During the summer months the revival meeting became a spiritual and social feast for those starved for human companionship. The same denominations popular on the Plains—Methodists, Baptists, Presbyterians, Episcopalians and Catholics—had significant numbers in the mining camps. Catholics in the mines outnumbered those on the Plains, and the Catholic sanctuaries were more often than not town landmarks. The mining camp environment was hardly conducive to religious activity and here as elsewhere the minister or priest was the key to success or failure. Many were unable to stand the physical and psychological pressures. They were expected to be tolerant of drinking, smoking, gambling, and prostitution even though such things were classified as sins by their church. The minister had to preach a gospel that was understandable and acceptable and at the same time be true to his convictions.

Both the farmer and the miner, often isolated and in need of companionship, eagerly sponsored organizations for social purposes. To escape the humdrum monotony of farm life, farmers joined the Patrons of Husbandry and at the periodic Grange meetings talked of crops, finance, and politics while the women exchanged ideas on running a household and raising a family. In the mining camp, in the early days, absence of family caused men to join the fire-fighting companies, the fraternal lodges such as the Masonic Order and the Odd Fellows, and the labor unions to obtain sympathetic friends in an otherwise impersonal and often disorganized world. The miners' union seldom struck for improved wages, hours, and working conditions, though when they did, such struggles with capital inevitably ended in disaster. Unions existed primarily to serve a social function—to care for the injured miner or to support his wife and children in case of fatal accident. Otherwise the union halls served as a gathering place where men with limited leisure time could talk over common concerns.

Among the earliest social activities of the Plains communities was the bee, an occasion when neighbors gathered to participate in a mutual endeavor, such as erecting a new school building, church, or bridge, or helping a family in distress or a neighbor at husking time. Once the work was done, the fun began. Dancing was the universal form of recreation and by all odds the most popular social activity. There were few women, and men traveled far and wide to obtain a partner for an important ball. Amateur theatrical performances were also held. In an attempt to get family participation in social activities, spelling and singing schools were encouraged. The big holiday celebration of the year was the Fourth of July, possibly because the weather permitted a large outdoor gathering with food, speeches, and games.

The miner's recreation was also limited, but masculine-oriented and far more crude. Drinking and gambling were an inseparable part of his life. Physical stamina was as important to his social life as to his work, and he demonstrated it in contests of physical strength, whether dancing in a saloon, running a footrace, or brawling. Prize-fighting was also a featured form of entertainment. Miners enjoyed competitive sports and many camps organized baseball clubs, track, and ski teams to compete with neighboring towns. The theater where professional dramatic players, musicians, and vaudeville stars performed was more popular than any other forms of entertainment in the mining towns. As the towns gained maturity, well-publicized dances were sponsored by the Hook and Ladder companies, the fraternal orders, or various ladies auxiliaries. Properly planned, these balls were reliable money-makers for the subscription library, church, or school.

Because of the diverse national backgrounds of the inhabitants, holidays were occasions for special celebration far more often than elsewhere on the frontier. When the Irish celebrated St. Patrick's Day with parades, fireworks, and drinking, patriotic Americans felt called upon to make the Fourth of July or Washington's birthday a bigger event. On no frontier did music play a greater part in the lives of the inhabitants. Choral groups and bands, often sponsored by Cornish men, gave concerts and participated in parades.

Immigrants taking up farms on the Plains were a homogeneous lot; many of them came from Germany and Scandinavia, and a sizable majority came from northern and western Europe. In contrast, the mining camp was far more cosmopolitan. In the first decade or two, white, northern Europeans usually were in the majority, with Cornish and Irish miners rubbing shoulders with French shopkeepers and German bartenders. In later decades corporate mining enterprises systematically encouraged the migration of Italian, Slavic, and Greek laborers. Each group, held together by customs and language, appears to have dominated the labor market for a period of five to eight years, moving on to be replaced by a new group with common national origins.

Race prejudice and discrimination against minorities prevailed in the mining camp as elsewhere in the nineteenth century where people were crowded together, but no group was treated more harshly than the Chinese. Segregated in a designated section of the camp, their occupations were usually limited to cooking, washing, and garden-tending. Language, customs, religions, and clannishness set them apart from the mainstream of the population and they were blamed for much of the crime and vice that existed. Chinese prostitutes were abused more than most and all drug problems were attributed to the Chinese habit of smoking opium. Chinese and Mexican-Americans were not permitted to work a mining claim in many districts until Anglo-Americans had concluded that it was not likely to produce enough gold or silver to warrant continued effort. Discriminatory taxes were levied against both groups. On occasions, when Mexicans or Chinese violated or protested the rules, riots broke out that were designated as "Chinese wars" or "Mexican wars" in the camp newspaper.

Apparently, there were few blacks in the mining camps. They were not segregated in residence, probably because of the small numbers, but they were only employed as personal servants, cooks, or waiters. Negroes were not taken seriously; they were expected to be a source of entertainment, and their antics were the subject for jokes and ridicule. Somewhat surprisingly they too demonstrated racial prejudice by participating in anti-Oriental meetings.

The frontier was turbulent, but frontier violence and law enforcement have received emphasis out of proportion to their importance. In the farming country the greatest concern was with the horse thief. If one was apprehended, his trial was likely to be speedy and informal. Jails were rare and insecure and the prisoner often escaped. During the Civil War years, gangs of outlaws operated in Kansas and Nebraska under the pretense of representing either the Union or the Confederate cause. Highwaymen robbing stagecoaches in the mining territories similarly rationalized and disguised their activities. In times of crisis informal vigilante groups were organized and occasionally continued to operate after their usefulness was over. During the boom times in the mining camp idlers, gamblers, prostitutes, confidence men, and reprobates mingled with laborers, shopkeepers, professional men, and investors. Drunkenness often resulted in accident and injury. Prostitutes were the cause of countless brawls, and there was endless petty theft and housebreaking, thought usually by the destitute. Only on rare occasions was a sizable amount of money taken, or a serious injury inflicted, or a life lost either in town or in hold-up of a stage. Homicides and murders occurred so infrequently that when they did the community was shocked and outraged. In such a society the town marshal's or constable's job was something less than glamorous and adventuresome. Much of his time was spent gathering up the drunks, interceding in fist-fights, and investigating petty thievery. He was criticized and abused by the taxpayers for not being more effective in maintaining order.

When the historian reflects upon the pattern of daily living of the Plains farmer and the far western miner, he cannot escape the conclusion that the similarities were far greater than the differences. As farmer or miner took up his homestead or claim, each launched a struggle with his environment. Both engaged in the hard physical labor necessary for survival day in and day out, whether working behind the plow or with pick and shovel. Both lived in primitive habitations where household furnishings were crude and meager, and diet exceedingly limited. Both battled against nature, determined to master the environment and to capitalize on the natural resources in the hope of economic gain.

The inevitable question is, "What was the legacy of the frontier in general, and the mining camp in particular, to American character and institutions?" If students of American character can agree upon any one thing it is that the migratory compulsion has been a principal heritage of pioneering.[4] The people of the United States are unique among modern people in believing that moving just for the sake of moving is a good thing and quite likely to lead to social and economic upward mobility. The sources of this belief lie in the character of the social life of the nation, which was, in the nineteenth century, undergoing rapid changes, transforming a previously stable society and at times creating an institutional vacuum in which there was little that was certain or predictable. While such instability led to anxiety and social disorganization, it was simultaneously associated with the growth of the nation and with individual well being, as the wide interest in the potential riches of the gold and silver rushes in the Far West demonstrated. If such processes reached extremes, they tended to be in the frontier areas of the West, which came to represent a national condition. The miners, perhaps more than any other group in the country, symbolized the precarious social and economic existence linked with the national habit of moving. Many years ago Hubert Howe Bancroft recognized this fact when he made an observation about Idaho miners that could be universally applied to mining areas: "The miners of Idaho were like quicksilver. A mass of them dropped in any locality, broke up into individual globules, and ran off after any atom of gold in the vicinity.[5]

Closely associated with the habit of mobility is the concept of the frontier as a "safety valve," as an avenue of escape from economic and social adversity. Historians have agreed that it did not work as such for the Eastern laborer, whose low wages never permitted him to save enough to transport his family to a homestead on the Plains or buy the machinery to work the soil competitively. Pioneer farmers usually had moved only a short distance to the Plains from an adjoining state or nearby county and had previously engaged in farming. In addition, they did not move in times of economic adversity because they could not afford the trip with a large family. The situation was entirely different on the mining frontier, however. Certainly the districts where wages were fixed and prices rising in an inflationary spiral were no haven for the unskilled and the poor. The typical prospector was a single man, or if married, was far removed from family attachments in the East, and he was free to wander with a minimum of baggage and less responsibility. Thus, reports from any other mining district where the prospects were rumored to be better gave him new hope. Perhaps his economic fortunes were not improved by his continuous mobility, but he lived in hope that the next move would bring improvement. From a psychological standpoint, if he believed that every move was going to provide an avenue of escape from poverty, the mining frontier offered him his big opportunity. Some held to this belief for a lifetime. A society that measured people by material success labeled the miners wanderers, but the miners believed that the diggings offered the road to that material success.

Enough has been written here to illustrate the absence of well-defined stages in the advance of the mining frontier.[6] Economic groups did not march westward through Cumberland Gap or South Pass or anywhere else in an orderly procession with long time intervals between. In the mining districts everything happened at once in a kaleidoscopic pattern. Within a matter of days after the news of the discovery of precious metal, experienced miners, shopkeepers, merchants, professional men, express and freight agents, saloon keepers, and entertainers of all sorts were headed for the new El Dorado. Scarcely had a district been formed and the first claims registered before at least one town, and possibly more, had been located, streets laid out, and business lots sold. All the surrounding grazing and arable lands were taken up to raise cattle, grain, and vegetables to feed the accumulating population. Both ranching and dairy frontiers quickly were interrelated with the mining frontier. All types of business and professional men were on the scene; bankers, engineers, and investors delayed for a time but were not far behind.

To ask whether miners in the frontier period imitated existing institutions or formed new ones is to invite a debate that will never end. Let it suffice that they did both. Certainly in the initial phases of mining they utilized the techniques they had found successful elsewhere; those without experience tried out what they had read about or observed from neighbors. In balance, it appears that miners had an initial tendency to imitate or recreate the social institutions they had known, but as the camp gained maturity there was an increasing tendency to innovate when dealing with legal institutions or technological improvements.

Both contemporary observers and later historians have talked much about the individualism that prevailed on the frontier but much of what they have said is wishful thinking. Mining certainly was never an individual enterprise. Men quickly sought out one or more partners to assist in working a claim, building a shelter, or providing subsistence. Cooperation was the traditional pattern not only in handling essential economic tasks but also in law enforcement, social concerns, and charitable endeavor.

The frontier experience has often been described as a stimulus to the growth of American democracy. In the first stages of the mining district when regulations were being established and any violation was punished by vigilante action, the young men in mass meetings all agreed with the principle of one man, one vote. As the community gained maturity, the qualifications for participating in politics became more restrictive. Property and residence requirements were established for voting, then age and race became factors. The average miner appears to have been politically apathetic, sufficiently concerned to vote only if his economic well-being was threatened. Concern with material success and the resulting fierce competition led inevitably to class lines being established based upon economic success or social position. Workers resented the idlers and hangers-on. Perhaps the important thing was that class distinctions were not quite as rigid as elsewhere; they could be more easily breached, and the ladder of success could be more easily climbed. But the all-pervading spirit of equality, of social democracy, which has been ascribed to frontiering was not universal. True, at first all men stood on a par at the threshold of opportunity. They lived alike, dressed alike, ate alike, and played alike. All traditional symbols of servitude were abolished among white men. Those whom they knew were addressed on a first name basis. The title of "Mr." was a mark of respect. As in other regions in the United States during the nineteenth century, however, this social equality did not extend to racial minorities. Democracy, then and now, meant many different things to many people.

Miners, like other frontiersmen, talked a great deal about the self-made man and rugged individualism in the economic field, but they (again like most frontiersmen) looked to the government for subsidies and assistance. Government geologists were expected to locate promising mineral deposits and mineralogists to provide technical expertise in recommending changes in milling and mining techniques. Congressmen were hounded to legalize the land claims of miners who were squatting on the public domain. Mail and freight deliveries were either directly subsidized or underwritten by contracts guaranteeing a specific amount of business by the government. Army engineers improved roads; telegraphs and railroads were aided by subsidies, land grants, and loans. The self-made mining mogul who attributed his success to luck and ingenuity should, in honesty, have recognized that he and all his less fortunate associates were, in the beginning at least, underwritten by their government.

Those who argue the leveling influence of the frontier have suggested that there customs and institutions from foreign lands were shed or minimized and that a composite Americanism emerged. This process took time and most mining camps just did not last long. In fact, a part of their charm was the diversity of language and cultural patterns.

Mining camps that survived for a decade or more and became integrated into the industry quickly minimized the importance of diversity and localism, and developed a national, even international, outlook in their concern for investment capital, technical assistance, and engineering skill. The term, "The American Mining Industry," slowly took on significance.

Above all else, miners, like other pioneers, were opportunistic and optimistic, so much so that they were in many respects dreamers. Bernard DeVoto some years ago noted, "Ours is a story made with the impossible. . . .it began as dream and it has continued as dream down to the last. . . ."[7] DeVoto, in *Treasure Hill: Portrait of a Silver Mining Camp,*[8] illustrated the theme that residents of the mining camp throughout their lifetime, no matter what the adversity, had a boundless belief in the future. More recently, T. H. Watkins in his study *Gold and Silver in the West* re-affirmed the importance of this concept when he subtitled his work, "The Illustrated History of an American Dream."[9]

Contemporary historians of the United States have a tendency to minimize the significance of the frontier experience in our national history. Some ignore it, others dismiss it with impatience, arguing that pioneering activity was limited to a rural America of the eighteenth and nineteenth century and has no legacy or lessons for twentieth century industrial America. Perhaps Duane A. Smith in *Rocky Mountain Mining Camps: The Urban Frontier*[10] has raised the mining camp to a new position of historical relevance when he suggests that the pattern of living there was a part of our urban, rather than our rural heritage. Certainly the goals, problems, anxieties, and opportunities of the residents appear to be identical to those of the modern urbanite. Moreover, historians of the Plains frontier who turn their attention from the farmer's homestead and focus on that region's supply towns are likely to discover economic and social forces at work that have relevance to our time. Lewis E. Atherton pointed the way in considering town life in *Main Street on the Middle Border.*[11] A recent worthy model is Robert R. Dykstra's study of *The Cattle Towns.*[12]

But the groundwork for these more recent studies was laid by earlier historical writing. Frederick Jackson Turner originally raised the questions when he wrote his famous essay, the aim of which was "simply to call attention to the frontier as a fertile field for investigation."[13] Everett Dick's *Sod-House Frontier* was among those books that first began to provide evidence and answers. Nothing that is done well is lost, and Dick's studies have repeatedly provided the background for answers to the questions Turner raised. It is on the basis of such scholarship as Dick's that subsequent generations of historians will be able to test general conceptions of frontier life more accurately, increasingly so with the aid of new methodologies, enabling yet more sophisticated comparisons of the social and economic consequences of rapidly changing societies.

NOTES

1. Charles A. Eastman, *Indian Boyhood* (New York, 1971), p. 246.
2. Everett Dick, *The Sod-House Frontier 1854-1890* (New York, 1937), p. 202.
3. T. H.Watkins, *Gold and Silver in the West* (Palo Alto, Calif., 1971), p. 11.
4. Ray Allen Billington, *America's Frontier Heritage* (New York, 1966), pp. 181-97.
5. Hubert Howe Bancroft, *Works: History of Washington, Idaho and Montana*, XXXI (San Francisco, 1890), p. 427.
6. Rodman Wilson Paul, *Mining Frontiers of the Far West, 1848-1880* (New York, 1963), pp. 2-3.
7. Bernard DeVoto to Catherine Drinker Bowen in Bowen, Catherine Drinker, Edith R. Mirrielees, Arthur M. Schlesinger, Jr., and Wallace Stegner, *Four Portraits and One Subject: Bernard DeVoto* (Boston, 1963), p. 25.
8. Tucson, 1963.
9. Palo Alto, 1971.
10. Bloomington, 1967.
11. Bloomington, 1954.
12. New York, 1968.
13. Frederick Jackson Turner, "The Significance of the Frontier in American History," *Annual Report of the American Historical Association for the Year 1893* (Washington, 1904), pp. 200-01.

CHAPTER 5

FRONTIER VIOLENCE:
Another Look

W. Eugene Hollon

> *Everett Dick and Gene Hollon met in the summer of 1969 when happenstance brought them and several other leading students of the American West to the Henry E. Huntington Library. There, over the luncheon table, on expeditions to neighboring libraries or historic spots, friendships deepened. Born and educated in Texas, and for many years a leading member of the University of Oklahoma faculty, Hollon since 1967 has been Ohio Regents Professor and Research Professor of History at the University of Toledo. He has, he estimates, written more than twenty articles, at least fifty minor papers, and 150 book reviews, as well as six books that have contributed significantly to our knowledge of the frontier. He is currently writing a book on frontier violence, and he takes a fresh look at the whole subject in the challenging essay that follows.*

The distinguished historian James Truslow Adams observed in an article published in *The Atlantic Monthly* in 1928 that the gang wars of that era were primarily the results of three hundred years of American frontiering. The same idea has been expressed innumerable times by writers, commentators, and historians—especially during the traumas of the past decade. That America has had a violent past and that the frontier has symbolized the nation at its most violent, are by now commonly accepted notions. They provide us with prefabricated "explanations" for events that we often do not understand and perhaps do not want to understand.

The literature on violence in America is so extensive that a mere catalogue of books relating directly to the subject fills more than four trays in the Library of Congress card index.[1] Approximately eighty of the listed titles have been published during the three years between 1967 and 1970. This does not include newspaper and magazine articles, or all studies relating to crime in general.

Why then another look at violence, if so much already has been written about it? Is there any point in trying to prove the accepted truisms that the nineteenth-century frontier was an invitation to violence or that it deserves primary responsibility for our violent society today? Was there another side of the coin, and was H. L. Mencken right when he observed that "something which everyone accepts as the gospel truth is invariably false"? These are questions I have asked myself thousands of times since beginning research in 1968 on the subject of frontier violence.

To the average individual, the phrase "frontier violence" conjures up a vision of characters such as Billy the Kid, "Wild Bill" Hickok, "Doc" Holliday, John Wesley Hardin, Ben Thompson, *ad infinitum*. These psychopaths have been so thoroughly enshrined into the Valhalla of heroes that serious scholarship has been unable to strip them of the ill-fitting halos invented by hack-writers, motion picture producers, and TV serials. Myths easily become reality. It was common knowledge, for example, that President Dwight D. Eisenhower was extremely fond of books relating to the exploits of his childhood hero, "Wild Bill" Hickok. In a nation-wide television address in 1954, the President of the United States referred to the former marshal of Abilene, Kansas, Eisenhower's hometown, as an example of courage and devotion to duty that all Americans might well emulate.

The facts about the real Hickok have been revealed so many times that some listeners were shocked that he would be used as a model of American manhood. As far as his devotion to duty was concerned, Hickok played both sides of the law, was fired from his job at Abilene after a few months, and throughout his adult life possessed many of the qualities of a mad dog. The same can be said for William Bonney's character. William, or "Billy the Kid," has been the subject of approximately four hundred book-length publications during the past century. A few of these have been objective, but the majority defend or tacitly approve of most of the acts of violence (including some twenty-two murders) that Billy committed during his brief outlaw career.

Most of the vast ocean of literature about other famous gunmen of the West also consists of narrations of events and deeds that often were more mythical than real. The professional outlaw-killer almost invariably was a drifter, unable to settle his personal problems or achieve fame except through violence. In relative numbers he represented a small minority of the frontier town or community population, but the publicity he has received has distorted the image of frontier violence. In reality, it often took the form of action by one group of residents against another, rather than that of individual man against man. And it was unleashed periodically against Orientals, Mexicans, Negroes, Indians, and other ethnic or racial minorities. The historical enmity toward Orientals has generally been explained as a product of American antipathy to color, or by vague references to the "black legend." For a considerable period of our history, Orientals remained the only people barred from migrating to the United States. Meanwhile, the frontier had accumulated considerable experience in violence against Indians and Mexicans before the first wave of Chinese reached the Pacific Coast in the middle of the nineteenth century.

Much that has been written about the Chinese in the Trans-Mississippi West is extremely poignant. Wherever they went, prejudice and violence followed them and the expression about not having "a Chinaman's chance" had a literal meaning. "The burden of our accusation against them is that they come in conflict with our labor interest," an official spokesman for the city of San Francisco explained to a Special Committee of Congress in 1876, "that they can never assimilate with us; that they are a perpetual, unchanging, and unchangeable alien, degraded labor class, without desire for citizenship, without education, and without interest in the country it inhabits, is an element both demoralizing and dangerous to the community within which it exists."[2]

It seems obvious from this and similar statements of the period that the anti-Chinese feeling stemmed from the white man's resentment of the willingness of the Chinese to work long hours for low wages. This undercurrent of tension between the two races exploded into violence so frequently in Western towns and mining camps that it often went unnoticed by the press, but now and then an event was so barbarous and tragic that newspapers and magazines reported it throughout the country. One such incident occurred in the Chinese section of Los Angeles on the night of October 24, 1871, when a large crowd was attracted to the area by the sound of gunfire. During the melee that followed, a white bystander was killed and two or three others were wounded. An armed mob, determined to avenge the murder, subsequently "went to work on Chinatown." The Chinese who initially started the disturbance had by this time left the city, a fact that did not deter the mob from lynching twenty-one or twenty-two innocent Oriental merchants and laborers, and inflicting several thousand dollars in property damage. After the massacre and looting, the Chinese government made a vigorous protest to the United States and subsequently received a large indemnity. Not one member of the mob was ever indicted.

Another disgraceful atrocity occurred at Rock Springs, Wyoming Territory, on September 2, 1885. White coal miners had grown increasingly bitter and felt that the Chinese were displacing them in the mines. A clash between the two groups eventually resulted in the slaughter of between twenty-two and fifty Chinese and the expulsion of the remaining four or five hundred.[3] Public opinion throughout the West overwhelmingly supported the white miners, and within a few days the incident at Rock

Springs had inspired similar acts against Chinese workers in Idaho, Montana, and Washington. As usual, no white participant in these and half a dozen similar riots of the period was ever brought to trial.

Discrimination against all Orientals remained strong in the Far West long after the end of the frontier period. It easily spilled over to include the Japanese and small numbers of Hindus who began arriving on the Pacific Coast around 1900. The "Japs" and "rag-heads" were never the victims of full-scale, bloody massacres of the type suffered regularly by the Chinese, but the verbal harassment, restrictive legislation, and physical violence that were practiced against them are equally shameful. They also were resented because of their willingness to work long hours for low wages. The Hindus never became the visible force that the Japanese did, but wherever they settled in small colonies, friction quickly developed between them and the established community.[4]

The treatment of the people of Japanese lineage, which culminated in the immigration restriction policy of the 1920s and the concentration camps during World War II, represented a continuation of the campaign of discrimination against the Chinese that started half a century earlier. For the most part, opposition was based upon fears that were largely irrational, and that made a mockery out of the so-called "promise of American life." It is an unhappy story of racial hatred that has subsided only recently, but it represents a clear-cut example of the perpetuation of a frontier attitude upon a modern industrial society.

Among other racial groups that felt the wrath of "frontier justice" from time to time were people of Latin American extraction, particularly Mexicans in Texas and California. Texans learned to hate Mexicans with pathological violence even before their war of independence in 1836. The massacres at the Alamo and Goliad committed by the Mexicans led to the massacre by the Texans at San Jacinto. Racial arrogance on both sides unquestionably contributed to the subsequent war between the United States and Mexico and the seizure in 1848 of more than half of Mexico's territory. For the next sixty years, Mexicans raided north of the Rio Grande, and the Texas Rangers ignored international boundaries as they pursued the enemy in the best frontier tradition. Each side referred to the other as bandits, or worse.

The Rangers were organized during the early days of the Texas Republic and quickly developed a reputation as efficient Indian fighters. They similarly considered Mexicans their natural enemies and seldom gave them the benefit of the doubt. These frontier law officers played a major role as scouts with the army of General Zachary Taylor as he invaded Mexico via Monterey and Buena Vista, and later with General Winfield Scott, who went via Vera Cruz to Mexico City. "Take them all together," a private in Taylor's army recorded in his diary, "With their uncouth costumes, bearded faces, lean and bronze forms, fierce eyes and swaggering manners, they were fit representatives of the outlaws who made up the population of the Lone Star State."[5] It is no wonder therefore that the Texans struck terror into the hearts of Mexican citizens who had the misfortune to get in their way.

One reason that the heritage of the frontier has extended into the twentieth century in Texas is that the physical frontier survived there much longer than in almost any other region. The Lone Star State's reputation for violence also rests upon a broader base than the perpetual warfare between Rangers and Mexicans. Particularly turbulent was the Reconstruction era, thanks mostly to political tensions, family feuds, range warfare, and the activities of the Ku Klux Klan. Such a climate provided the necessary conditions for general lawlessness and the emergence of the professional killer.

Like thousands of other Americans, Texans took their prejudices with them to the California gold fields. One such individual was Thomas Jefferson Green, who subsequently was elected to the first California legislature and promoted the infamous "Foreign Miners' Tax Law," which required Chileans, Peruvians, Mexicans, and other foreigners to pay a twenty-dollar monthly fee for the right to pan gold. Although Green maintained that the law was designed to raise revenue to bolster the bankrupt state treasury, he regularly issued tirades against all things Mexican and Negro, and boasted that he personally could "maintain a better stomach at the killing of a Mexican than at crushing a body louse."[6]

Evidently there were many others who felt the same way and who were not particularly displeased when, for one reason or another, Latins refused to pay the discriminatory tax. Americans regularly formed posses and scattered the foreign-born residents of the mining camps in all directions. Not infrequently they resorted to ear cropping, whipping, and even lynching. The victims sometimes took to the road as professional bandits and made travel in parts of California extremely hazardous. One native of Sonora who became famous as the leader of a daring gang of desperados was Joaquin Murieta. Some maintain that Joaquin was merely a legendary figure who provided the Latins with a Robin Hood symbol, but unquestionably, the cruel treatment received from the brutal element among the Americans drove many a foreigner to a criminal career.

An Easterner named William Perkins who spent three years in California during this period summed up the popular attitude when he recorded:

The 'Greaser' has all the characteristic vices of the Spaniard, jealous, revengeful, and treacherous, with an absorbing passion for gambling; and he has a still greater likeness to the inferior tribes of Indians; the same apathetic indolence; the same lounging thieving propensities; never caring for the morrow, and alike regardless of the past as to the future.

He observed also that "the summary execution of . . .a few Mexicans has had a more wonderful effect than could have been anticipated."[7] Most of the Mexicans, Chileans, and Peruvians who arrived in 1849 had been driven back to their homelands within two or three years. Although Perkins did not disguise his prejudices against them, he realized that the Latins served as convenient scapegoats for rough men looking for excitement.

Frontier Violence

Moverover, racial conflicts constituted only one part of the general state of lawlessness that existed in early California. Again Perkins wrote in his journal:

> It is surprising how indifferent people become to the sight of violence and bloodshed in this country. Here we have almost daily rows, attended with loss of life, and we look upon these scenes with the greatest callousness of feeling, at the same time being well aware that in any of these rows, one's own life is just as much in danger as another's. A man now fires his pistol on the slightest motive or quarrel, with the same readiness that in another country he would strike a blow with his fist.[8]

When the Forty-Niners began to arrive, the Mexican population of California probably numbered ten thousand or more. For the most part they had a peaceful, prosperous life, which some early visitors compared to an Utopian paradise. At first the Yankees gave the impression of treating the Californios as equals, particularly the wealthy "rancheros." But some quickly declared open season on the natives and took what they wanted, using various pious excuses—"progress has its price;" "the Californios are culturally unsuited to the new order;" "they brought it on themselves;" and "the race goes to the strong." The disintegration of the Mexicans' world was so rapid that almost immediately they became a tiny minority in Northern California. In Southern California they held their own in numbers for about twenty years, but they could not compete with the more aggressive Yankees. Many of Mexican origin went back to Mexico, while all but a handful of the descendents of the original Spanish residents were absorbed into the main population stream before the end of the century.

A far more tragic experience befell the California Indians, or "Diggers," whose numbers were estimated to be 150,000 in 1850. The miners fell upon them with savage fury, drove them from their homes, and enslaved or murdered their warriors. By 1875, less than one-fourth of their original number were still alive; those not destroyed by outright violence had for the most part succumbed to the white man's diseases and alcohol.

The story of violence practiced against the California Indians is a microcosm of three hundred years of Indian–white relationships in America. Wherever and whenever Indians were in the way, they were removed, often violently. Although there never was an organized campaign of genocide against the Indians, it would be difficult to find a more macabre story of the destruction of one race by another. Since the Colonial period, an estimated 1,200,000 Indians have been massacred in the United States, while even more have been killed by alcohol and pestilence. In addition, the United States has made and broken approximately four hundred treaties with the Indians, suppressed or destroyed their culture and religion, and taken most of their lands. All of this has been done in the name of "manifest destiny," even though the phrase was not coined until the middle of the nineteenth century. A young newspaperman put it more bluntly in his Marion, Ohio *Weekly Star*. On June 20, 1881, Warren G. Harding, future President of the United States, editorialized as follows: "As there is no room for Indians and no food, let them be killed off."

Such an attitude typified that of thousands of others throughout the nineteenth century. It is doubtful if Harding had ever read any of the essays by Dr. Samuel Johnson or that he would have been bothered by the question which the editor of *The Literary Magazine* raised in 1756. Concerning relations between the American colonists and the Indians during the Seven Years' War, Dr. Johnson wrote:

And indeed what but false hope, or resistless terror can prevail upon a weaker nation to invite a stronger into their country, to give their lands to strangers whom no affinity of manners, or similitude of opinion, can be said to recommend, to permit them to build towns from which the natives are excluded, to raise fortresses by which they are intimidated, to settle themselves with such strength, that they cannot afterwards be expelled, but are for ever to remain the masters of the original inhabitants, the dictators of their conduct, and the arbiters of their fate?[9]

Perhaps no subject relative to the development of the American West has inspired more publication than the violent aspects of

Indian—white relationships, particularly warfare. From the time of James Fenimore Cooper the vicarious killing of Indians has provided enjoyment for millions of readers and motion picture viewers. Cooper made "another redskin bit the dust " into a romantic and patriotic phrase. Recently there has been healthy reaction as writers have sought to show another side of the coin. An example of this trend is Dee Brown's best-selling volume, *Bury My Heart at Wounded Knee* (1971).

A mere listing of the battles with Indians, from the Pequot War in the early seventeenth century to the massacre at Wounded Knee in South Dakota in 1890, would cover more than a hundred pages in small type. Brown therefore concentrates on the thirty year period that witnessed our worst Indian conflicts, 1860-1890, to select incident after incident of the white man's atrocities. During these three decades, the once great Cheyenne were ruined, along with the Ute, Sioux, Apache, Comanche, Kiowa, and all the other tribes who had something that the pioneers wanted. However guilty the author might be of selecting evidence to suit his argument, his book has brought home to thousands of readers the fact that the Indians were human beings, more sinned against than sinful, that killing them *did count,* that even if some of their adversaries considered them animals, shooting their innocent women and children was not romantic, patriotic, or sporting.

Just as there is nothing new about violence throughout the course of American history—only our sudden awareness of it—so there is nothing new in Brown's descriptions of the massacres at Sand Creek, Washita, Wounded Knee, and elsewhere. Why, then, the popularity of his book? Perhaps the reviewer in the February 1, 1971 issue of *Newsweek* answered that question when he wrote: "Nothing I have ever read has saddened and shamed me as this book has. Because the experience of reading it has made me realize for once and all that we really don't know who we are, or where we came from, or what we have done, or why."

If Americans are only now beginning to recognize the distortions in their history, they are also more and more aware that it is easier to look at the symptoms of violence than to explain the deeper causes. The average historian is better trained to deal with the chronology of events and their relationship to one another than with human behavior. Even the psychiatrists are not in agreement as to why man is by nature violent. So the historian faces an almost impossible challenge in seeking in frontier violence a cause of the violence of today.

That the rough life of the frontier prior to 1900 did not foster respect for the law as law seems indisputable. Frequently remote from the courts of authorities of established communities, the frontiersmen not only enforced their own law, they chose which laws should be enforced and which should be ignored. Thus, without exception, the history of every western territory and state was replete with violence and lawlessness, with the most intense and prolonged examples found in Texas and California. Involved were a wide range of individualistic types and classes: miners, cowboys, claim jumpers, Indian fighters, buffalo hunters, border ruffians, banditti, soldiers, trail drivers, mule skinners, railroad workers, highwaymen, Texas Rangers, United States marshals, and professional gunmen. Even the most orderly types—ranchers, farmers, bankers, town builders, railroad owners, politicians, and mine owners—did not hesitate to take the law into their own hands, either as individuals or as self-appointed members of local vigilance committees. Generally these committees were formed to apprehend road agents, horse thieves, and murderers, but westerners frequently vented their emotions against innocent Chinese, Mexicans, and Indians.

That violent acts by individuals and groups on the western frontier were directed less often against Negroes, Jews, or Mormons was scarcely to the frontiersmen's credit. Few Jews lived beyond the Mississippi in the nineteenth century, the Mormons were concentrated in Utah where they formed an overwhelming majority, and most of the Negroes in the West were confined to Texas, Arkansas, and some of the border states. There are several isolated examples of whippings and two or three lynchings of Jews in early California and elsewhere in the West, but they were never the victims of a full-scale massacre.

The Mormons had gone through their most violent years by the time they were forced out of Illinois in the 1840s. Prejudice against them continued for many decades after they had established their Kingdom of Zion in the valley of the Great Salt Lake, but the much-talked of war of extermination never materialized. The Negroes constituted a different story, however, and individuals and small groups were sometimes whipped or lynched by the Ku Klux Klan, especially in Texas and Arkansas, during Reconstruction. The practice continued long after the Klan disbanded and well into the twentieth century.

The reasons that the frontier might have been an open invitation to violence are far more complex than the availability of guns, although the casual wearing or possession of side arms, rifles, and shotguns long after the traditional dangers had disappeared definitely made violence more likely. Similarly the glib assumption that our tendency toward violence is the result of a frontier heritage ignores the fact that many of the Western gunmen and outlaws were veterans of the Civil War and operated in mining or cattle towns, and especially in the cities. The monumental report of the National Commission on the Causes and Prevention of Violence published in 1969[10] makes it clear that violence has traditionally been more of an urban than a frontier problem. In fact, no major city in the United States and only a few small towns managed to escape one or several major riots during the nineteenth century. The urban historian Richard Wade reaches the same conclusion in *Violence in the Cities: A Historical View* (1969), while John Hope Franklin in *The Militant South* (1956) cites the violence in that region—shootings, duels, lynchings—that took place at the same time that the western frontier was experiencing its most violent period.

In literature the frontier has always appeared larger than life, from the early writings of Captain John Smith to the present. The openness of the country—particularly beyond the eastern forests—its extremes in climate and geography, scarceness of people, and abundance of game, contributed to a natural tendency to exaggerate the truth and emphasize the exception.

For every act of violence by individuals or groups in the American West during the pioneer period, there were thousands of examples of kindness, generosity, and sacrifice. More often than not people worked together harmoniously for the good of the community. The majority practiced the biblical adage about being their "brother's keeper:" they donated their time, money, and sometimes their lives for friends or total strangers in moments of misfortune or extreme danger. Most were friendly, hard working, and fair-minded individuals. But these simple virtues, along with poor food and shelter and general boredom, are not the stuff upon which exciting narrative is ordinarily written.

Often when there was no violence or excitement, writers or newspaper reporters invented it. The first "land rush" into Oklahoma in 1889 has generally been described by on-the-spot reporters as an orgy of claim jumping, quarreling, and homicide. Yet there is no record of, or an authentic witness to, a single fight or serious dispute during the first few days. On the contrary, the fifty thousand participants in the initial "run" had an organized government functioning within thirty-six hours.

Except for one or two attacks by small bands of Apaches, the Butterfield Stage that operated between Missouri and California and across the Southwest for three years prior to the Civil War was never interfered with by professional or amateur road agents. Moreover, not a single shoot-out took place on main street at Dodge City or any of the other Kansas cowtowns in the manner of the face-to-face encounter presented thousands of times on television. A western historian recently examined the files of all of the newspapers published in Abilene, Ellsworth, Wichita, Dodge City, and Caldwell for the years 1870–1885. He found evidence of only forty-five men dying by violence during the fifteen-year period, most of them cowboys and gamblers shot by town marshals. The average number of homicides per cattle

Frontier Violence

town trading season amounted to only one and one-half per year, a record which few towns of comparable size could match today.[11]

Of the many faults that the individualistic frontiersmen possessed, petty thievery was rarely included. Locks symbolized to them an impeachment of public honesty and integrity and they frequently did not secure the doors of their homes or places of business. A stranger was considered honest until proved otherwise, and it was taken for granted that a traveler was welcome to help himself to a man's food or lodging if he were in need and no one was at home. He either left the price for what he had taken or a note of explanation or promise to pay later. Generally, a man's word was as good as his bond.

Most cow towns, mining camps, and boom towns of all varieties did bear a close resemblance to Sodom and Gomorrah during their early days when practically everyone carried guns and when saloons, gambling houses, and brothels were the principal centers of entertainment. Yet in many frontier settlements, schools and churches sprang up and the "dens of iniquity" were regulated or put out of business within a remarkably short time. Bancroft concluded in his two-volume work on violence in the California gold fields that, under the circumstances, it was miraculous that mob law and failure of justice were as infrequent as they were. Moreover, wherever miners gathered, they organized local society swiftly and efficiently.

> In this respect the morals of the Californian miners were far purer than those of the Machiavellian school. They would shoot their enemy, or hang the enemy of their camp, but they would not deceive him. They found a way to rule themselves and their little societies without Jesuitical cunning. They were the sons of their father Adam whose eyes had been opened to know good and evil, and when they saw wickedness coming into the camp, warned by the folly of their primogenitor, they lifted their heel and crushed it.[12]

Almost everything that has been said about frontier violence at one time or another contains large elements of the truth. On the other hand, contradictions and exceptions make impossible any final conclusions on the exact relationship between frontiering and lawlessness. No more profound conclusion can be reached than the observation that the frontier merely preserved, refined, and passed on a heritage for violence that began when the European set foot on American soil. It deserves no more credit or blame for what we are today than does Cain, who killed his brother Abel.

NOTES

1. There are many concepts of violence, including psychological warfare or violence to a person's psyche or livelihood. As herein used, the word "violence" generally refers to physical aggression.

2. Quoted in Elmer Sandmeyer, *The Anti-Chinese Movement in California* (Urbana, Illinois, 1939), p. 25.

3. Figures on the number of Chinese killed at Rock Springs vary greatly from source to source. Several articles have been written on the incident, but the most complete account is Isaac Hill Bromley, *The Chinese Massacre at Rock Spring, Wyoming Territory, September 2, 1885* (Boston, 1886).

4. An influx of Hindus into the bustling lumber center of Bellingham, Washington, to fulfill a demand for contract labor in that city's sawmills, produced a wave of hostility that soon resulted in their being expelled. An editorial in the *Bellington Reveille,* September 6, 1907, had a familiar refrain: "From every standpoint it is most undesirable that these Asians should be permitted to remain in the United States. They are repulsive in appearance and disgusting in their manners. They are said to be without shame, and while no charges of immorality are brought against them, their actions and customs are so different from ours that there can never be tolerance of them. They contribute nothing to the growth and upbuilding of the city as a result of their labors. They work for small wages and do not put their money into circulation."

5. Samuel E. Chamberlain, "My Confessions," Part I, *Life Magazine*, July 23, 1956, p. 75.

6. Quoted in Leonard Pitt, *Decline of the Californios: A Social History of the Spanish Speaking Californians* (Berkeley, 1966), p. 60.

7. *William Perkins' Journal of Life at Sonora, 1849 – 1852,* with an introduction and annotation by Dale L. Morgan and James R. Scobie (Berkeley, 1964), pp. 143–44, 237.

8. Ibid., pp. 159–160.

9. Quoted in E. L. McAdam, Jr. and George Milne, eds., *A Johnson Reader* (New York, 1964), p. 191.

10. Hugh Davis Graham and Ted Robert Gurr, eds., *A History of Violence in America: Historical and Comparative Perspectives* (New York, 1969).

11. Robert R. Dykstra, *The Cattle Towns* (New York, 1968), p. 146.

12. Hubert H. Bancroft, *Popular Tribunals* (San Francisco, 1887), I, 142–43.

CHAPTER 6

THE TOWN MARSHAL AND THE POLICE

Philip D. Jordan

When Philip D. Jordan retired from his professorship at the University of Minnesota, he returned to Burlington, Iowa, where he had been born in 1903, and found himself surrounded by historical source materials destined to keep him even busier than he had been during his distinguished teaching career. The author of a dozen books and some 450 articles and reviews on popular American culture, he turned now to local records as the basis for case studies of law breaking and law enforcement on the Mississippi Valley frontier. His last book, Frontier Law and Order, *published in 1970, testifies to the richness of his findings and his skill in interpreting them. His essay in this volume, exploring the role of the western marshal and the nature of the crimes he sought to control, again demonstrates the importance of his investigations. Everett Dick, his life-long friend, will find in it evidence of the germinal effect of his own writings on later studies.*

The town marshal has become a western legend. He swaggered into saloons, served process, and shot bad men dead. His star cloaked him with awesome authority, and its glitter mirrored and reflected the strength, boldness, and stern resolve of its wearer. The marshal was the lord of a legal domain, and his castle was the jail. Deputies and posse members were his liege men. At times the marshal strictly observed statute and ordinance, at times he flaunted and flouted the law, at times he made his own law without benefit of legislature or town council. Some marshals epitomized rascality and others personified the peace officer at his best. Although much has been written about individual marshals and their violent episodes, little, indeed, has been set down in western literature about the office itself—its basis in law, its duties and obligations, its methods and techniques. Curiously, few persons are aware of the evolution of the modern police department from the office of town marshal.

Marshals striding America's Middle Border were the inheritors of an ancient office. It would be difficult for some slovenly, semi-literate town marshal, exercising authority in a village situated between the twisting Mississippi and the muddy Missouri rivers, to appreciate his legal heritage. His life and duties were acted out not only in the heartland of the river country but also on the great plains, the verdant foothills of mountain ranges, and the distressing dryness of desert reaches. Haunch-squatted in a protective gulch close to a warming fire, marshals were unaware that they were marshals only because night watchmen and marshalmen had walked their rounds in old London. A cowtown marshal, laying heavy hand upon a vagrant, seldom, if ever, realized that eighteenth-century English officers had done the same thing long before.

Nor did many marshals comprehend that their office since colonial days had faithfully followed successive frontiers westward as had explorers, emigrants, and settlers themselves. The people carried the law with them just as they took rifles and Bibles and livestock on the long trek. By the time the Ohio country was reached and probing fingers of settlement were pushing toward the Mississippi River, the office of town marshal was as firmly fixed in the American tradition as was Jethro Wood's cast-iron plow. One dug into the motives of men, and the other into the soil. Each was equally necessary if settlements were to survive.

The Town Marshal and the Police

The process of rooting and establishing a community was both haphazard and calculated. Struggling settlements originally were politically unorganized, but it was not long before residents demanded elementary controls. Although individually they might hold the law in contempt, collectively they desired legal institutions. Unincorporated hamlets did not have to appoint or elect local officials, including a peace officer, but it was mandatory for incorporated communities to do so.

Specific requirements, stipulated by state statute, must be met. This was normal practice from New York to California and from Minnesota to Florida. Acts of incorporation clearly stated that qualified voters should elect mayors, selectmen, recorders, treasurers, coroners, and marshals. Councilmen, in turn, passed ordinances, again in conformity with state statutes, which prescribed the duties of town officers, set license fees, regulated public health, prohibited nuisances, and enumerated misdemeanors. The marshal, bonded and under oath, was charged with the onerous task of transforming the abstract legal phrases of ordinances into a concrete pattern conditioning the behavior of townspeople. He was the servant of the mayor's or recorder's court, just as the sheriff was the handmaiden of the county court and the United States marshal the agent of federal courts.[1]

A rudimentary description of the office of marshal and its duties, such as that in the *Revised Code* of North Dakota in 1895, defines the village marshal as a peace officer who possesses the powers and is subject to the liabilities possessed and conferred by law upon sheriffs, and that he executes the orders of trustees and enforces the by-laws and ordinances of a village. To the layman, this probably is less than satisfactory. A more detailed description would add that the marshal was the chief ministerial officer of the municipal corporation, that he executed and returned all processes, that he attended the sittings of his court, that he was obligated to repress all riots, disturbances, and breaches of the peace, and that he apprehended persons charged with offenses. In essence, that was how the marshal's duty was defined in New Jersey in 1821 and in New Mexico fifty-nine years later. Indeed, when a mid-western marshal arrested a happy-go-lucky reveler for shooting out the lamps in some nineteenth-century saloon, he was following in the footsteps of marshals in eighteenth-century New York, who were charged to apprehend those "evil-minded persons" who broke, took down, or carried away "the gas lamps hung out or fixed up before the dwelling houses. . .or have extinguished the lights therein."[2]

Marshals were drawn almost always from lower and lower-middle-class social and economic groups. One has only to attempt to decipher the arrest books of marshals and their deputies to realize how unlearned and uneducated many were. They could scarcely spell or write. Few cities specified, as did St. Louis, that officers must read, write, and speak the English language. Even if such criteria appeared on paper, they were not followed. Marshals' reports were apt to be a mass of misinformation and contradictions. Too many did not even know the law they were supposed to enforce.

Unfortunately, the practice of keeping personnel records was unheard of in most places during the nineteenth century, but information may still be pieced together that sheds light upon the national origins and occupations of peace officers. The qualifications of many a frontier marshal consisted of his alleged ability to use a gun, of his dexterity with his fists, of his political influence, or of his happening to be in the right town at the right time. In short, no consistent standards were applied. If any one quality was looked for, it was brute force. The Metropolitan Police of Washington, D. C. recruited bricklayers, carpenters, bookbinders, and, among others, tailors and printers. Historically, New York's Police Department hired clerks. Seattle expressed a preference for longshoremen and ex-sailors. San Francisco favored preliminary fighters and amateur pugilists.[3]

Musclemen, indeed, represented not only by town marshals but also by their successors, characterized the make-up of law-enforcement agencies. They were, as delineated by Edgar Lee Masters in his *Spoon River Anthology*, "grim, righteous, strong, courageous." Unfortunately, their righteous indignation was based upon a set of values which prevented them from distinguishing between what was true and good and what was evil and wicked. To them, might was right, and all too often they used the law only as an excuse to use that might. It was simpler to swing a sap than to understand a statute.

Yet, when it is understood that the principal duty of nineteenth-century local officers was quieting saloon brawls, subduing pugnacious drunks, and handling disorderly persons dedicated to assault and battery or assault to kill, the muscle marshal, with fists, billy, and loaded cane, was an asset. It is equally true that of all the misdemeanors, drunkenness stood first. The saloon, however romantically it may appear on stage or screen, was the primary breeding place of both petty and major crimes.

The proof of the effects of "four-fights-in-a-drink" whiskey is plainly set down in scores of marshals' arrest books, police blotters, and dockets of local courts. Month after month, throughout the Middle Border and beyond, more arrests were made for intoxication and for crimes resulting from drinking than for any other reason. Like Abou Ben Adam, the sot lead all the rest. He was the bane of the marshal's existence, for the tipsy individual was not only a threat to himself but also a menace to his family and the community. When he wore a gun or carried a knife, he could be terrifying. Marshals in river towns dreaded the arrival of steamboats, which discharged drunken and quarrelsome passengers and put ashore staggering roustabouts who had assaulted deckhands and officers.

Thousands of emigrants, traders, preachers, and travelers journeyed into the interior on steamboats. Tons of freight moved on river queens, flatboats, keelboats, and barges. River fronts and levees, generally squalid and packed with debris and the dregs of humanity, were headaches for marshals. Almost every "Front Street" was lined with saloons. Marshals were charged with keeping the peace and, in early days, served as wharfmasters. In addition to collecting wharfage fees from vessels that stopped to discharge or take on passengers and freight, marshals saw to it that levees did not become shanty towns or hideaways of petty thieves.

They prohibited unauthorized persons from using public landings as wood yards. Occasionally, they assisted duly appointed wharfmasters with the keeping of steamboat registers, entering the name of each boat that arrived or departed. St. Louis, as early as 1843, authorized the harbormaster to make arrests. The corpses of passengers or crews, whether dead from natural or other causes, were handed over to local marshals, who turned them over to the coroner.[4]

When they were otherwise engaged, marshals busied themselves with peddlers, vagrants, gamblers, and painted ladies. They looked in stores, shops, empty rooms, and deserted buildings to find, if possible, males dallying with the girls. Any person found in the Fort Madison cemetery in 1866 in company with a common prostitute, at any time during day or night, was subject to a jail term of thirty days and a fine of a hundred dollars plus court costs.[5]

Despite ordinances against prostitution, lawmen in frontier communities followed the practice of not bothering prostitutes if the ladies plied their calling with discretion and did not create a public disturbance. Madames and operators of cribs and "rooming houses" expected, as a matter of custom, to be hauled into court periodically, pay minimum fines, and return to business. This satisfied purer portions of the public, poured funds into school budgets, and, as the saying went, "didn't clip th' hair offen nobody." It seldom, however, quieted editors who bellowed for reform and castigated marshals for their laxity in enforcing the law.

Gamblers, like streetwalkers and bedroom solicitors, were as slippery and colorful as goldfish in a bowl and as equally exposed to public view. And, like guppies, they multiplied mightily despite constant and vigilant efforts to reduce their number. Generally speaking, local marshals tolerated games of chance by local, professional gamblers. Only when aroused citizens raised a fuss or when shills and shysters invaded a community to both gamble and disturb the peace did the law intervene except for periodic, token raids and arrests.

In 1839, citizens of Springfield, Illinois, sought ways to rid the town of a gang of gamblers who were a nuisance at home and a disgrace abroad. Eighteen years later, a marshal in Oquawka, Illinois, arrested thirteen gamblers armed with pistols, slungshots, and Bowie knives. As early as 1836, residents of St. Louis and of Vicksburg, Tennessee, campaigned actively against gamblers, idlers, and other unsavory characters "whose influence was pernicious to society." In dozens of communities, indignant townspeople attacked houses of ill fame, breaking windows, destroying furniture, and chasing thinly clad girls from the warmth of companionship into the chilly out-of-doors. The same treatment was accorded gamblers. Card sharks, on each advancing frontier, sooner or later, faced retribution. Faro Harry, a Virginia City gambler, even though sinuous as a snake, quick as a cat, and deadly with a pistol, was smart enough to be cautious. A ranchman, who knew Harry, explained:

But from observation of his perfect physique and some knowledge of the high esteem in which he was held by Virginia's undertakers, Harry's real motive for absenting himself from the rich pickings of mine owners' private rolls and pay rolls, and contenting himself with a packer's modest pay, was surmised by our party to lie in the fact that the local Virginia "Boot Hill" (especially reserved to the occupancy of gentlemen who passed out of this life with their boots on) was full to overflowing, suggesting a temporary suspension of his recreations until a contemplated addition to the "Hill" could be made ready.[6]

The odds against a marshal's suppressing either prostitution or gambling were about as great as were the odds against an untutored innocent trapped in a crooked game of dice or cards. Contrary to general belief keno frequently was a more popular pastime than was poker. Five-card stud poker and other variations symbolized the great American game not so much because more persons played poker, but because poker received more publicity. Hundreds of tales of the game appeared in sporting papers such as the *Spirit of the Times* and in Beadle's dime novels. On the other hand, local newspapers throughout the Middle Border and the western country were filled with pungent remarks decrying the presence and practices of keno manipulators. Three-card monte ran a close second. Six keno players were arrested in one week in Lincoln, Nebraska, in November, 1869, and a three-card monte man from Omaha operating there fleeced a visitor from Chicago of almost two hundred dollars some years later. In 1879, a notorious three-card monte expert was described as looking more like a clergyman than a gambler. Such examples could be multiplied a hundred fold. Gambling reached such a point in Denver that local law could not keep up with the comings and goings of professionals.[7]

Marshals and their deputies again and again were ordered by mayors to close all keno houses. Again and again, weary officers struck at such establishments. "Yesterday," said a Nebraska editor, "we understand Marshal Hollins received a note from his honor ordering him to close up the keno houses. Keno is dead in this community." However, the resurrection came quickly. In Omaha, in 1888, officers confiscated some three thousand dollars' worth of gambling equipment, including faro, roulette, and poker tables and check boxes, counters, wheels, faro boxes, and some two bushels of chips. Jail records for Lincoln, Nebraska, from 1886 to 1889 indicate far more arrests on charges of prostitution, intoxication, fighting, and vagrancy than for gambling, and Lincoln at that time might well have been considered a gambler's paradise.[8] These figures should be neither surprising nor startling, for they were typical of the arrest pattern throughout the country. St. Louis arrests, for example, for 1865, showed 2,371 charges of drunkenness, 1,900 of disturbing the peace, 560 of vagrancy, thirty-six of keeping a bawdy house, and forty-five of gambling.[9]

Yet such statistics must not convey the impression that marshals consistently gave scant attention to gambling. Much depended upon the marshal's temperament, the attitude of town and city officials, and, obviously, public opinion. As a rule enforcement in river towns was rather lax. Vigorous reform periods were followed by months of neglect. During the autumn of 1870 and the spring of 1872, St. Louis officers, spurred by criticism, closed some seventeen faro and five keno establishments in thirty-eight raids, carting off thousands of cards, chips, faro boxes, keno urns, balls, and check racks.[10] Such bursts of activity normally were sporadic and designed primarily to lull a sin-conscious public and to prevent preachers from sermonizing on a favorite topic. Once reformers and clergymen were quieted, the balls clattered and rolled again.

In the eyes of the law, prostitutes and gamblers were at least semi-respectable and entitled to some consideration. The madame of a whore house frequently was a lady of considerable political influence. A first-rate gambler, running a quiet, more-or-less honest establishment, frequently was an entrepreneur who, in large measure, boosted the local economy. Prostitutes and gamblers, as a result, were handled with care by marshals who knew who buttered some of their bread.

This was not true of the vagrant. He had no money, power, or influence and was victimized everywhere. Nobody cared who arrested him or why. The vagrant was the frontier's patsy. Everyone was his nemesis. To all he was a dirty, low-down, no-good sonofabitch. He had been prey of vicious injustice for centuries both in England and the United States. No ordinances placed greater and more far-reaching power in the hands of marshals than did those defining vagrancy. State statutes and local laws, following almost word for word English statutes relating to idle and disorderly ruffians, rogues and vagabonds, and incorrigible persons, wove a net that could be thrown over almost anyone. Local vagrancy ordinances were apt to be relatively brief, stating that any person convicted of being a vagrant, mendicant, street beggar, or common prostitute was subject to a fine. But such local laws rested upon state vagrancy statutes, which, in almost every instance, were lengthy and specific and read as if written by an Elizabethan or penned by a self-righteous clergyman with no conception of compassion. It must not be forgotten, even though it has been said before, that marshals were obliged to enforce all local ordinances that harmonized with state and federal law.

The South Dakota vagrancy statute of 1919 is typical of vagrancy statutes of the time.

All persons without visible occupation or means of support, loitering around houses of ill-fame, gambling houses or places where intoxicating liquors are drank (sic), all male persons who solicit or invite fornification or unlawful sexual intercourse by any person with any female, or who accepts the gratuities of any common prostitute; all common gamblers and all persons who shall attend or, operate any gambling device of apparatus; all persons commonly known as fortune tellers; any person who shall be engaged in practicing any trick or device to procure money or other thing of value; or shall engage in any unlawful calling; any able bodied married man who shall, without lawful excuse, neglect or refuse to provide for the support of his family; all persons tramping or wandering around and lodging in freight cars, barns, out houses, tents, wagons or vehicles, and having no visible calling, business or means of support; all persons begging in public places or from house to house or inducing children or others to do so; all persons found representing themselves as collectors of alms for charity institutions; all persons playing or betting in any street or public open space, at any game or pretended, game of chance, or at tables or other instruments of gambling; and all persons without a fixed abode within the state, camping on or along any public highway for the purpose of trading horses, whether as owner or owners of such horses, or otherwise.

All those enumerated, if found guilty of vagrancy, were subject to imprisonment in the county jail for not less than five days or more than thirty days, or by a fine of not less than five dollars or more than a hundred dollars, or by both fine and imprisonment.[11]

Local marshals, almost without exception, found the omnibus vagrancy laws more effective tools than hickory billies. Public endorsement supported enforcement. "The West has never been and should never be allowed to be," wrote a Minnesota editor in 1867, "a harbor for a class of individuals who are sufficiently able but too lazy to work for a living." A few years earlier, Dubuque citizens chained vagrants to a heavy block of timber sunk in the basement floor of the Market House. During 1888, 2,608 persons in Omaha were arrested on vagrancy charges. Despite examination of available statistics and of marshals' arrest books, it is today impossible to learn how many persons ran afoul of vagrancy acts, but one thing is certain: vast numbers of arrests were made on vague, blanket charges, such as "vagrancy" and "disorderly conduct" which were used loosely by marshals to "cover a multitude of sins which are not crimes." Many such arrests resulted in illegal detentions. The narrative of the law's treatment of the "vagrant" is, indeed, sordid.[12]

Vagrants were put to work breaking rock, repairing streets, and sweeping gutters while a marshal or a deputy stood over them with a loaded cane. A rather unusual punishment meted out to those convicted of vagrancy and other offenses, including grand larceny, occurred in Lincoln, Nebraska. There, during 1889, such offenders were, as the saying went and as entered in the jail records of the police department, "shipped to the front." This meant that prisoners, apparently unable to pay fines, in lieu of being sentenced to jail, were ordered to do manual labor for the Kilpatrick Construction which then was responsible for the construction of the Burlington and Missouri Railroad through northwestern Nebraska and Wyoming.[13]

A town marshal, supervising a chain gang, walking his weary rounds, rattling store doors to determine whether or not they were locked, snooping into saloons and livery stables, intervening in drunken brawls, and, now and again, shooting it out, in true western fashion, with some desperado, equipped himself during the early days of enforcement as best he could. His uniform was apt to be the normal garb of his community. If he were a river-town officer, the marshal might wear a black satinet coat, grey pants and vest, and coarse plough shoes. In cattle country, he donned broad-brimmed hat, woolen shirt, nondescript trousers, and, of course, boots and spurs. A mining-camp officer looked like a miner. Indeed, it was difficult to distinguish between citizens and officers in most places before the 1850s because the latter wore no badges. An eight-point, copper star was worn by New York City police in 1845. In 1850, St. Louis police adopted a metallic star, and in 1856 Chicago officers pinned on a six-point brass star. By 1868 badges were in general use.

Marshals ordered them by mail from a number of companies and from traveling salesmen who manufactured badges on the spot.[14]

Like sheriffs and constables, marshals selected and purchased pistols of their choice. Colt and Smith and Wesson were favorites. Officers frequently made their own billies from seasoned oak or hickory, or, after drilling a hole through the length of a nightstick, asked a local blacksmith to fill the hole with lead. Nashville, Tennessee, on May 6, 1871, purchased a supply of Smith and Wesson pistols, thirty-one holsters, and forty billies. In 1881, the Lincoln police department, headed by Marshal I. L. Lyman, owned six badges, two billies, one set of handcuffs, three nippers, and three whistles. An effective homemade sap might be purchased in saddleshops or leather establishments. The saps were oval-shaped and filled with shot. Handcuffs and nippers, although available, were not in general use much before 1880. Although George Rogers Clark on July 5, 1778 purchased four pairs of hand-forged handcuffs for ten dollars, supply houses did not furnish commercially made cuffs on a large scale until the 1870s.[15]

Contrary to some popular opinion—created perhaps by authors and script writers—most town marshals were not good shots. Indeed, there were officers who could throw a rock more accurately than they could aim a handgun and hit a target.

Closeup work was far more effective. "The muzzle of my gun was very busy against his ribs," said one officer, "and he was coming pretty fast." On the other hand, Dallas Stoudenmire, El Paso marshal, once killed two men in a shootout which was over almost before it began. James Butler Hickok (Wild Bill), when marshal of Abilene, shot and killed Phil Coe plus an innocent bystander. Apparently, Wyatt Earp, when marshal of Dodge City handled a gun fairly well, but he was far from being an expert shot. Ed Masterson, judging from his experiences when marshal at Dodge City, was less than competent. Now and again, as in the case of Marshal Tom Pollock of Denver, an officer was caught without weapons and was forced to rely upon blasphemous verbal threats. And sometimes, as in the case of Marshal Morgan of Burlington, and Joseph Beard of Lexington, Kentucky, marshals were killed in line of duty.[16]

In almost every community, at one time or another, the marshal was criticized either for shooting too much or too little or either not enforcing the laws adequately or being overzealous in upholding them. A typical blast appeared in 1858 in a Wisconsin newspaper:

> If the city marshal is afraid to do his duty—if he is fearful of another re-election and desires to keep the right side of rowdies and villains to effect it—he better appoint an efficient and wide-awake deputy. Drunkenness, fighting, house breaking and rowdyism are running riot in the city and not a man arrested! And it is reported that a counterfeiter was warned to leave town, by the city Marshal, or he would be arrested! Is it a fact? Are any of the officers linked with the villains? What is the trouble? We are opposed to mob violence and vigilance committees, but the people and their property must and will be protected. Will the city marshal do his duty or will he resign? These villains and drunken rowdies ought to be jerked up, and the law wants them to be executed with promptness and energy—without fear! Will Mr. Chambers [the marshal] do it? The people demand it and will sustain him in it![17]

Marshals received generous compliments only if town folks and editors believed them worthy. "I. L. Lyman—and nobody dare deny it—makes a good City Marshal and Street Commissioner. . . . He deserves the thanks of the entire community," said a Nebraska editor. Lyman and his deputies, on another occasion, were characterized as prompt, full of energy, and such rapid workers that they did not permit "any outside duffers to light in here and run the town to any appreciable extent." Peace officers, whether good or bad, seem to have received less newspaper space than did the soiled doves and gamblers they arrested or the bandits and evil ones they gunned down. Purple prose far too frequently was reserved for those outside of the law. Thus a "biographer" could say that Billy the Kid never showed a yellow streak, adding that "Every hour in his desperate life was a zero hour, and he was never afraid to die." Few such exaggerated tributes were paid even to outstanding marshals.[18]

Marshals not only enforced the law but also became involved with the law, as dozens of cases show. Some were serious, others comical, yet each settled a disputed point. The Portland, Oregon, city council on July 31, 1867 elected as marshal an individual named A. Rosenheim. His election was a sore disappointment to Marshal Henry L. Hoyt, who had held office since June 1866. Hoyt not only refused to relinquish the marshalship but also withheld books, papers, and property pertaining to the office. The election of Rosenheim, he maintained, was illegal because Rosenheim had been a member of the city council when he was chosen. This was clear proof that Rosenheim had voted for himself. The dispute, dragging through lower courts, finally reached Oregon's Supreme Court which vindicated Hoyt, holding that the offices of city councilman and city marshal were incompatible and could not be held by the same person. Furthermore, it was contrary to the policy of the law for an officer to use his official appointing power to place himself in office.[19]

Another case involved a local ordinance that proscribed the running at large of dogs, hogs, mules, horses, and cows. Marshals, under such an ordinance, were justified in picking up strays or unattended animals. Alamosa, Colorado, had such an ordinance upon its books and looked to a Marshal Hyatt to enforce it. One day a cow was ambling down the street, and Hyatt took up the cow, and later, in conformity with the law, detained and sold it. Although the money from the sale had been given to him, Mr. Brophy, the animal's owner, entered suit against the marshal for trespass, for unlawfully taking his cow away, and for selling a good milch animal, valued at a hundred dollars, for a considerably smaller sum. Brophy's attorney discovered that the record of Hyatt's appointment as marshal in the town minutes was interlined. The attorney argued that the interlineation was an error and that Hyatt's appointment was invalid; therefore, he had acted without authority when he confiscated Brophy's cow. The case went to the Supreme Court of Colorado, which held that Hyatt's appointment was valid and

The Town Marshal and the Police

that he had acted within his authority. Hyatt kept his star, Brophy lost his cow, and the town trustees learned to keep cleaner records.[20]

Somewhat more serious was a decision in 1894 handed down by the Kansas Supreme Court. It held that the marshal and police of a city and any persons aiding and abetting them were liable in damages for unnecessary cruelties and indignities inflicted upon prisoners in their charge. The following year, justices of the Texas Supreme Court held that a town marshal could lawfully arrest a person accused of a felony committed within the county, although not within the town. Once again, the court declared that a village marshal possessed the same powers as a county sheriff in the matter of prevention and suppression of crime and the arrest of offenders. In Iowa, the Supreme Court in 1894 held that an illegal arrest by a marshal was a breach of a bond to "faithfully . . . and without oppression discharge all duties. . . required by law."[21]

As can be seen a marshal's duties were so great that as hamlets grew into towns and as towns developed into cities more than one local officer was needed. A day marshal requested and usually succeeded in having a night watchman appointed. He might be classified as a deputy marshal, a night watchman, or a special policeman. When a local marshal discovered that he was unable to handle enforcement during daylight hours by himself, town selectmen and city councils aided him by appointing one or more deputies or special officers. The next step was to confer on the marshal the additional title of chief of police; thus a marshal was both marshal and police chief. Finally, the term "marshal" was dropped in favor of the new title. Such is the genealogy of many a modern police department. The functions of the chief remained the same, but to these were added the burdens of administration.[22]

Not all marshals became chiefs and commanded departments, however. Scores of communities preferred to keep the title of marshal and the marshal system, although sometimes a local marshal actually served as chief, but without the title. If this is somewhat confusing, one has only to keep in mind that it was not uncommon for citizens both to fear and resent what they believed to be the centralized authority of a chief; that they suspected that a chief was more susceptible to political influence than was a marshal; and that a marshal, like an old glove, was more comfortable to have around. Some of these objections were irrational, but others had some validity. Public whim and a sense of tradition also played a role. A marshal might *act* as if he were chief, but he was not one unless the office had been created by ordinance and he, under that ordinance, had been appointed or elected.

Even such long-established eastern cities as Baltimore, Maryland, and Worcester, Massachusetts, were still using the title of marshal in 1890. So were the Middle Border towns of Keokuk, Iowa, and Rock Island, Illinois. Throughout the Trans-Mississippi country and beyond the Missouri River, marshals, in 1890, headed well-organized or loosely knit departments in, for example, Des Moines, Iowa; Beatrice and Lincoln, Nebraska; Hutchinson, Kansas; and East Portland, Oregon. It is quite incorrect to say that, as a general rule, as communities grew bigger, the marshal always was replaced by a chief, although this was the trend. To illustrate: Baltimore's population in 1890 was 434,439, and its police department numbered 129 officers and 639 men. Beatrice's population at the same time was 13,836, and its force consisted of three officers and three men. This should shatter forever the common belief that a local officer always was a hick, small-town marshal.[23]

By the turn of the century, heads of departments, whether marshals or chiefs, had dressed officers and men in blue uniforms of varying design, ranging from those patterned after infantrymen's uniforms to ill-fitting sack suits. Patrolmen were equipped with revolvers, clubs, and whistles. Handcuffs, nippers, and "come-alongs" were in general use. Badges, in the shape of stars and shields, but usually without numbers by which to identify wearers, were commonplace. The three-shift system of eight hours per shift had been adopted in larger communities.

Today town marshals and police officers repeat age-old practices and face traditional dangers. They also symbolize a heritage. Throughout the hazardous history of law enforcement, it was the town marshal who, at the grass roots level, met as best he could the challenge of crime in a free society. Most did the best they could, even though the best was mediocre. Many who wore the star were inept and unfit, although not dishonest. Some were out-and-out rascals. A few were outstanding. All were conditioned by their times. Perhaps more significant is the fact that local marshals, although not always realizing it, provided, in so many instances, the stimulus, and the know-how for the development of modern police departments.

NOTES

1. For examples of state statutes on incorporation, see *Nebraska Statutes, 1867*, p. 696; *New York Laws, 1784—1813*, II, 493; *Combined Laws of the State of California, 1850—1853*, pp. 106—107; *Alabama Acts, 1839—1841*, p. 58; *Public Statutes of the State of Minnesota, 1849-1858*, pp. 301, 307, 310. An unusual variation, written into Kentucky law by the General Assembly, December Session, 1836, relating to the town of Mayslick, stipulated that instead of town trustees appointing a constable or marshal, they appoint a town sergeant, "who shall report to one member of the town board all persons who commit a breach of the peace and see to it that this act and all regulations in pursuit thereof be carried into effect."

2. *Laws of the State of New-Jersey, 1821*, p. 539; *General Laws of New Mexico, 1880*, p. 181; *New York Laws, 1784-1813*, II, 539—540.

3. *Evening Star* (Washington, D. C.), September 10, 1861; Laurence Veysey, ed., *Law and Resistance: American Attitudes Toward Authority* (New York, 1970), p. 279; for evaluation of police "professionalism," see Arthur Neiderhoffer, *Behind the Shield: The Police in Urban Society* (Garden City, New York, 1967).

4. Fort Madison Ordinance Book, p. 103; St. Louis, *Revised Ordinances, 1843*, p. 220.

5. Fort Madison Ordinance Book, 1865—1873, p. 21.

6. *Iowa Sun and Davenport and Rock Island News*, June 5, 1839; *Oquawka* (Illinois) *Spectator*, December 4, 1857; J. Thomas Scharf, *History of St. Louis City and County* (2 vols., Philadelphia, 1883), II, 18—35; *Vicksburg* (Tennessee) *Register*, September 24, 1835; Edgar Beecher Bronson, *Reminiscences of a Ranchman* (Lincoln, Nebraska, 1962), pp. 6—7.

7. Plattsmouth *Nebraska Herald*, November 11, 1869; Lincoln *Daily State Journal*, August 20, 1876, March 30, 1879. For gambling odds, see *Handbook*

on *Craps Containing Rules for the Inside Playing of the Game* (Cleveland, 1928) and Martin Gardner, "Mathematical Games—On the Ancient Lore of Dice and Odds Against Making a Point," *Scientific American,* CCXIX (November 1968), 140—145. For general discussions of prostitution and gambling, see Philip D. Jordan, *Frontier Law and Order* (Lincoln, Nebraska, 1970), chaps. 4, 8; Sandra Dallas, *Cherry Creek Gothic: Victorian Architecture in Denver* (Norman, Okla., 1971), chaps. 6, 7. For dime novels, see, for example, Edward Willett, *Flush Fred's Full Hand; or, Life and Strife in Louisiana* (No. 289, May 7, 1884); Willett, *Fred Flush, the River Sharp; or, Hearts for Stakes. A Romance of Three Queens and Two Knaves* (No. 483, January 25, 1888).

8. Plattsmouth *Nebraska Herald,* October 29, 1869; *Omaha Municipal Reports, 1888,* p. 256; Lincoln City Jail Register, 1886—1889, Nebraska State Historical Society, RG832.

9. Plattsmouth *Nebraska Herald,* October 29, 1869; *Omaha Municipal Reports, 1888,* p. 256; Lincoln Jail Register; *St. Louis Mayor's Message, May, 1865,* "Report of Chief of Police," n. p.

10. *St. Louis Mayor's Message, 1872,* pp. 102—103.

11. *South Dakota Revised Code, 1919,* s. 4403—4404.

12. *Winona* (Minnesota) *Daily Republican,* June 5, 1867; *Dubuque* (Iowa) *Miners' Daily Express,* August 13, 1852; *Omaha Municipal Records, 1887,* pp. 278—281; Alan Barth, *The Price of Liberty* (New York, 1961), p. 44.

13. Lincoln Jail Register, 1886—1889, July 25, 1889; Lincoln *Daily State Journal,* August 27, 28, 1889; Duane Reed, Nebraska State Historical Society, to the author, March 12, 1969.

14. George E. Virgines, "Badges of Law and Order," *The Westerners Brand Book* (Chicago, Ill.), XXIII (September 1966), pp. 49—51, 55—57; St. Louis, *Revised Ordinances,* 1850, p. 326; Raymond B. Fosdick, *American Police Systems* (New York, 1930), p. 70.

15. Robert J. Neal and Roy G. Jinks, *Smith and Wesson, 1857-1954* (New York, 1966), p. 154; James A. James, ed., *George Rogers Clark Papers, 1781-1784* (Springfield, Illinois, 1926), p. 255; Lincoln *Daily State Journal,* April 19, 1881. Among popular models were the Colt '72, the .44—40 Frontier Colt, and the Colt .45. Smith and Wesson favorites were, among others, Model 1869, Model 1875 (Schofield Patent), and the Wells Fargo variation of Model 1875. The Smith and Wesson Model 1899 (army and navy), in various barrel lengths, won enthusiastic endorsement among peace officers. The Remington New Model 1874 was less popular. The literature pertaining to handguns is so extensive, and, in certain areas, so provoking, that this author prefers to cite for introductory, general reference Charles Edward Chapel's *Guns of the Old West* (New York, New York, 1961), knowing full well that some gun experts and historians would prefer not only another title but also a lengthy bibliography.

16. Joe LeFors, *Wyoming Peace Officer* (Laramie, Wyoming, 1953), p. 150; Leon C. Metz, *Dallas Stoudenmire El Paso Marshal* (Austin, 1969), p. 46; Wayne Gard, *Frontier Justice* (Norman, 1949), p. 239; Dale T. Schoenberger,

The Gunfighters (Caldwell, Idaho, 1971), chap. 5; Stanley W. Zamonski and Teddy Keller, *The Fifty-Niners A Denver Diary* (Denver, 1961), pp. 74–75; *Oquawka Spectator,* September 11, 1850; J. Winston Coleman, Jr., *Retribution at the Court-House* (Lexington, Ky., 1957), pp. 5–6.

17. *La Crosse* (Wisconsin) *Independent Republican,* May 12, 1858.

18. Lincoln *Daily State Journal,* July 17, 1879, October 23, 1880; Walter Noble Burns, *The Saga of Billy the Kid* (New York, 1925), pp. 57–58.

19. State of Oregon *ex rel.* A. Rosenheim, Appellant, v. Henry L. Hoyt, Respondent, 2 Ore. 247 (1869).

20. Brophy v. Hyatt, 10 Col. 223 (1887).

21. The City of Topeka *et al* v. D. W. Boutwell, 53 Kan. 20 (1894); Geary Newburn v. B. A. Durham *et al,* 88 Tex. 288 (1895); John F. Yount, Appellant, v. M. J. Carney *et al,* 51 Iowa 559 (1894).

22. For the development of two major, urban police departments with histories involving marshals, see Roger Lane, *Policing the City Boston 1822-1885* (Cambridge, Mass. 1967) and James F. Richardson, *The New York Police Colonial Times to 1901* (New York, 1970).

23. Frederick H. Wines, *Report on Crime, Pauperism and Benevolence* (Washington, 1895), III, pt. 2, pp. 1024–1034.

CHAPTER 7

INDIAN POLICY REFORM AND AMERICAN PROTESTANTISM 1880-1900

Francis Paul Prucha, S.J.

> *Of the many friendships formed by Everett Dick during the 1969 summer at the Huntington Library, none was more treasured than that of Francis Paul Prucha, S.J., professor of history at Marquette University. This was understandable, for Paul Prucha has won the respect of the entire profession since he launched his academic career twenty years ago. During those two decades he has written more than a half-dozen books and some two-score articles, most of them stemming from his early interest in the army in the West or his recent concern with Indian policy. Few historians have done so much to correct our misapprehensions on both of those subjects, but particularly the latter. The multi-volume history of Indian policy on which he is now engaged promises to be one of the classic works of our generation. In the article written to honor Everett Dick, Father Prucha reveals the role of evangelical Protestantism in shaping relations with the Indians during the last two decades of the nineteenth century, thus opening a new vista on that important subject.*

The Trans-Mississippi West in the years after the Civil War was marked by scattered Indian reservations, the remnants of vast areas once claimed exclusively by the native Americans. With the aggressive expansion of the whites in the post-war years these reservations and their Indian inhabitants came under severe pressure. The Indians were considered a barrier to the advance of civilization and to the exploitation of the resources of the Great West. Their resistance to the invasion of their homelands by miners and settlers and to the devastating inroads into their cultural patterns that came with the wanton destruction of the buffalo led to wars that dominated the dozen years after Appomattox and dragged on for a dozen more. An abortive "Peace Policy" during President Grant's administration proved the existence of widespread sentiment in favor of just and peaceful dealings with the Indians, but only after military subjugation of the tribes did humanitarians have a free hand to develop a solution for the abiding "Indian problem."

Indian policy reform in the last two decades of the nineteenth century was led by a tight little group of dedicated men and women, who were convinced that at last they had discovered a proper answer to the question of what to do about the Indians. By insistent propaganda to awaken and inform the national conscience and thereby bend Congress and federal officials to their will, the reformers successfully shaped government policy and gave new drive and a new orientation to Indian–white relations in the United States.[1]

They were able to achieve so much because they were united and well organized. Organizations, indeed, sprang up spontaneously in several places at once as Indian affairs received public attention. In Boston a group of leading citizens, disturbed by the forced removal of the Ponca Indians from their lands in Dakota to Indian Territory, formed the Boston Indian Citizenship Committee in 1879 to fight for Indian rights and for the recognition of the Indian as a person and a citizen. At the same time a similar organization was getting under way in Philadelphia, led by a group of women who were aroused by injustices to the Indians and who hoped to stir up the people of the United States to demand reform in Indian affairs. Their organization began informally in 1879 but quickly acquired formal structure as the Women's National Indian Association, with branches throughout the nation. In 1882 a number of Philadelphia men, led by Herbert Welsh, founded the Indian Rights Association, which became the most important of the reform groups. Closely associated with these organizations was the official Board of Indian Commissioners. Originally established in 1869, it was made up of a group of humanitarian businessmen appointed to bring rectitude into Indian affairs by supervising the financial operations of the Indian Office. The Board eventually gave up direct participation in governing Indian relations and turned its efforts toward influencing public opinion.[2]

The work of these separate organizations was coordinated at an annual conference held each year at a resort hotel on Lake Mohonk, near New Paltz, New York. Here in a sylvan setting the self-denominated "Friends of the Indian" met to discuss Indian reform, to hear speakers on matters of concern, and to formulate resolutions that could be broadcast to the public and used to lobby for specific goals with Congress and government officials. The instigator of the Lake Mohonk Conferences and a continuing presence behind them was the owner of the resort, the Quaker Albert K. Smiley, who in 1879 had been appointed a member of the Board of Indian Commissioners. Dissatisfied with the brief meetings of the Board in Washington, he decided to invite its members and other interested persons to spend three days each year as his guests at Lake Mohonk. The first group assembled in 1883, and soon the meetings became the chief forum for the reformers. Their aim, as Smiley saw it, was "to unite the best minds interested in Indian affairs, so that all should act together and be in harmony, and so that the prominent persons connected with Indian affairs should act as one body and create a public sentiment in favor of the Indians."[3]

Their harmony was based on a common philanthropic and humanitarian outlook expressed in Christian terms, for the reform organizations had a strong religious orientation. The Women's National Indian Association was established under Baptist auspices, and although assuming a non-denominational posture, it consciously drew on church support. Its executive board in 1884 listed members from eight Protestant denominations—Baptist, Presbyterian, Episcopal, Congregational, Methodist, Quaker, Reformed, and Unitarian—and in the previous year had included Lutherans also. In 1883, moreover, the women specifically added missionary and school work to their efforts, and the Association took on many of the characteristics of a home missionary society. The leaders quoted with approbation in their publications a remark made by the Reverend Joseph Cook in 1885: "The first motto of all Indian reformers should be Indian evangelization. . . .Let us not depend on politicians to reform the Indian. We cannot safely depend even on the Government schools to solve the Indian problem. The longest root of hope for the Indians is to be found in the self-sacrifice of the Christian Church."[4] The Indian Rights Association, too, acknowledged the Christian motivation of its work. Herbert Welsh asserted that the Indian needed "to be taught to labor, to live in civilized ways, and to serve God." "The best Christian sentiment of the country," he said, "is needed to redeem the Indian, to stimulate and guide the constantly changing functionaries of the government who are charged with the task of his civilization."[5]

The atmosphere of deep religiosity in which the reformers worked was most notable at the Lake Mohonk Conferences. Each began with an invocation, and the discussions were redolent with religious spirit terminology. Part of this was due, no doubt, to the influence of the Quaker host; part, also, to the participation of many religious leaders. Of the names listed in the membership rosters, 1883–1900, more than a fourth were ministers, their wives, and representatives of religious groups, and a great many others were prominent lay leaders in their churches. The editors of the leading religious journals and papers, too, were regularly on hand. Presiding over the meetings in the 1890s was Merrill E. Gates, president of Rutgers and then of Amherst, a fervent promoter of the Christian spirit. His remarks at the opening of the conference in 1899 were not unrepresentative of the mood. He noted the beauty of the natural surroundings at Lake Mohonk and then continued:

> We believe in the government of a God whose will is at once beauty in the material world, and moral order in the world of will and action. We believe in the moral government of the universe; and we rejoice in the beauty of the physical earth as part of God's ordained order. We assemble as those who have faith in Him; and believing the reign of His holy will we delight in the beauty with which He surrounds us. But we come with earnest purpose, too. We recognize that we are not here for pleasure alone. We believe that we have a duty to the less-favored races; and in considering together the problems connected with these people we are touching almost every question of social reform and governmental administration.[6]

The conviction that they were engaged in Christian work was repeatedly expressed and universally assumed. "It may be taken for granted," the Reverend Lyman Abbott observed at Lake Mohonk in 1885, "that we are Christian men and women; that we believe in justice, good-will, and charity, and the brotherhood of the human race." And President Gates declared in 1891:

> This is essentially a philanthropic and Christian reform. Whatever may be our views, our slight differences of view or differences that may seem to us profound, we all gather here believing that the Lord of the world is the Lord Jesus Christ; believing that, ever since God himself became incarnate, for a man to see God truly, he must learn to see something of God in his fellow-man, and to work for his fellow-men. We come in the spirit of service.[7]

The word "Christian" dropped unselfconsciously from the lips of the reformers as they set about to do God's will, to guide the Indian "from the night of barbarism into the fair dawn of Christian civilization," as Herbert Welsh expressed it in 1886. The only hope for a solution to the Indian problem, Gates declared at the end of nearly two decades of organized humanitarian effort, was to bring the Indians "under the sway of Christian thought and Christian life, and into touch with the people of this Christian nation under the laws and institutions which govern the life of our States and Territories." As he welcomed the members of the Lake Mohonk Conference in 1900, he recalled again the Christian foundation of their work for Indian reform. "Nothing less than decades of years of persistent effort," he said, "years of effort prompted by that love of one's fellow-men which has its perennial root in the love of Christ for us, can do the work which here we contemplate and discuss." He welcomed especially the devoted missionaries who labored so diligently for their charges, but he gave a clue to the pervasive Christianity of the age when he turned to welcome, too, representatives of the Indian Bureau, whom he described as "Christian men of high purpose, whose aim in the issuing of regulations and the administration of Indian affairs is identical with the aims of the Christian workers in the field, and the Christian friends of the Indian who gather here."[8]

Sentiments such as these gave the tone to their public meetings, but the unity of the reformers was of a more fundamental nature than these pious expressions of Christian good will. Although there were debates and differences of opinion among the prominent men and women working for reform in Indian affairs in the 1880s and 1890s, there was strong underlying agreement in outlook and in goals. If we seek the foundation of this agreement, we find it principally in American evangelical Protestantism, which defined what the term "Christian" meant to these Friends of the Indian.

This was not surprising, for the history of the United States throughout the nineteenth century was marked by a strong evangelical movement.[9] So dominant was this force that one historian of American religion has asserted that the story of American Evangelicalism is "the story of America itself in the years 1800 to 1900, for it was Evangelical religion which made Americans the most religious people in the world, molded them into a unified, pietistic-perfectionist nation, and spurred them on to those heights of social reform, missionary endeavor, and imperialistic expansionism which constitute the moving forces of our history in that century."[10] The evangelicals, in fact, sought to create what has been called a "righteous empire" in America. They set out with considerable success "to attract the allegiance of all the people, to develop a spiritual kingdom, and to shape the nation's ethos, mores, manners, and often its laws."[11]

This religious motivation had important consequences for the nation's dealings with the Indians from 1800 to 1900; witness the continuing efforts, beginning early in the century, to educate, civilize, and Christianize the Indians and thus bring them into the national fold.[12] What marked the last decades of the century, however, was an intensification of the desire for unity, a new energy in the "quest for a Christian America," and an increasing emphasis on a secularized, as opposed to a theological, formulation of goals and activities. And it was exactly at this time that the "Indian problem" demanded a long overdue solution. The coincidence of an ultimate crisis in Indian affairs, brought about by the overwhelming pressure of aggressively expanding white civilization and the intensified religious drive for a unified American society, led to a new program of Indian policy reform. The consequences for the Indians and for the United States were as significant as the dramatic military encounters with the plains tribes that electrified the nation after the Civil War.

The distinguishing mark of American Evangelicalism was its insistence on individual salvation; the conversion and reformation of individuals would, evangelists believed, correct the evils of society. The Indian reformers eventually realized the fundamental conflict between this principle and the communal life and customs of the Indians. Their solution was to ignore the wishes of the Indians, and insist on their individualization and acculturation freed from bondage to the tribe. "The Indian as a savage member of a tribal organization cannot survive, ought not to survive, the aggressions of civilization," the Indian Rights Association declared in a typical statement in 1884, "but his *individual redemption* from heathenism and ignorance, his transformation from the condition of a savage nomad to that of an industrious American citizen, is abundantly possible."[13]

"The philosophy of the present [Indian] policy," Senator Henry L. Dawes, chairman of the Senate Committee on Indian Affairs, said in 1884, "is to treat him as an individual, and not as an insoluble substance that the civilization of this country has been unable, hitherto, to digest, but to take him as an individual, a human being, and treat him as you find him." Thomas Jefferson Morgan, a former Baptist minister and public school educator who was appointed Commissioner of Indian Affairs in 1889, urged that the tribal relation be broken up, socialism destroyed, and "the family and the autonomy of the individual substituted." Merrill Gates saw in individualism "the key-note of our socio-political political ideas of this century" and thought he could find sympathetic vibrations of it even among the Indians.[14] He epitomized the sentiments of the reformers as he summed up their two decades of work in 1900:

We have learned that education and example, and, pre-eminently, the force of Christian life and Christian faith in the heart, can do in one generation most of that which evolution takes centuries to do.

But if civilization, education and Christianity are to do their work, they must get at the individual. They must lay hold of men and women and children, one by one. The deadening sway of tribal custom must be interfered with. The sad uniformity of savage tribal life must be broken up! Individuality must be cultivated. Personality must be developed. And personality is strengthened only by the direction of one's own life through voluntary obedience to recognized moral law. At last, as a nation, we are coming to recognize the great truth that if we would do justice to the Indians, we must get at them, one by one, with American ideals, American schools, American laws, the privileges and the pressures of American rights and duties.[15]

The fight for individualization was carried on on many fronts by the evangelical reformers. Most important was the movement to break up tribal ownership and substitute the allotment of land in severalty.[16] Communal land holding was considered to be the substructure upon which tribal power rested. If it could be destroyed, the way would be clear for treating the Indian as an individual and absorbing him into American culture.

Allotments of land in severalty had been advocated from the days of Thomas Jefferson, and piecemeal legislation had authorized allotments for a number of tribes. Now such a process was too slow and uncertain to satisfy the new reformers. The panacea they sought was a general allotment law that would turn all Indians into individual land owners and break up traditional tribal relations. Allotment, said the Commissioner of Indian Affairs in 1881, would have the effect "of creating individuality, responsibility, and a desire to accumulate property" and would teach the Indians "habits of industry and frugality." It would be "the entering-wedge by which tribal organization is to be rent asunder," the Indian Rights Association declared in 1884.[17]

By concerted effort the reformers persuaded Congress to enact the Dawes Severalty Act of February 8, 1887, authorizing the President to allot portions of reservations to individual Indians, with the provision that the allotments be inalienable for twenty-five years. The Indians were to be made citizens when they received their allotments, and the surplus lands of the reservations were to be opened to white settlement.[18] Humanitarians hailed the Dawes Act as the "Indian Emancipation Act" and spoke of the beginning of a new epoch in Indian affairs. The importance attached to the principle embodied in the measure can be seen in Merrill Gates's paean to it in 1900:

The supreme significance of the law in marking a new era in dealing with the Indian problem, lies in the fact that this law is a mighty pulverizing engine for breaking up the tribal mass. It has nothing to say to the tribe, nothing to do with the tribe. It breaks up that vast "bulk of things" which the tribal life sought to keep unchanged. It finds its way straight to the family and to the individual. It recognizes and seeks to develop personality in the man and in the woman.[19]

The principle was further extended by a drive to treat the Indians as individual citizens before the law. Tribal jurisdiction, which hindered absorption into American life, was an abomination, and every effort to destroy it carried its own justification. "Acknowledge that the Indian is a man," said Henry S. Pancoast of the Indian Rights Association, "and as such give him that standing in our courts which is freely given as a right and a necessity to every other man." Professor James B. Thayer of Harvard Law School, the most vigorous of the reformers seeking to incorporate the Indians into the legal system of the United States, declared in 1886 that it was high time to put an end to "the monstrous situation of having people in our country who are not entitled to the full protection of our national constitution, who are native here and yet not citizens." He cared little about whether or not the Indians wanted to abandon their tribal relations; the United States could simply ignore the tribes and deal directly with individuals. "There is little harm in men associating together," Thayer said, "whether in tribes of Shakers or Oneida communities, or Odd Fellows, or Masons, or Germans, or colored men, or Indians, if they like; but as we do not carry on a separate commerce with the tribes of Shakers we had better stop doing it with the Indians."[20]

The individualism of the evangelical Protestants was tied closely to the Puritan work ethic. Hard work and thrift were virtues that seemed to be at the very basis of salvation. The reformers could conceive of no transformation for the Indians that did not include self-support. Annuities to the tribes and rations to subsist the Indians were blocks that prevented realization of the ideal. Until these were abolished and the Indians made to labor to support themselves and their families, there would be no solution to the Indian problem. Allotment of land in severalty was insisted upon because the reformers believed that without the labor needed to maintain the private homestead the virtue of hard work could never be inculcated.

Reformers commonly saw in labor a fulfillment of an essential command of God, as Merrill Gates did in 1885, when he criticized past efforts to aid the Indians. "Above all else we have utterly neglected to teach them the value of honest labor," he said. "Nay, by rations dealt out whether needed or not, we have interfered to suspend the efficient teaching by which God leads men to love and honor labor. We have taken from them the compelling inspiration that grows out of His law, 'if a man will not work, neither shall he eat!' "[21] The precepts of work and thrift reechoed again and again in Gates's addresses to the Lake Mohonk gatherings. In 1896 he explained once more the common goal and spoke of wakening in the Indian broader desires and ampler wants:

> To bring him out of savagery into citizenship we must make the Indian more intelligently selfish before we can make him unselfishly intelligent. We need to *awaken in him wants*. In his dull savagery he must be touched by the wings of the divine angel of discontent. Then he begins to look forward, to reach out. The desire for property of his own may become an intense educating force. The wish for a home of his own awakens him to new efforts. Discontent with the teepee and the starving rations of the Indian camp in winter is needed to get the Indian out of the blanket and into trousers,—and trousers with a pocket in them, and with a *pocket that aches to be filled with dollars!* [22]

Without personal property, Gates argued, there would be no strong development of personality, and he noted that the Savior's teaching was full of illustrations of the right use of property.

Individual development and the stimulation of honest labor, in the evangelical Protestant worldview, were possible only in the perspective of the family. Glorification of hearth and home was an essential element in their program for Christian living, for the Christian purity and virtues that they extolled could take root and be nurtured to full maturity only within the Christian family.[23] What the reformers saw of Indian life, therefore, seriously offended their sensibilities. Not understanding a culture that differed so markedly from their own, humanitarians saw only heathen practices, which they were obliged to stamp out as quickly and as thoroughly as possible. Polygamy was a special abomination, and the whole tribal arrangement was thought to create and perpetuate un-Christian modes of life. Gates's lengthy attack upon tribalism in 1885 was premised on the belief that it destroyed the family. "The family is God's unit of society," he declared. "On the integrity of the family depends that of the State. There is no civilization deserving of the name where the family is not the unit in civil government." But the tribal system, he believed, paralyzed both "the desire for property and the family life that ennobles that desire." As allegiance to the tribe and its chiefs grew less, its place would be taken "by the sanctities of family life and an allegiance to the laws which grow naturally out of the family."[24]

The goals envisaged for the Indians were deemed possible because the humanitarians believed in the unity of mankind. If the Indians were basically no different from other human beings—except for the conditioning coming from their environment—then there could be no real obstacle to their assimilation. "Let us forget once and forever the word 'Indian' and all that it has signified in the past," Charles C. Painter, lobbyist for the Indian Rights Association in Washington, told the Lake Mohonk Conference in 1889, "and remember only that we are dealing with so many children of a common Father." The doctrine of the brotherhood of man was a cardinal principle of the reformers, who wanted to erase all lines of distinction that separated the Indians from the rest of the nation. In the process traditional Indian customs were to be simply pushed aside as unimportant. In speaking of the proposal for severalty legislation, Philip C. Garrett said in 1886:

If an act of emancipation will buy them life, manhood, civilization, and Christianity, at the sacrifice of a few chieftain's feathers, a few worthless bits of parchment, the cohesion of the tribal relation, and the traditions of their race; then, in the name of all that is really worth having, let us shed the few tears necessary to embalm these relics of the past, and have done with them; and, with fraternal cordiality, let us welcome to the bosom of the nation this brother whom we have wronged long enough.

Commissioner of Indian Affairs Morgan, in speaking of Indian children, stressed first of all "their kinship with us." "They, too, are human and endowed with all the faculties of human nature," he observed; "made in the image of God, bearing the likeness of their Creator, and having the same possibilities of growth and development that are possessed by any other class of children."[25]

What especially marked the development of evangelical Protestantism and gave it its peculiar flavor during the last decades of the nineteenth century, however, was the subtle transformation that brought about an almost complete identification of Protestantism with Americanism. This shift culminated a movement extending through the century. During the early 1800s the coordination of the two elements, indeed, had been very close; Americanism and Protestantism protected each other. "So close was the bond, so deep the union," says one scholar, "that a basic attack on American institutions would have meant an attack on Protestant Christianity itself. Positively, defense of America meant a defense of the evangelical empire."[26] This "ideological amalgamation of Protestant denominationalism and Americanism," was not simply an acceptance of evangelical religion by the officials of the state. It came increasingly to be a complacent defense of the social and economic status quo by the churches. "Protestants, in effect," notes one writer, "looked at the new world they had created, were proud of its creator, and like Jehovah before them, pronounced it very good." Ironically, despite warnings of the necessity of separation of church and state, the churches gave a religious endorsement to the American way of life. Thus, under a system of official separation, Protestants eventually became "as completely identified with nationalism and their country's political and economic system as had ever been known in Christendom."[27] The perceptive English observer Lord Bryce noted in 1885: "Christianity is in fact understood to be, though not the legally established religion, yet the national religion."[28]

As the nineteenth century drew to a close, two forces intensified the union between Protestantism and Americanism. One was the weakening of traditional theological interest, so that the principles of Americanism became in large part the religious creed. The other was the growing threat to the dominance of the "righteous empire" by new forces in the United States, principally the influx of millions of European immigrants who did not fit the Anglo-Saxon Protestant pattern of America, and the growing industrialization and urbanization of the nation, which upset the foundations of the traditional rural Protestant outlook.

Afraid that the unity of America was being weakened, the churches promoted new measures to strengthen union and conformity. None of these was more important than a universal public school system, which, while reflecting and continuing evangelical Protestant virtues (under a cloak of "nonsectarianism") would instill the Americanism that had become a basic religious goal.[29] Typical was the stand taken by Thomas A. Morgan in his *Studies in Pedagogy,* published in the same year that he assumed direction of government Indian affairs. The "free schools of America," he wrote, would create a universal Americanism. The goal of teachers should be to bring about a common life among the various peoples who made up the nation. He considered the public schools to be "safeguards of liberty," the "nurseries of a genuine democracy," and "training schools of character." "They are American," Morgan declared. "Nothing, perhaps, is so distinctly a product of the soil as is the American school system. In these schools all speak a common language; race distinctions give way to national characteristics. . . ."[30]

The Indians were engulfed in this flood of Americanism. Their Americanization, indeed, became the all-embracing goal of reformers in the last two decades of the century. "The logic of events," Commissioner Morgan declared in his first annual report, "demands the absorption of the Indians into our national life, not as Indians, but as American citizens."[31] Nor were the Indians to be allowed to stand in the way of American progress. The reformers were convinced of the divine approbation of the spread of American culture, and the development of the West as an indication of that progress was part of the Protestant American mission. Tribal rights that would obstruct the fruitful exploitation of the nation's domain had to be sacrificed. The reform-minded Secretary of the Interior, Carl Schurz, saw that the advance of an enterprising people could not be checked, and he hoped to persuade the Indians to accept individual allotments of land that could be protected. "This done," he said, "the Indians will occupy no more ground than so many white people; the large reservations will gradually be opened to general settlement and enterprise, and the Indians, with their possessions, will cease to stand in the way of the 'development of the country.' " He hoped to maintain peace and to protect the Indians "by harmonizing the habits, occupations, and interests of the Indians" with those of the nation.[32]

Whereas Schurz lamented the inability of the government to protect the Indians against the march of progress, more radical reformers advocated absorbing the Indians as a matter of principle. "Three hundred thousand people have no right to hold a continent and keep at bay a race able to people it and provide the happy homes of civilization," Lyman Abbott told his colleagues at Lake Mohonk. "We do owe the Indians sacred rights and obligations, but one of those duties is not the right to let them hold forever the land they did not occupy, and which they were not making fruitful for themselves or others." The Indian reservations should be abolished, letting the full blast of civilization rush in upon the Indians. "Christianity is not merely a thing of churches and school-houses," Abbott insisted. "The post-office is a Christianizing institution; the railroad, with all its corruptions, is a Christianizing power, and will do more to teach the people punctuality than schoolmaster or preacher can." Morgan put it just as bluntly: "The Indians must conform to 'the white man's ways,' peaceably if they will, forcibly if they must. They must adjust themselves to their environment, and conform their mode of living substantially to our civilization. This civilization may not be the best possible, but it is the best the Indians can get."[33]

The reformers acknowledged their obligations to educate the Indians and to provide them, as much as possible, with the tools of civilization. But then individualism was to take its course. Once the doors were opened and the new light shown to the Indians, it would be up to them as individuals to make their own way; the law of the "survival of the fittest" would take over.

The means for their Americanization seemed to be at hand. Building on the foundation of individualism supplied by the land-in-severalty legislation and the provisions for granting American citizenship, reformers envisaged a universal national school system, which would do for the Indians what the public school system of the states was doing to assimilate other alien groups into the republic. The government and the humanitarian reformers joined hands to educate the Indians as individual Christian patriotic American citizens.

As early as 1880 the Board of Indian Commissioners remarked: "If the common school is the glory and boast of our American civilization, why not extend its blessings to the 50,000 benighted children of the red men of our country, that they too may share its benefits and speedily emerge from the ignorance of centuries?"[34] After the enactment of the Dawes Act Indian education loomed as ever more important, for reformers realized at last that neither the individual homestead nor the citizenship that went with it would transform the Indians into real Americans unless they had education that would fit them to meet the responsibilities of their new status.

The Lake Mohonk Conference of 1888 devoted most of its time to a discussion of Indian education. The conference began with a formal paper read by Lyman Abbott, who in his usual forthright manner called for a plan "for solving the educational problem of the Indian race,—for converting them from groups of tramps, beggars, thieves, and sometimes robbers and murderers, into communities of intelligent, industrious, and self-supporting citizens." He insisted that this was the responsibility of the national government and could not be relegated to voluntary associations (that is, in the main, to missionary groups). The conference, following his lead, adopted a platform that condemned the "ill-organized and unsystematic educational methods of the Government" and called for a "well-organized system of popular education, framed in accordance with the principles of our American institutions, and competent to provide the entire Indian race with adequate education." It noted that the cost of education was only a fraction of the cost of war, that the expense of educating the Indian for self-support was less than one-tenth the cost of keeping him in pauperism, and it pledged its cordial cooperation in efforts "to remove at once the National dishonor of supporting ignorant and barbaric peoples in the heart of a Christian civilization."[35]

A blueprint for a systematized universal school system for the Indians was soon provided. Only three months after Thomas J. Morgan entered upon his duties as Commissioner of Indian

Affairs he presented the Lake Mohonk Conference with a ready-made plan. Morgan began with a stance of humility, seeking the counsel of those present. "When President Harrison tendered me the Indian Bureau," Morgan related, "he said, I wish you to administer it in such a way as will satisfy the Christian philanthropic sentiment of the country. That was the only charge that I received from him. I come here, where the Christian philanthropic sentiment of the country focuses itself, to ask you what will satisfy you." He had but one motive, he told the conference: "to embody in administrative work the highest thought which you elaborate in regard to the treatment of the Indians." [36]

Morgan outlined a school system modeled upon the public schools, with special provisions for high schools, grammar schools, and primary schools. The education was intended for all Indian children and was to be compulsory, and although special stress was placed on industrial training that would fit the Indians to earn an honest living, Morgan asked also for "that general literary culture which the experience of the white race has shown to be the very essence of education," for which command of English was indispensable. Elements in his proposal strikingly reflected the goals of the Christian America he and the Lake Mohonk philanthropists idealized.

"The chief thing in all education," he asserted, "is the development of character, the formation of manhood and womanhood. To this end the whole course of training should be fairly saturated with moral ideas, fear of God, and respect for the rights of others; love of truth and fidelity to duty; personal purity, philanthropy, and patriotism. Self-respect and independence are cardinal virtues, and are indispensable for the enjoyment of the privileges of freedom and the discharge of the duties of American citizenship." The Protestant emphasis on the virtues of hard work and regularity was evident. "Labor should cease to be repulsive, and come to be regarded as honorable and attractive," Morgan insisted. And the students were to learn the virtue of economy and to understand that waste was wicked. The grammar schools were to be organized and conducted so that they would accustom the pupils to systematic habits. "The periods of rising and retiring, the hours for meals, times for study, recitation, work and play," he directed, "should all be fixed and adhered to with great punctiliousness." His goal was to replace the "irregularities of camp life" with "the methodical regularity of daily routine." Such routine would develop "habits of self-directed toil," and teach the students "the marvelous secret of diligence." "When the Indian children shall have acquired a taste for study and a love for work," he proclaimed, "the day of their redemption will be at hand."[37]

Morgan's proposed educational system would strengthen home and family life, as the reformers understood it. "Owing to the peculiar surroundings of the mass of Indian children," he declared, "they are homeless and are ignorant of those simplest arts that make home possible." So the schools he proposed were to be boarding schools wherever possible, schools that would draw the Indian children away from "the heathenish life of the camp." The grammar school years, especially, were looked upon as a period in which it would be possible "to inculcate in the minds of pupils of both sexes that mutual respect that lies at the base of a happy home life, and of social purity." And it was Morgan's aim for the children to be taken into the schools "at as early an age as possible, before camp life has made an indelible stamp upon them."[38]

To all these goals of Indian education was to be added inculcation of American patriotism. Indian children were to be "instructed in the rights, duties, and privileges of American citizens, taught to love the American flag, . . . imbued with a genuine patriotism, and made to feel that the United States and not some paltry reservation, is their home." They were to be educated, not as Indians, but as Americans. "In short," Morgan noted, "the public school should do for them what it is so successfully doing for all the other races in this country,—assimilate them." [39]

The exclusively Protestant character of the Americanism represented by the Indian reformers was demonstrated by the growing attack upon Roman Catholicism in the 1880s and 1890s. The increased immigration of Catholics from southern and central Europe, the unfortunate emphasis and interpretation given to the declaration of papal infallibility, and the impolitic appointment of Monsignor Satolli as Apostolic Delegate gave great concern to Protestants, whose domination of American society appeared to be threatened. "Patriotic" organizations, which preached a "pure" Americanism, began to thrive and eventually coalesced into the nativistic American Protective Association at the very time that Indian reform reached a climax. The school question was the center of much of the bitterness, as Catholics, objecting to the Protestant Christianity that pervaded the "non-sectarian" public schools, established parochial schools and then sought to win support from public funds.[40]

The Indians were to be victims of this conflict. A system of mission schools supported in part by government funds had emerged in the 1870s and 1880s. These so-called "contract schools" fit well into the traditional cooperation between the federal government and missionary societies for the education of Indian youth. Churches supplied the school buildings and the teachers, and the government paid an annual amount to the school for each child enrolled. By the end of the 1880s, however, Protestants discovered with alarm that the great bulk of the contract school funds were going to Roman Catholics. In 1889 $347,672 out of a total of $530,905 was distributed to Catholic schools; the Presbyterians with $41,825 ran a poor second.[41] Thomas J. Morgan, who had lashed out at Catholics when he was principal of a school in Rhode Island, did not shed his views about the sanctity of the public school system when he became Commissioner of Indian Affairs in 1889. Catholic fears were increased when Daniel Dorchester, who had previously condemned the Catholic school system in Boston, was appointed Superintendent of Indian Schools in Morgan's department. Catholics worked zealously to prevent Senate confirmation of the two appointments, but without success. The two men, it is true, maintained a careful objectivity in their public acts, but the dominant atmosphere of Indian reform was hostile to government support of the Catholic contract schools.[42]

Foremost among the critics of the Catholic mission schools was the Reverend James M. King, secretary of the National League for the Protection of American Institutions, who spoke at Lake Mohonk in 1890 on "The Churches: Their Relation to the General Government in the Education of the Indian Races."[43] Over the next years his attack gained intensity. In 1892, he referred to an "unscrupulous" attack made by a Catholic missionary on the government schools "because they have the Protestant Bible and gospel hymns in them." Then he went on to make his point: "In this Columbian year it becomes us to remember that our civilization is not Latin, because God did not permit North America to be settled and controlled by that civilization. The Huguenot, the Hollander, and the Puritan created our civilization. Let us not put a premium by national grants on a rejected civilization in the education of a race who were here when Columbus came." King concluded that "much Roman Catholic teaching among the Indians does not prepare them for intelligent and loyal citizenship. The solution of the Indian problem consists in educating them for citizenship as we educate all other races."[44]

Although Catholic action against Morgan's administration of Indian affairs helped to defeat President Benjamin Harrison in 1892, and Morgan and Dorchester left office, the pressure against the contract schools was too widespread to overcome. The Protestant denominations quietly withdrew from the program, preferring to lose their own meager benefits rather than to see the Catholics profit. And little by little Congress wore away the contract school system. In 1896 the funds were reduced to 80 per cent of the previous year's, and by 1900 the government support of church-run schools for the Indians was cut off altogether. The Catholics won a favorable decision in regard to money that came from the Indians through treaty rights, rather than by direct appropriation, but the position of the Protestant reformers won the day.[45] The Indians were to be educated in government schools, in order to become exemplary American citizens in the Protestant tradition of the nation.

The opposition to contract schools did not mean that Christian influences upon the Indians were eliminated. Great emphasis continued to be placed on Christian endeavor outside the formal school system. When President Edward H. Magill of Swarthmore College had addressed the Lake Mohonk gathering in 1887, he had noted that the Dawes Act opened the way to the civilization of the Indians but had added, "for the realization of all our highest hopes for the Indian, for his education and training, for his introduction as an equal among a civilized people, and for his preparation for the high and responsible duties of American citizenship, we must look largely, if not chiefly, to the religious organizations of our country." Commissioner Morgan, while fighting government appropriations for missionary schools, had admitted the need for "the influence of the home, the Sabbath-school, the church, and religious institutions of learning" and for "consecrated missionary work."[46] In 1893 Merrill Gates turned again to his oft-repeated theme. He told the people at Lake Mohonk:

Only as men and women who are full of the light of education and of the life of Christ go in and out among these savage brothers and sisters of ours, only as the living thought and the feeling heart touch their hearts one by one, can the Indians be lifted from savagery and made into useful citizens. . . .As we get at them one by one, as we break up these iniquitous masses of savagery, as we draw them out from their old associations and immerse them in the strong currents of Christian life and Christian citizenship, as we send the sanctifying stream of Christian life and Christian work among them, they feel the pulsing life-tide of Christ's life.[47]

This "pulsing life-tide" found eager transmitters in the committed Christians working as teachers within the government Indian schools, for it was understood that these schools would reflect the Protestant Americanism that had been the goal of their founders. Lyman Abbott outlined the pattern when he spoke against the contract schools in 1888: "Religion is, after all, a matter of personal influence more than of catechetical instruction. If the Government will come to the churches for Christian teachers, the churches may well agree to leave the catechisms out of the schools in which these Christian teachers do their work."[48]

Clearly the Indian reformers of the late nineteenth century were not, as they have sometimes been depicted, a small, peripheral group of men and women, who by clever machinations and unjustified propaganda foisted a program of reform upon Congress and the Indian service.[49] Neither the men nor their impact can be understood in that narrow perspective. Rather, they represented or reflected a powerful and predominant segment of Protestant church membership, and thereby of late nineteenth century American society. When they spoke, they spoke for a large majority of the nation, expressing views that were widely held, consciously or unconsciously. They were the chief channel through which this Americanism came to bear upon the Indians.

It was the fate of the Indians that the "solution" of the "Indian problem" that had troubled the national conscience throughout the nineteenth century should have been formulated when such a group was in command. The Friends of the Indian set out with good intentions to stamp out Indianness altogether and to substitute a uniform Americanness; to destroy all remnants of corporate existence or tribalism and to replace them with an absolute rugged individualism that was foreign to the traditions and hearts of the Indian peoples. Through land ownership, citizenship, uniform legal status, and above all through education, the Indians were to be turned into patriotic Americans. If the reformers were wrong in both goals and methods (as subsequent events demonstrated that they were), they erred because the America they represented was so satisfied with its vision of the world that everyone was expected to accept and conform. The humanitarians who so confidently devoted their energy and good will to solving the Indian problem simply mirrored the tenets of American civilization and gave them the added force of religious endorsement.

NOTES

1. The Indian policy of the United States in the period after the Civil War has been studied in Loring Benson Priest, *Uncle Sam's Stepchildren: The Reformation of United States Indian Policy, 1865-1887* (New Brunswick, 1942); Henry E. Fritz, *The Movement for Indian Assimilation, 1860-1890* (Philadelphia, 1963); and Robert Winston Mardock, *The Reformers and the American Indian* (Columbia, Missouri, 1971). These books provide a general background for the reform movement in Indian affairs from 1880 to 1900.

2. General information on these organizations can be found in the books by Priest, Fritz, and Mardock cited above. For details about the programs and activities of the Women's National Indian Association, see the annual reports of the Association, the numerous pamphlets published by the group, and its periodical, *The Indian's Friend,* begun in 1888. The Indian Rights Association reported its activities in its annual reports and published a great many informational and hortatory items in pamphlet form. The Board of Indian Commissioners also issued substantial annual reports.

3. *Lake Mohonk Conference Proceedings,* 1885, p. 1. The *Proceedings* of the Lake Mohonk Conferences appeared under varying titles. Ultimately the standard form was *Proceedings of the Fifth Annual Meeting of the Lake Mohonk Conference of Friends of the Indian.* Throughout this chapter a simplified citation, with the year, will be used. The *Proceedings* were also printed in the annual reports of the Board of Indian Commissioners.

4. The missionary work is reported in the annual reports and in special pamphlets published by the Association. See *Missionary Work of the Women's National Indian Association, and Letters of Missionaries* (Philadelphia, 1885); and *Sketches of Delightful Work* (Philadelphia, 1893). The statement of Cook appears on the title page of *Missionary Work.*

5. Herbert Welsh, *The Indian Question Past and Present* (Philadelphia, 1890), pp. 15, 18.

6. *Lake Mohonk Conference Proceedings,* 1899, p. 9.

7. *Lake Mohonk Conference Proceedings,* 1885, p. 50; *Lake Mohonk Conference Proceedings,* 1891, p. 11.

8. Herbert Welsh, "The Needs of the Time," *Lake Mohonk Conference Proceedings,* 1886, p. 13; *Lake Mohonk Conference Proceedings,* 1900, pp. 13, 21.

9. I have learned much about evangelical Protestantism from Robert T. Handy, "The Protestant Quest for a Christian America," *Church History* XXII (March 1953), 8−20; Robert T. Handy, *A Christian America: Protestant Hopes and Historical Realities* (New York, 1971); Martin E. Marty, *Righteous Empire: The Protestant Experience in America* (New York, 1970); William G. McLoughlin, ed., *The American Evangelicals, 1800-1900: An Anthology* (New York, 1968); and Sidney E. Mead, *The Lively Experiment: The Shaping of Christianity in America* (New York, 1963).

10. McLoughlin, *American Evangelicals,* p. 1. He concludes: "The history

of American Evangelicanism is then more than the history of a religious movement. To understand it is to understand the whole temper of American life in the nineteenth century." Ibid., p. 26.

11. Marty, *Righteous Empire,* Foreword.

12. For examples of these efforts, see Robert F. Berkhofer, Jr., *Salvation and the Savage: An Analysis of Protestant Missions and American Indian Response, 1787-1862* (Lexington, Kentucky, 1965); Francis Paul Prucha, "American Indian Policy in the 1840s; Visions of Reform," in John G. Clark, ed., *The Frontier Challenge: Responses to the Trans-Mississippi West* (Lawrence, Kansas, 1971), pp. 81–110; and the accounts of Grant's Peace Policy in Priest, *Uncle Sam's Stepchildren,* and Fritz, *Movement for Indian Assimilation.* The religious aspects of the Peace Policy are fully treated in Robert H. Keller, Jr., "The Protestant Churches and Grant's Peace Policy: A Study in Church-State Relations, 1869–1882," Ph.D. dissertation, University of Chicago, 1967.

13. *Report of the Indian Rights Association,* 1884, p. 5. Emphasis added.

14. *Report of the Board of Indian Commissioners,* 1883, p. 69; Report of Morgan, October 1, 1889, in *House Executive Document* No. 1, 51st Cong., 1st Sess. (Ser. No. 2725), p. 4; Merrill E. Gates, "Land and Law as Agents in Educating Indians," *Report of the Board of Indian Commissioners,* 1885, p. 26.

15. *Lake Mohonk Conference Proceedings,* 1900, p. 14.

16. The movement for land in severalty that culminated in the Dawes Act of 1887 is carefully traced in Priest, *Uncle Sam's Stepchildren,* Section IV. See also, D. S. Otis, "History of the Allotment Policy," in *Adjustment of Indian Affairs* (Hearings before the Committee on Indian Affairs, House of Representatives, 73rd Cong., 2nd Sess., in H. R. 7092, Washington, 1934), Part 9, pp. 428–489; and J. P. Kinney, *A Continent Lost—A Civilization Won: Indian Land Tenure in America* (Baltimore, 1937).

17. Report of Hiram Price, October 24, 1881, in *House Executive Document* No. 1, 47th Cong., 1st Sess. (Ser. No. 2018), p. 17; *Report of the Indian Rights Association,* 1884, p. 6.

18. 24 U.S. *Statutes at Large,* pp. 388–390 (1887). A good contemporary account of the Dawes Act is James B. Thayer, "The Dawes Bill and the Indians," *Atlantic Monthly,* LXI (March 1888), 315–22.

19. *Lake Mohonk Conference Proceedings,* 1900, p. 16.

20. Henry S. Pancoast, *Impressions of the Sioux Tribes in 1882, with Some First Principles in the Indian Question* (Philadelphia, 1883), p. 22; James B. Thayer, *Remarks Made at a Meeting in Cambridge, Mass., Called by the Women's Indian Association of That City, May 3, 1886* (n.p., n.d.).

21. "Land and Law as Agents in Educating Indians," *Report of the Board of Indian Commissioners,* 1885, p. 18.

22. *Lake Mohonk Conference Proceedings,* 1896, p. 11.

23. McLoughlin, speaking of the middle third of the century, notes: "It is difficult to find a collection of Evangelical sermons in this period which does not devote at least one sermon to 'The Christian Home' and another to 'Motherhood.' It was the Evangelicals who made home and hearth the central features of American sentimentalism." *American Evangelicals,* p. 17.

24. "Land and Law as Agents in Educating Indians," *Report of the Board of Indian Commissioners,* 1885, pp. 27–29.

25. Charles C. Painter, "The Indian and His Property," *Lake Mohonk Conference Proceedings,* 1889, p. 88; Philip C. Garrett, "Indian Citizenship," *Lake Mohonk Conference Proceedings,* 1886, p. 11; Thomas J. Morgan, *A Plea for the Papoose: An Address at Albany, N.Y., by Gen. T. J. Morgan* (n.p., n.d.), pp. 2–3.

26. Marty, *Righteous Empire,* p. 89.

27. Mead, *Lively Experiment,* pp. 142, 156–157.

28. Quoted in McLoughlin, *American Evangelicals,* p. 26. See also, John Edwin Smylie, "National Ethos and the Church," *Theology Today,* XX (October 1963), pp. 313–21.

29. Robert T. Handy notes: "The cultural dominance of Protestantism was illustrated in the transition to a public tax-supported school system; this transition was palatable to Protestants because the schools were rather clearly Protestant in orientation, though 'non-sectarian.' " "The Protestant Quest for a Christian America," p. 11. See also Handy, *A Christian America,* pp. 101—05.

30. Thomas J. Morgan, *Studies in Pedagogy* (Boston, 1889), pp. 327–28, 348–50.

31. Report of Morgan, October 1, 1889, *House Executive Document* No. 1, 51st Cong., 1st Sess. (Ser. No. 2725), p. 3.

32. Carl Schurz, "Present Aspects of the Indian Problem" *North American Review,* CXXXIII (July 1881), 17, 23.

33. *Lake Mohonk Conference Proceedings,* 1885, pp. 51–52; Report of Morgan, October 1, 1889, *House Executive Document* No. 1, 51st Cong., 1st Sess. (Ser. No. 2725), p. 3.

34. *Report of the Board of Indian Commissioners,* 1880, p. 9.

35. *Lake Mohonk Conference Proceedings,* 1888, pp. 11, 94–95.

36. *Lake Mohonk Conference Proceedings,* 1889, p. 16. Morgan's address at Lake Mohonk was submitted on December 1, 1889, to the Secretary of the Interior as a "Supplemental Report On Indian Education," and printed in *House Executive Document* No. 1, 51st Cong., 1st Sess. (Ser. No. 2725), pp. 93–114.

37. "Supplemental Report on Indian Education," pp. 98–101.

38. Ibid., pp. 99–101, 103.

39. Ibid., p. 96.

40. The best account of anti-Catholicism in the late nineteenth century is Donald L. Kinzer, *An Episode in Anti-Catholicism: The American Protective*

Association (Seattle, 1964). See also, John Higham, *Strangers in the Land: Patterns of American Nativism, 1860-1925* (New Brunswick, 1955), Chapters III and IV.

41. The figures are given in Report of Morgan, September 5, 1890. *House Executive Document* No. 1, 51st Cong., 2nd Sess. (Ser. No. 2841), p. xvii. An excellent history of church–state cooperation in Indian schools is R. Pierce Beaver, *Church, State, and the American Indians: Two and a Half Centuries of Partnership in Missions Between Protestant Churches and Government* (St. Louis, 1966).

42. Information on the conflict over contract schools is in Harry J. Sievers, "The Catholic Indian School Issue and the Presidential Election of 1892," *Catholic Historical Review,* XXXVIII (July 1952), 129–55.

43. *Lake Mohonk Conference Proceedings,* 1890, pp. 51–58.

44. *Lake Mohonk Conference Proceedings,* 1892, pp. 63–64. A strong Catholic attack upon the sectarian nature of the government Indian schools was made by the Reverend J. A. Stephan, Director of the Bureau of Catholic Indian Missions, in 1893. The attack brought sharp reaction from the Protestants. See *Report of the Board of Indian Commissioners, 1893,* pp. 112—13.

45. The official actions of the Presbyterians, Baptists, Episcopalians, Congregationalists, and Methodists are appended to Report of Morgan, August 27, 1892, *House Executive Document* No. 1, 52nd Cong., 2nd Sess. (Ser. No. 3088), pp. 177–182. See also Beaver, *Church, State, and the American Indians,* p. 167, and Laurence F. Schmeckebier, *The Office of Indian Affairs: Its History, Activities, and Organization* (Baltimore, 1927), pp. 212–13.

46. *Lake Mohonk Conference Proceedings,* 1887, p. 60; Morgan, "Supplemental Report on Indian Education," p. 97.

47. *Lake Mohonk Conference Proceedings,* 1893, p. 12. This personal and persuasive approach, which marked Protestant missionary effort, contrasted with the more sacramental approach of the Roman Catholics. For an excellent comparison of the two groups of missionaries on a single reservation, see Howard L. Harrod, *Mission Among the Blackfeet* (Norman, 1971).

48. *Lake Mohonk Conference Proceedings,* 1888, p. 15.

49. This view is taken, for example, by George E. Hyde in *A Sioux Chronicle* (Norman, 1956). In a chapter entitled "The Brethren" he ridicules the work of the humanitarian reformers.

CHAPTER 8

CORPORATION FARMING IN CALIFORNIA

Paul Wallace Gates

> *No volume honoring Everett Dick would be complete without an essay on land policy, a subject to which he has contributed significantly and about which he wrote in his latest book, the* Lure of the Land *(1970). That Paul Gates, until his retirement in 1971 one of Cornell's most distinguished professors, should be invited to contribute such an essay was natural, for no scholar has contributed more to our understanding of the nation's land laws and their administration. From the day thirty years ago when his* Wisconsin Pine Lands of Cornell University *appeared to the publication in 1968 of his monumental* History of Public Land Law Development, *his many books and articles have revolutionized our knowledge of land disposal. The essay that he has prepared for this volume is in his best tradition, for it not only explores a little-known topic but shows how giant corporations have distorted well-intended land laws for their personal gain.*

For many years critics of the United States Department of Agriculture have maintained that it, like the agricultural colleges, was primarily concerned with the welfare of the large commercial farmer and neglectful of that of the small man getting a meager income from his limited acreage. They have pointed to the slowness with which the department became alerted to the forces contributing to the rapid increase in tenancy between 1920 and 1935 in the more commercial sections of the corn, wheat, and cotton belts; share croppers and tenants did not benefit from the crop reduction program of the Agricultural Adjustment Administration which tended to deprive them of their livelihood; the later crop control programs gave and are still giving an impetus to the elimination of hundreds of thousands of small farmers from agriculture. Critics might also have scored department officials for their opposition to restrictions on the size of benefit payments and to efforts to limit them to $55,000 or less.[1] Critics have also charged that the department made no effective effort to challenge the enormous, non-reimbursable Federal expenditures on irrigating the dry lands of the West that have underminded many aspects of agriculture in older sections of the country; that it has watched complacently while the Department of the Interior has failed to make effective efforts to enforce the land limitation in the reclamation legislation; and that it has shown little concern about corporation farming, which, some authorities fear, threatens the continuation of the family farm.

The Government and Corporation Farms

Some of the benefits corporate farm enterprises were receiving from the public purse came to light in 1969 when Representative Paul Findley of Illinois and Senator John J. Williams of Delaware had the statistics published in the Congressional Record.[2] Under the Agricultural Stabilization and Conservation Program, 6,536 corporations, partnerships, and family and individual farmers were paid more than $25,000 each in 1967 for withholding land from producing certain surplus crops. Findley inserted additional data showing the great gulf between the payments to the upper 20 percent of cooperating "farmers" and the lower 40 percent.[3]

PAYMENTS FOR LAND WITHDRAWAL

	Percentage of total payments received by upper 20% of cooperating farmers	Percentage of total payments received by lower 40% of cooperating farmers
Sugar Program	83%	2.9%
Cotton Program	69%	6.6%
Wheat Program	62%	8.1%
Feed Grains	56%	4.9%

More shocking were the details of payments. Heading the list for the entire country for 1967 was J. G. Boswell of California, who received $7,643,303 for partial land withdrawal on his ranches in San Joaquin Valley, on his Rancho San Antonio in Fresno County, and on his South Lake Farms in Kings County. Next on the list came two sugar-producing companies in Florida and Hawaii, which were each paid more than a million dollars for reducing their sugar output. Sixth on the list was the Kern County Land Company, whose payments came to $838,130. Other companies that received large payments for reducing their crops in California were the Salyer Land Company, $789,910, Miller & Lux, $237,271 (plus $126,049 for the Bowles Farming Co.), the Irvine Company, $179,696, and the Tejon Ranch Company, $115,802.[4] The payments for 1968 were also breathtaking[5]:

Program	Payments
Cotton acreage and diversion	$ 786,518,386
Feed grains diversion and support payments	1,366,034,710
Wheat support	747,407,190
Sugar Act	83,394,126
Wool Act	69,435,004
Agricultural conservation	208,160,824
Crop land adjustment	80,533,040
Soil Bank	108,396,418
Miscellaneous	13,008,293
Total Payments	$3,462,887,996

Corporation Farming in California

In 1969 and 1970 price-support payments to the larger holders of land and allotments were even higher, presumably as a result of continual consolidation of both holdings and allotments. In 1969 eight payees received more than a million dollars each, twenty-one received more than half a million and seventy-five more than a quarter million. Again the largest payments were made to J. G. Bosworth $4,400,000 to him directly and $677,225 to the Boston Ranch Company, which he owned, making a total of $5,077,225. Six of the first eight payments in excess of a million dollars were to California companies, including Bosworth and the Boston Land Company: Giffen Inc., $3,412,867; South Lake Farms, $1,807,697; Salyer Land Co., $1,637,961; Mt. Whitney Farms, $1,152,294; Kern County Land Co., $1,080,533. Seventy-one of the first 178 payments in excess of $150,000 were to Californians. Other interesting payments were to Vista del Llano (Anderson, Clayton & Company), $778,624; Newhall Land & Farming Company, $299,641; Miller & Lux, $292,961; Irvine Company, $226,574; Eastland Plantations (Senator Eastland of Mississippi), $146,792; Amana Society, $149,172 (Iowa); and Tejon Ranch Company $137,963. As Senator John Williams drily said: "These are not small farmers." At the other end of the scale 45 percent of the participating farmers received a total of less than 2 percent of the payments.[6]

In 1970 there were further increases in payments to the top nine "farmers," who each drew more than a million dollars[7]:

J. G. Boswell Co.	
(plus $677,225 to Boston Ranch Co.)	$4,400,000 (California)
Giffen Inc.	4,095,104 (California)
South Lake Farms (Bangor Punta)	1,875,454 (California)
Salyer Land Co.	1,547,174 (California)
Tenneco (Kern Co. Land Co.)	1,317,061 (California)
Hawaiian Commercial & Sugar Co.	1,232,166 (Hawaii)
Waialua Sugar Col., Ltd.	1,111,060 (Hawaii)
Vista del Llano (Anderson, Clayton & Co.)	1,105,702 (California)
U.S. Sugar Corp.	1,073,980 (Florida)

The S. A. Camp Company of California was next with $903,650.

The publication of this information on the major beneficiaries of the various acts to limit crops and bolster farm prices brought opposition to the larger payments and a demand that they be limited to somewhere between $5,000 and $55,000. For a time the chiefs of the Department of Agriculture and the powerful farm lobby successfully resisted any reduction, as both Democratic and Republican leaders yielded to the latter's demands. But the tremendous disparity between the payments made to the few very large land owners and those received by the great bulk of cooperating farmers weakened the lobby. The *New York Times* declared on April 5, 1970, that the land retirement and production control programs, by the expenditure of billions of dollars, "helped to create a class of wealthy land owners while bypassing the rural poor," and "continued to widen the gap between the rich and the poor. . . ." Seventy percent of the allotments were for less than ten acres and the average payment to small operators was $63. One critic put it a little differently: "The windfalls of the wealthy may well be politically sustained by the pittances to the poor."[8] The 1971 Nader Task Force study, *Power and Land in California,* by Robert C. Fellmeth and associates, made this remarkably clear. In addition it revealed how the California Water Project and state planning, tax, and real estate laws further benefited the large land owners at the expense of the small.

Efforts to have Congress limit benefit payments at the upper level were resisted by representatives of cotton and sugar-producing states until 1970 when the cries of outrage against the huge handouts reached such proportions that a compromise was reached. A maximum of $55,000 was established.[9] The Department of Agriculture seems to have been reluctant to reveal how this restriction is working and in the first year of its application there were complaints that it was being evaded.

On January 13, 1971, the *Wall Street Journal* revealed that the major cotton producers in Kern County—one of the leading cotton-producing areas in the country—were planning to escape

Corporation Farming in California

the $55,000 limitation, by planting enough cotton to get the top $55,000 subsidy and leasing the balance of their land with allotments to tenants for payments of six to seven cents for each pound of cotton produced on the leased land. This might net the land owners from $69 to $80 an acre on the leased land. The tenants, in turn, could receive up to $55,000, thus nicely evading the provisions or the intent of the law.

The two largest Federal subsidies to large-scale and corporation farming in California have been the low-cost water for irrigation provided directly or indirectly by the Bureau of Reclamation and the various crop-control programs enacted since 1933 and administered by the Department of Agriculture. They were responsible for astonishing results. While the acreage planted in cotton in the United States dwindled from 43,000,000 acres in 1929 to 13,918,648 acres in 1964, the acreage in cotton in California expanded during the same years from 300,881 to 759,422 acres, notwithstanding all efforts to control production. Over the same period the production of cotton for the entire country remained practically stationary, but the California crop increased sevenfold, from 253,881 bales to 1,761,509 bales. By buying up the best and most productive irrigable land and by making heavy applications of liquid nitrogen and weed killers, California cotton growers brought their yield to 2.3 bales to the acre, in contrast to 1.1 bales for the entire country. The average size of California farms increased in these years from 224 acres to 476 acres (627 acres in 1969), while the number of farms declined from 135,676 to 80,852.

California beet sugar producers also fared well in the period 1929-1964 under a combination of government subventions and controls. While the number of growers in the United States diminished from 35,155 to 22,185 the acreage in sugar beets increased from 643,797 to 1,376,026; in California the number of producers increased from 352 to 2,334, the acreage from 39,884 to 354,377. During these years the value of the United States crop increased 29 times.[10]

The more liberal farm organizations watched with increasing

alarm the intrusions of corporations into agriculture, fostered, as they saw it, by federal income tax and subsidy measures. The data made available by Representative Findley and Senator Williams provided fuel for the fire of their complaints, which reached a white heat when President Richard Nixon, in November 1971, nominated Earl L. Butz to replace Clifford Hardin as Secretary of Agriculture. True, there seemed to be little difference between the views of the outgoing and incoming secretaries, as both were conservative, and both were friendly to corporate farming. Butz was a director of Ralston-Purina, one of the corporations most frequently excoriated for its intrusions into farming and Hardin resigned his cabinet position to become vice-chairman of the company.

Earl Butz, Dean of Agriculture at Purdue University and well known authority on farm credit, had been Assistant Secretary of Agriculture in the Eisenhower administration, an officer of American Farm Economics Association, and had lectured at the University of Wisconsin and Rutgers University. He listed himself in *Who's Who* as a director of three industrial companies, all largely interested in agricultural production: J. I. Case (a big farm machinery company controlled by the Kern County Land Company), Ralston-Purina (pet foods and breakfast cereals), and International Minerals and Chemicals (chemical fertilizers, animal feeds, and pesticides). In 1970 he was made a director of Stokely-Van Camp (a fruit and vegetable canning company which owns and leases substantial farm acreage in Tennessee). From these companies he drew a combined income of $29,800 in addition to his salary at Purdue. In the past Butz had revealed himself as concerned with efficiency in farm production, with eliminating or reducing dependence upon farm labor, and with the advantages of large-scale operations. The *New York Times* found that Butz had actually predicted a further decline of a million farms during the 1970s. It described him as "an unabashed apologist for corporate power."[11] There was little in .the public record that reflected any concern on Butz's part about the rapid decline in the number of farmers and farm families

Corporation Farming in California

or about the increased amount of capital needed to support a family farm.

Four major developments set off the attacks upon Earl Butz and the Nixon farm policy: 1) the 1969 census of agriculture, which showed an alarming decline—20 percent—in the number of farms during the previous decade; 2) a bumper crop of corn and wheat and a sharp decline in prices farmers were receiving for their grain without any move in administrative circles to offset this decline; 3) the attention being paid in newspapers and conferences of agricultural economists to the rapid rise in farm land values and stories of investments in farm land by great and small corporations; and 4) the great increase in capital requirements for farming. All these developments coming together produced a groundswell of rural opposition to corporate farming and demands for government action to protect the family farm and rural communities.

Butz was attracted by the honor the President had extended to him, though he doubtless was aware that confirmation by the Senate of his nomination might not be easy. In his public statements and before the Senate Committee on Agriculture he showed himself to be adaptable, even to the point of recognizing that small farmers might still have a place in rural life.[12] He displayed an acute awareness of the political character of the position and made marked gestures toward conciliating those who felt that the small farmer deserved more consideration than he had been receiving in high circles in the Department of Agriculture. In a surprising speech to the National Farm Institute in February 1972, after his confirmation, the former director of three or four corporate farm conglomerates was reported to have "lashed out at conglomerated farms, labor unions and low farm prices." Conglomerate farms that "get low interest rates, easier access to capital, tax advantages and more direct access to markets than many individual family farmers can" were a matter of concern to him.[13]

This concern, and that of liberal farm organizations, was justified. In June 1971 the results of a Department of Agriculture study were made available. The statistics were for 1968 and did not reflect the later moves of corporations into farming operations, and the Department tried to minimize the importance of corporation farming by stressing that many corporations were essentially family-owned enterprises and that the total amount of land farmed by corporations and the value of their products constituted a small part of the whole. Yet the statistics for California, Florida, and Hawaii gave advocates of the family farm little comfort.

The number of corporate farms in 1968 was 13,313, and their land totalled 60,056,000 acres, or 1 percent of the commercial farms and 7 percent of the land in commercial farms. Corporations owned 36 percent of the commercial farm land in Hawaii, 31 percent in Florida, 28 percent in Utah, 22 percent in Nevada, 19 percent in California and 17 percent in Colorado and New Mexico. Sixty corporations in Hawaii produced 95 percent of the sugar and pineapples, Hawaii's principal crops.[14]

Agrarian-minded members of Congress were not long in alerting the public to these issues. Senators Fred R. Harris of Oklahoma, Harold Hughes of Iowa, Adlai E. Stevenson III of Illinois, and Gaylord Nelson of Wisconsin all announced plans for investigating corporation farming through Senate subcommittees. Representative James Abourezk of South Dakota declared that his Antitrust Subcommittee of the House Judiciary Committee would hold hearings on a bill to prevent "further excursion into food production by these corporate giants and to require them to divest themselves of their present production holdings." Senator Nelson got the jump on his colleagues when, as part of his very active campaign for reelection in 1968, his Subcommittee on Monopoly of the Senate Select Committee on Small Business held a series of hearings in the West to sound out public opinion on corporation farming. Out of these came an important report, a model for later committees. Included was information concerning the number of corporations engaged in farming in North Dakota and data which was not easy to acquire concerning their holdings. Other testimony bore on the inefficiency of corporate farms, the harmful effects of integration in the broiler industry, and, fully as important, the loss of business in small towns.[15]

The National Farmers Organization (NFO) and the Farmers Union both directed their attention to "this alarming development," while the American Farm Bureau denied that any significant increase in corporate farming was discernible.[16] Among the corporations prominently mentioned as engaged in agriculture were Libby, McNeill & Libby, Pillsbury, and Central Soya (beef and chicken industries); Swift, Textron, Heinz, the Burlington Northern, Penn-Central and Southern Pacific railroads, Ralston-Purina, Ford, United Fruit, and Purex (lettuce, celery, onions); DuPont, Shell, Jewell Tea, Gulf & Western, Del Monte, American Cyanamid, and John Hancock (corn, wheat and soybeans); Goodyear Rubber, Continental Oil, Lockheed, International Harvester, International Systems and Controls, Boeing, Utah & Idaho Sugar, International Telephone, Standard Oil, Kaiser Aluminum, Dow Chemical (growing catfish), American Brands, and Tenneco. Most of these instances of corporate agricultural operations were of recent origin, but lumped in with them were some companies that had long engaged in agriculture and were currently doing little really new in this field.

The existence of large agricultural operations was not shocking to Californians, who were aware that Americans had grabbed up Mexican ranchos at an early date and retained them, if not intact, in great blocks. As late as 1929 nineteen original Mexican grants were still intact, twelve had a least two-thirds of their area in single ownerships, and six, had one-third to one-half of the original acreage in single ownerships.[17]

Best known of the Mexican grants, which, in whole or in part, continued in limited ownership in the twentieth century were those held by Miller & Lux, the Kern County Land Company, the Tejon Ranch Company, the Newhall Land and Farming Company, and the Irvine Foundation. Both these latter holdings had been extensively used for grazing or irrigated farming, specializing in sugar beets, lima beans, citrus fruits, and grain. New large holdings emerged in the twentieth century through transfers and through the partial breakup of the huge Miller & Lux holding. Examples are the 52,000-acre California holding of the great cotton firm, Anderson, Clayton & Company of Houston, Texas; the 54,000-acre South Lake Farms owned by Bangor Punta through its control of Producers Cotton Oil Company; Purex's 30,000-acre holding; Penn Central Railroad's 120,000-acre holding; and Standard Oil Company's 306,000 acres. Conglomerate agribusiness is well rooted in California.[18]

California Land Policy

The huge holdings acquired through Mexican land grants were added to, in many cases, through subversion of federal and state acts originally meant to enable the ordinary settler to get a small tract for a farm. The Homestead, Preemption, Timber Culture, Desert Land, and Swamp Land Acts, some scrip acts, and the school and agriculture land grant acts were supposed to limit entry to public land. Under the Swamp Land Act and some college land grant acts, land could be purchased from the state in 160- and 320-acre lots. The Desert Land Act allowed the purchase of as much as a section, while others permitted individuals to acquire one or two quarter-sections. Unfortunately, the settler measures, as they were planned by Congress, were never carefully drafted. The result was that capitalists took advantage of loopholes and perpetrated frauds on a gigantic scale in acquiring huge holdings. Many people of small means aided and abetted them by entering land which they agreed to convey when the title was secured. By acting as a dummy entryman the small man made his little profit.

California might well have escaped the blighting effect of the government policy of opening public land to unlimited entry had it not been for the mistaken policy of President James Buchanan and his Secretary of the Interior, Jacob Thompson, who sought to bolster federal revenue during the depression years following 1857 when settlers could not raise the money to buy their preemptions. Once land had been offered by the government it could be purchased without limit at $1.25 an acre or with bounty land warrants and other forms of scrip.

Not until 1858 was any land in California so offered and then times were so bad that practically none was sold. From that time on, however, the 10,000,000 acres thus offered remained subject to unlimited purchase. Most of this was in the Sacramento and San Joaquin valleys. In the 1860s, when conditions improved, speculators and land developers descended on the land offices to snap up the most likely tracts. To the state already burdened with the concentration of ownership resulting from the Mexican heritage there was thus added further large ownerships.

Apologists for stockmen, lumbermen, and speculators in land who were responsible for subverting the public land system after 1862 have long maintained that the 160-acre limitation in the Homestead, Preemption, Timber Culture, and Timber and Stone Acts induced, if it did not compel, the use of dummy entrymen to secure viable land units. The same criticism was voiced of the Desert Land Act with its 640-acre limitation. It cannot be too strongly emphasized that these measures were not enacted for the large landlords but for the actual settlers on the land. But men of capital and political influence had always in the past enjoyed easy access to the public domain and were not to be deterred from continuing that privilege. They utilized the many loopholes in the land legislation that careless framing had left, continued their close personal and business relations with the registers, receivers, and surveyors of the local land offices, and placed on their payrolls the ablest men who had served in responsible positions in the General Land Office. These latter, whose compensation while in public office had been small, had, as insiders, seen how contested claims advocated by influential people were manipulated. Now on their own as lawyers and lobbyists, they could exact high fees for their expertise. Through these means and the willingness of employees and others to act as dummies, large estates were built up and the settler legislation perverted. Notwithstanding these practices, which became well known, congressmen continued to prate about the opportunity the public lands offered the man of small means and their desire to retain the land for the benefit of the landless.

California's state land laws compounded the errors and weaknesses of federal legislation, for while they embodied the limitations on the size of entries of the federal laws, they were made meaningless by allowing the use of dummy entrymen. Insiders in the state land office managed to acquire vast estates, amounting in one instance to 300,000 acres. Provisions also allowed the selection of state lands by private individuals on unsurveyed tracts, and permitted buyers of state warrants the inestimable advantage of a prior choice. The net effect of state administration of its swamp, school, lieu, internal improvement and agricultural college grants, amounting to 8,430,738 acres, was to make them the prey of political spoilsmen and aggressive capitalists.[19] The stage was thus set for those "land crazy" who were possessed of influence and capital to add to their possessions, already large through their purchases of Mexican claims and public offered lands.

History of Two Corporation Farms

The two largest and oldest of the 1,673 corporation farms in California are the Tejon Ranch Company and the Kern County Land Company.[20]

Tejon Ranch Company

Tejon's holdings were put together chiefly by the acquisition of several huge Mexican grants. The grants included Tejon, 97,616 acres, the fourth largest in California, granted in 1843; Castaic, 48,799 acres, granted the same year; and Alamos y Agua Caliente and Liebre of 26,626 acres and 48,799 acres respectively. The two latter could qualify as midnight grants for they were given in the dying days of Mexican control in 1846. As there was little, if indeed any, evidence of improvements or occupation on any of these grants by the claimants or their representatives, as Mexican law provided, they were subject to denunciation and rejection because of non-fulfillment of the requirements. Furthermore, in view of the numerous instances of fraudulent antedating of grants, the last two should have been given the most critical examination before they were confirmed. More than one shrewd observer, both at the time and after, contended that the United States might better have rejected these undeveloped claims for non-fulfillment and made the lands subject to preemption entry by settlers. Or they could have been purchased at the going price of a few cents an acre and added to the public domain.

Since there was no evidence of improvement on Tejon, the Superintendent of Indian Affairs for California, Edward F. Beale, determined in 1852 to locate an Indian reservation there as a home for the natives of southern California. He seemed aware that someone might have a claim to the land, but he knew that if it were to be upheld by the courts the claim could be bought for a small sum.[21] During his term as Superintendent of Indian Affairs he received an appropriation of $250,000 with which he began to carry out his extensive plans for the reservation. Large sums were expended in building adobe granaries, workshops, stables, and residences for officers and Indians. Three thousand acres were planted to wheat, barley, and potatoes. After Beale's dismissal in 1856, the plan for a large reservation at Tejon was abandoned.[22]

Beale was not to be without patronage for long. Between 1857 and 1861 he was kept busy searching out routes for wagon roads in the Southwest and in 1861 was appointed Surveyor General for California. In this important position he not only had much patronage to dispense but could learn what areas of land could be most profitably acquired and developed. More than one surveyor general used knowledge he gained in the General Land Office to build a fortune for himself.

In 1855 Beale had acquired for $1,500 the La Liebre grant, on which he was making his home. In 1865 and 1866 he committed himself further to his ranching operations by purchasing Tejon, Alamos, and Castaic, bringing his holdings to

195,219 acres. These ranchos plus a considerable quantity of livestock that was included seem to have cost him $89,200. Beale also bought from John C. Fremont an undivided half of adjacent San Emigdio (17,709 acres), which had been granted in 1842. This richly endowed tract was not retained and later fell into the hands of the Kern County Land Company.[23]

Beale bought numerous homestead claims from misguided settlers who thought that somehow or other they could make productive farms on dry land that was only suitable for grazing or irrigation. A contemporary observer, Mary Austin, believed that Beale had not been responsible for initiating these homestead entries, an accusation frequently brought against those who acquired settlers' homesteads to build up large estates. Beale showed friendliness to the settlers and was quite willing to buy them out after title had issued. By his death in 1893 his acreage at Tejon had increased by 100,000 acres through purchase of settlers' holdings and, doubtless, the use of swamp, desert land, school, agricultural college, and other scrip entries.[24]

Here on his hacienda, Beale pastured as many as 125,000 sheep, which produced enormous quantities of wool for the Boston market.[25] When disastrous droughts struck in the eighties, Beale, like most other owners of great ranchos, was badly hurt by loss of stock. He gradually shifted from sheep to cattle. His improved grade stock and the Herefords in which he began to specialize brought him good prices at his annual sales, which in some years amounted to 7,000 animals. He made some effort to diversify his farming operations on Tejon by setting out orange, lemon, and pear trees. By 1891 he had 55 acres in fruit and 45 in alfalfa, 25,000 cattle, 7,500 sheep and 350 horses. In the latter days of Beale's management the gross earnings of the rancho averaged $100,000 a year. Without irrigation, the land offered little opportunity for more intensive development. As early as 1862 Beale had the foresight to purchase an eighty-acre tract around springs that might be needed in the future.[26]

In 1893 Tejon fell to Beale's son, Truxton, who continued, like his father, as a livestock rancher. In 1912 the land, stock,

Corporation Farming in California

and improvements were sold for $3,000,000 to a group of Los Angeles capitalists, chief of which was the Chandler family, owners of the *Los Angeles Times*. Beale's initial attempt at diversification had accomplished little and had not been continued, but now with capital and expanding markets Tejon became a modern corporate farm. Millions of dollars, mostly from oil royalties, were invested in a water development and irrigation program, and the Tejon Ranch Company, through its tenants, became deeply involved in the large-scale production of cotton, potatoes, other vegetables, alfalfa and alfalfa seed, and fruit. Cattle continued to be a major part of the operations, for a large portion of the land was not suited to any other purpose. In 1970 the land holdings amounted to 295,000 acres, of which 140,000 were managed by the Company and 100,000 by twelve tenants. Of the 19,841 acres of irrigated land, 4,406 acres were in cotton, 3,759 in potatoes, and 7,061 in grain and vegetables. The Company reported for 1970 a livestock income of $1,269,128, range rent of $88,685, farming rent of $1,120,733, and water sales of $25,880.[27]

The large owners of irrigated or potentially irrigable farm land in California who use, or intend to use, federally supplied water have not been notably favorable to the provision of the Federal Reclamation legislation that requires the sale of irrigable lands in excess of 160 or 320 acres. Some, however, have disposed of their excess lands, a notable example being the Di Giorgio Fruit Company. In 1970 the Tejon Ranch Company sold 197 acres of its table-grape land and 2,225 acres of its irrigated land, all but eighty acres of which were subject to this limitation, for $877 an acre and $233 an acre respectively. These sales enabled the company to double its income in 1970. It declared that it now held only 160 acres receiving federal water, and that both it and those of its lessees raising cotton were able to adjust to the $55,000 maximum payments for cotton land "without undue hardship."

The billion-dollar California Water Project, by which water from the upper Sacramento and Feather River in the northern part of the state is to be conducted south by a series of canals, tunnels, syphons, and pumps, is expected to change operations on Tejon greatly. The company does not have adequate supplies of water to enable it to farm some of its level land every year and especially to plant crops that are most water demanding. It has therefore contracted to use great quantities of the water the state and federal government are to make available. This will make it possible to produce oranges and other citrus fruit, grapes, and perhaps vegetable crops, on land that now can only raise crops in alternate years or crops that demand less water. Between 1972 and 1986, 27,236 acres of the company's land will be thus enhanced in value by this boon provided by the federal and state governments.[28]

Kern County Land Company

The group of men who acquired the huge holding later conveyed to the Kern County Land Company continued business careers throughout their lives and built up great fortunes. Most prominent among them were James Ben Ali Haggin and Lloyd Tevis, both Kentuckians. Neither Haggin nor Tevis quite made Bancroft's *Pioneer Register* for they reached California too late for that honor but they were among the earliest to become big landowners in the turbulent new state. They joined others like Henry Miller and Charles Lux in the rush for Mexican land claims and for hundreds of thousands of acres of public land, when it became open to entry. Within a few decades they and other well-established capitalists had acquired the best of the federal and state lands and Mexican land claims and formed a dominant landed aristocracy more powerful than any the South could boast in the ante-bellum period.

James Ben Ali Haggin (1827–1914) and Lloyd Tevis (1824–1899) mined for a time, practiced law, and formed a partnership in 1850 or 1851, lending money at California interest rates of 1-1/2 to 3 percent a month, and promoting water, telegraph, express, and railroad companies, and mining operations. The public record suggests that Haggin's investments rarely ended in failure. Returns from the Wells Fargo Express,

Southern Pacific Railroad, and the enormously rich Comstock lode, Homestake mine, and the Anaconda Copper mine enabled him to build up a fortune of fifteen million dollars.

Through loans on Mexican ranchos, Haggin and Tevis and William B. Carr acquired large acreages in the Sacramento and San Joaquin valleys and along the coast. Del Paso, a ten-league, 44,371-acre grant to Captain Eliab Grimes, a native of Massachusetts, in December, 1844, descended to his nephew, Hiram Grimes, and from him to Samuel Norris who mortgaged it to Haggin and Tevis in 1859, to whom it passed. Del Paso was located just north of Sacramento but was kept out of the hands of the small farmers for whom it appeared to be well adapted and instead was made into the largest horse-breeding farm in the world. Because the ranch had few employees and did not contribute to the economic growth of the valley, those who withheld it from farming use were criticized.[29]

Next to be acquired was the nearby San Juan Rancho of four and a half leagues, 19,982 acres, on which Haggin held a mortgage of $10,000 with interest of 3 percent a month which had accumulated to $29,905. Possibly because it was more easily irrigated, this rancho was farmed in small tracts. Rio de Jesus Maria, a 26,637-acre rancho in Yolo and Napa Counties was foreclosed by Haggin and Tevis in 1859. Portions of San Buenaventura—the 26,632-acre rancho of Pearson B. Reading in Shasta County—the 22,193-acre Cuyama Rancho of the de la Guerra family in San Luis Obispo County, the 7,000-acre Livermore Rancho nine miles north of Bakersfield, and the 17,709-acre San Emigdio Rancho in Kern County, once owned by Beale, all fell to Haggin and Tevis.[30] Of these extensive holdings only the Livermore and San Emigdio tracts were to become part of the Kern County Land Company acreage, and San Emigdio was the only Mexican ranch it owned.

Henry Miller and Charles Lux consolidated parts or all of fifteen Mexican land claims for 174,844 acres, including Sanjon de Santa Rita in Merced and Fresno Counties, Tequesquite, Lomerias Muertas, San Justo, Aromitas y Agua Caliente, and Bolsa de San Felipe in San Benito County, Buri Buri in San

Mateo County, Salsipuedes in Santa Cruz County, Orestimba in Stanislaus and Merced Counties and Animas in Santa Clara County. They also bought 80,350 acres of state swamp land, 9,738 acres of state internal improvement land, 28,897 acres of school and lieu land, and 3,360 acres of smaller grants given the state for public buildings.

In all they used scrip, military warrants and cash to secure from the United States 181,000 acres. Still more was purchased from others who either acted as dummy entrymen or were taking advantage of the government's bargains in land to resell as soon as they could do so profitably. The total acreage of Miller and Lux in California was well over half a million acres, some of the best of which was on the Kern River in the upper San Joaquin Valley. Their acquisitions of partially developed ranches in northwestern Nevada and southeastern Oregon brought their total acres to more than a million. Their cattle numbered far more than 100,000, justifying, after the death of Charles Lux in 1887, application of the title "The Cattle King" to Miller.[31]

Haggin and Tevis, William S. Chapman, and other well-endowed speculators also set about to accumulate state and federal land with gusto. Haggin and Tevis acquired 12,000 acres of offered land which could be purchased in unlimited amounts, 34,000 acres of state swamp land through the use of dummies, 8,844 acres of agricultural college land, 59,000 acres of Southern Pacific Railroad land, 16,869 acres of school and lieu land with the aid of dummies, and quantities of land from individuals, including the 30,000-acre Whim rancho in eastern San Luis Obispo County. The Desert Land Act was a favorite device for acquiring dry land that was susceptible of irrigation. According to the *San Francisco Chronicle* and the *Visalia Delta* this act was pushed through Congress by Senator Aaron A. Sargent at the behest of William B. Carr, Haggin's associate in building up the San Joaquin empire. Haggin had filed on 30,000 acres along the proposed Calloway Canal using Soldiers Additional Homestead Scrip. When this proved defective and therefore invalid the entire entry faced cancellation, since this was not offered land and could not be purchased. The Desert Land Act seemed a happy solution to Carr and Haggin, so goes the *Chronicle* and *Delta* story, and Sargent was easily persuaded to sponsor and to push it vigorously in Congress.[32]

Within a week after the adoption of the measure, Sargent's friends were alerted and they entered 50,000 acres in Kern County with dummies for which all that was required at the outset was 25 cents an acre. The outcry against this flagrant abuse of an act that had been commonly regarded as a measure to assure land to small settlers may have led to the cancellation of some entries, but Haggin seems to have been successful in securing the land he desired. If Desert Land entries were suspended he could use his many employees as dummies to file for the land under the Homestead, Preemption, and Timber Culture Acts, or could acquire them with California agricultural college, school, or lieu script. All these procedures were common in the San Joaquin Valley and in the Redwood region north of San Francisco.[33]

In his own defense Haggin conceded that he had invited his friends, and presumably his employees, to enter land in the vicinity of canals and irrigation ditches he was building in order that they would pay a portion of the construction costs. He emphasized the extent of the improvements he was making, including housing for many hands, fencing, drainage of the overflowed lands, and the building of diversion dams and irrigation ditches. The land he and his associates were acquiring, he testified, was truly desert land which had been surveyed and open to entry for more than twenty years without a taker. The affidavits of his associates stressed that Haggin and Tevis were attempting to settle the land in 320-acre tracts, that great sums of money were expended on improvements in addition to housing and irrigation works including the digging of wells, that seed was provided, and that free rent for both land and water for a year was allowed. Thereafter one quarter of the crop was to be paid as rent. As a further inducement settlers were supposedly promised that they could purchase their tracts but either Haggin and Tevis changed their mind about this or the tenants never found it possible to raise the needed funds. Three years after the statement was made the census of 1880 shows that for all of Kern County there were only 282 farms, one for every nineteen people, whereas in counties in which the concentration of ownership was much less the ratio was one farm to eleven or twelve people.[34]

Haggin was not the only empire builder to develop or attempt to develop great tracts by draining the wet areas and irrigating the desert lands, then settling upon them buyers of small tracts or tenants or laborers.[35] Of all those who undertook such activities in the 1870s Haggin and Tevis and Miller and Lux were the only ones to succeed on a large scale, because they were abundantly supplied with capital from their other investments and could afford to wait for profit. Hence they became the focus of attacks in the eighties, not only because of the way in which they had acquired their land but because their operations prevented the settlement of yeomen farmers in sufficient numbers to advance the prosperity of Bakersfield and other ambitious hamlets. A revival of concern for the preservation of the family farm and fear of the dangers of land monopoly came to the fore in the eighties. Alien ownership of great cattle companies, some claiming to control a million or more acres, was also attacked. In California the Haggin and Tevis, Miller and Lux, and Beale holdings were not to escape. The *Kern Gazette* in 1887, fearing that they intended to preserve their holdings, struck hard at the first two, declaring that they were a misfortune to the county, as bad as a "plague of grasshoppers" in that they kept out a population of yeomen farmers.[36] The *Kern Echo* of June 2, 1887, averred that people were angry at the large ownerships, the "monopolists," and the ease with which the owners could dominate the operations of the local land offices and prevent actual settlers from getting land.[37] The *San Francisco Chronicle* of March 25, 1887, included the Beale holdings among those it condemned.

Political attacks against "monopolistic" holdings and the need to centralize scattered operations and make them less dependent on one man led to the incorporation of the Kern County Land Company in 1893. To this concern were conveyed the 350,000 acres of Kern lands of Haggin and associates, with improvements, livestock, and equipment. Capitalization was established at $10,000,000. Since its incorporation the company has enjoyed success almost beyond imagination. Rich oil fields have been tapped and the flow in income has made possible development of the company into one of the most successful livestock, fruit, vegetable, and fiber producers in the country. The company has acquired vast acreages in Arizona and New Mexico where ranching operations are conducted on an even larger scale, oil fields in Canada and Australia, a successful electronics subsidiary, control of a manufacturer of mufflers and other automobile parts, and the J. I. Case Company, producers of farm machinery. Generous dividends and stock splits (40 for 1) and appreciation of the market value of its stock made Kern County a most satisfactory investment.

In 1939 the Company owned 413,500 acres in California, 517,000 acres in New Mexico, and 105,000 acres in Oregon.[38] In 1958 it sold its Oregon ranch property, consisting of 171,000 acres, related grazing leases totalling over 1,000,000 acres, and 18,000 cattle, receiving as part of the contract the 6,000-acre Santa Anita rancho and the 500-acre Alliance Rancho near Paso Robles, California. It listed its owned lands in 1966 as 1,826,000 acres in California, Arizona, and New Mexico and its leased land as 794,000 acres. Its irrigated land in Kern County amounted then to 113,851 acres, of which 101,256 were "leased to independent farmers" and 12,595 farmed by the company. Construction of additional ditches made it possible to irrigate 128,954 acres in 1970, of which the company operated 42,030.[39] The company's herds of cattle over the years ranged from 55,000 to 145,000 and were valued in 1966 at $19,745,000. Cotton, whether through production or government payments to prevent production, was the largest source of income from farming. Other crops were also grown as acreage statistics for 1955 testify:[40]

Cotton	13,191	Corn	3,846
Potatoes	7,082	Milo	1,579
Alfalfa	8,661	Onions	135
Sugar beets	1,861	Wheat	866
Barley	11,845	Other	372

In 1966, when an effort was made by the Johnson administration to compel the large landowners of California who were using water from government projects to dispose of their lands in excess of 160 acres, as the reclamation legislation required, the Kern County Land Company assumed the leadership of the opposition. It was estimated that fifty-one owners of farms then held 150,000 acres of excess lands, of which the Kern County Land Company had 60,000 acres. The company's defense was that it had used the waters of the Kern River for seventy-five years before the Isabella Dam was built, that the dam did not create a new source of water but merely dammed a stream, and that the users of the water had paid quite a part of the cost of the dam, which did not store government water. Able political leadership and the fact that the powerful economic interests of the state were disinterested in, if not hostile to, the enforcement of the excess-lands provision prevented all efforts to compel the large owners to disgorge their possessions.

In 1967 two large conglomerates came into a classic conflict when they both tried to gain control of the Kern County Land Company. Tenneco, a Texas corporation with interests in oil, gas transmission, chemicals, and packaging, defeated Occidental Petroleum, which had huge oil-producing wells in Libya and was heavily involved in chemicals, plastics, coal, fertilizers, pesticides, and real estate. Though victorious, Tenneco, to gain complete control of its captive company, had to pay a huge bonus to Occidental for the stock it had purchased as part of its campaign to gain control. Whether the emergence of Tenneco which with its control of J. I. Case, one of the major farm machinery companies, and of Kern County, one of the great producers of cotton, fruit, and cattle and owning huge land resources susceptible of further intensive development through the application of water to be provided by the state is a cause for alarm to opponents of agribusiness and the much feared vertical integration of agriculture remains to be seen. In 1970 Tenneco purchased 3,060 acres said in the public announcement to be "mostly citrus orchards" from the S. A. Camp Farms whose land withdrawal payments of $489,641 in 1968 were second in

Kern County only to those of the Kern County Land Company.[41]

In summary, the large land company or corporation farm is in no sense a new development in California. In one form or another they have been in existence since the first years of American control. Though they were highly unpopular in the years from 1870 to 1910 these large land companies have survived and are today a feature of America's big business. They have long conducted a vendetta against organized labor and through the Associated Farmers of the nineteen thirties used their power to deny civil liberties to labor leaders by a combination of crude vigilantism and pliant local officials and courts. They have successfully resisted the enforcement of the 160-acre excess-land provision of reclamation legislation and are partly responsible for the huge California Water Project that promises much to the large land owners at the expense of the tax payer. A reading of the Nader-Fellmeth report, *Power and Land in California,* suggests that through their alliance with the utilities, the railroads, the real estate lobby, and the oil companies, the great land companies are in effective political and economic control of California.

NOTES

1. When the Food and Drug Administration was part of the Department of Agriculture, the Secretary and other high officials had virtually emasculated legislation giving it real authority by relaxing standards, listening only to commercial lobbyists, and virtually allowing self-regulation of commercial food processors. Department officials have also shown extreme tolerance to the continued use of insecticides long after their dangers were made clear. James G. Turner, *The Chemical Feast* (New York, 1971), chapter 6.

2. Findley was particularly troubled by the fact that in many of the counties where large individual payments were concentrated there were no provisions for making available the Federal Food Program for the poor. This was most true of Texas and a number of other southern states. *Congressional Record,* 91st Cong., 1st Sess., May 21 and June 26, 1969, pp. 13287–326 and 17553–58.

3. *Congressional Record,* 91st Cong., 1st Sess., June 16, 1969, p. 15867.

4. Anderson, Clayton & Company of Houston, Texas, owner of the Vista Del Llano land, does not appear in the list for 1967, but for 1968 it was paid $745,647. Members of Congress were deeply disturbed at the payments of

$653,252 ($814,616 in 1970) to the Delta & Pine Land Company of England for land owned in Bolivar County, Mississippi, $157,930 to Senator James O. Eastland of Mississippi, $177,207 to the Arkansas Board of Penal Institutions, and payments of from $100,000 to $554,000 to 63 individuals and companies on heavily subsidized irrigated land in Arizona.

5. *Congressional Record,* 90th Cong., 2nd Sess., September 9, 1968, pp. 26045 ff.: *Department of Agriculture and Related Appropriations,* "Senate Hearings before the Committee on Appropriations, 91st Cong., 1st Sess., 1969, pp. 1704−5.

6. *Congressional Record,* 91st Cong., 2nd Sess., March 21, 1970, pp. 8843−50; Robert C. Fellmeth, *Power and Land in California, The Ralph Nader Task Force Report on Land Use in the State of California* (2 vols., processed, 1971), I, 80.

7. *New York Times,* April 9, 1971, and Fellmeth, *Power and Land in California* I, 9. Twelve of the 23 "farms" receiving more than $500,000 were in California. We do not have the acreage for which these payments were made because the Department of Agriculture has refused to release the data.

8. R. J. Hildreth, ed. *Readings in Agricultural Policy* (Lincoln, Nebraska, 1968), p. 89.

9. Senator Birch Bayh hoped to reduce the limit to $10,000 or $20,000 and won considerable support. In the House there was strong feeling that the limit should be even less. However, administration opposition defeated the lower limit. In the Senate vote on the amendment for a deeper cut the votes of Edmund Muskie and Margaret Chase Smith of Maine and Aiken of Vermont in opposition, and the absence of Edward Kennedy and Edward Brooke of Massachusetts and Prouty of Vermont are not easy to understand. *Congressional Record,* 92nd Cong., 1st Sess., July 15, 1971, pp. S1187, 11206; *Public Law* 91-524, November 30, 1970, p. 1.

10. *1964 United States Census of Agriculture,* II, 432 and I, part 48, *California,* pp. 454−65. Arizona, like California generously provided with low-cost water for irrigation by the Bureau of Reclamation, had a similar development. Between 1929 and 1964 Arizona increased its acreage in cotton from 211,178 acres to 365,937 acres and its production from 149,488 bales to 761,233 bales.

11. Editorial, *New York Times,* December 28, 1971. See also *Nomination of Earl Lauer Butz before the Senate Committee on Agriculture and Forestry.* 92nd Cong., 1st Sess., November 17−19, 1971, p. 14.

12. Commenting on Butz's effort to convince the Senate Committee on Agriculture that he would "protect and preserve the small 'family farm,' " the *Wall Street Journal* of December 21, 1971, said, "if he succeeds he will serve the interests of neither agriculture nor the nation."

13. *Kansas City Times,* February 12, 1972.

14. The Department of Agriculture made three reports: "Corporations having Agricultural Operations: A Preliminary Report," "Preliminary Report ii," and

"Corporations with Farming Operations," *Agricultural Economic Report*, nos. 142, 156 and 209 (1968, 1969 and 1971). Only for Hawaii are the seven largest corporate farm operations mentioned. A report by Howard Tolley of the Bureau of Agriculture cites a report of the U. S. Chamber of Commerce that the capital value of corporate farms in 1924 was 2.9% of the total value of all farms. Cited in Emy K. Miller, "Corporation Farming in Kansas," M.A. thesis, University of Wichita, 1933, p. 8. This study is a unique achievement in that it centers on two corporations organized for producing grain in western Kansas in the late 1920s and by 1930–1932 were functioning on a large scale, one owning 70,000 acres and the other 21,000 acres. Their yields ranged widely from most productive to partial crop failures, depending on the amount of rainfall. The size of their operations and their practice of plowing up sod and dirt roads and destroying houses no longer needed and the removal of farm population resulted in much criticism when their extensive operations came to light, and action by the Kansas legislature in 1931 to outlaw corporation farming followed. "Ouster" suits were brought against both companies.

15. Announcements of the committee hearings to be held appear regularly in the *NFO Reporter* in 1971 but see especially the *Reporter*, XVI (February, 1972), 5, 7, 13; "Corporation Farming," *Hearings before the Subcommittee on Monopoly of the Select Committee on Small Business*, United States Senate, 90th Cong., 2nd Sess., 1968, p. 193; *Senate Report*, 91st Cong., 1st Sess., No. 628, December 20, 1968; *Congressional Record*, 91st Cong., 1st Sess., April 1, 1969, pp. 8266ff.

16. Following are some of the headlines that appeared in the *NFO Reporter* in 1971: "USDA Shrugs off Loss of 48,000 more Farms," "Raiders tell how Agri-Giants Engulf Farmers Standing Alone," "Metcals Blasts Corporate Secrecy; Seeks Investigation of Ownership," "Probe Corporate Moves into Farming," "Broiler Integrators Move in; USDA Turns Chicken," "USDA Experts conclude Hog Integration Coming," "Meet the Family of a Big Poultry & Hog Integrator," "Keep Big Biz off Farms; We'll Do Bargaining, NFO Tells Congress," "Collective Bargaining only way to Deal with Marketplace Giants," "Boeing Aircraft Starts Farming." It does not seem necessary to clutter up this note with the pages for they appear in every issue on two or three or more occasions.

17. Carey McWilliams, *California the Great Exception* (New York, 1949), 93.

18. Robert Glass Cleland, *The Irvine Ranch of Orange County 1810-1950* (San Marino, Calif., 1952), and Ruth Waldo Newhall, *The Newhall Ranch, The Story of the Newhall Land and Farming Company* (San Marino, 1958). The Southern Pacific Railroad Company holdings of two to four million acres were what remained of over 11,000,000 acres the United States had given it for the building of that portion of the first transcontinental railroad from San Francisco to the Nevada line, for a line down the San Joaquin Valley to Fort Yuma on the Colorado River and for a line north from Sacramento to the Oregon border.

Much of the remaining land was timbered and mountainous but the acreage on the west side of the Valley in the Westlands district when irrigated by water from the California Water Project promises a very large return. Southern Pacific sold to a subsidiary of the Standard Oil Company 259,000 acres of oil bearing land in this same district, in 1921. Stuart Daggett, *Chapters on the History of the Southern Pacific* (New York, 1966), 449.

19. Gerald D. Nash, "The California State Land Office, 1858-1898," *Huntington Library Bulletin*, XXVII (August 1964), 354, and *State Government and Economic Development. A History of Administrative Policies in California* (Berkeley 1964), 124-136.

20. "Corporations with Farming Operations," *Economic Research Bulletin*, June 1971.

21. Beale was informed in 1853 that he would probably "have a fight with the pretended owners,... but it can't be avoided." See Paul W. Gates, *California Ranchos and Farms, 1846-1862, Including the Letters of John Quincy Adams Warren* (Madison, 1967), 48. Beale is best known to history for his spectacular dash across the continent in 1848 bearing news of the discovery of gold and for his part in driving seventy camels to the Pacific coast where they were to be used experimentally on mail routes.

22. *Senate Executive Documents*, 33rd Cong., 1st Sess., serial no. 290, doc. 1, pp. 471–5. Also useful is Earle Crowe, *Men of El Tejon; Empire in the Tehachapis* (Los Angeles, 1957). For the letdown of operations at Tejon following the dismissal of Beale see Malcolm Edwards, ed., *The California Diary of General E. D. Townsend* (Los Angeles, 1970), p. 129.

23. Crowe, *Men of El Tejon*, 67, 154–7.

24. Hubert Howe Bancroft, *History of California* (7 vols., vols. 18-24 of *The Works*, Hubert Howe Bancroft, 39 vols., San Francisco, 1882-1890) VII, 55, said that the ownership of 200,000 acres at Tejon, including all available water, made possible the use and control of 300,000 acres. We know that Beale and his wife Mary entered 1,626 acres of school land with dummies and acquired a smaller acreage with the expensive agricultural college scrip. Paul W. Gates, "California's Agricultural College Lands," *Pacific Historical Review*, XXX. (May, 1961), 121. Mrs. Austin describes the efforts of her brother and mother and a number of other persons who attempted to make a living on the dry land they were homesteading near the Tejon ranch, and which one may guess were ultimately added to the Tejon holdings.

25. Charles Nordhoff, *California: For Health, Pleasure, and Residence* (New York, 1874), 191 ff., was entertained by Beale on Tejon. He noted the nearly 200,000 acres, over 100,000 sheep, "a peasantry of its own" of 300 Indians, and the routine of ranching operations. He speaks of the plowmen, indicating some cultivation but it appears the fruit trees, grape vines and other planting were mostly on small allotments allowed the natives. Beale is given credit for the advance the Indians had made from savagery to civilization, as advanced as that of many immigrants landing in New York.

26. Crowe, *Men of El Tejon*, 89, 157 n.

27. Tejon Ranch Company, *Annual Report*, 1971.

28. In theory the excess land was to be sold at the appraised value of the land without the water privilege but the $833 per acre price does not reflect this. Report of Howard H. Leach, President, to the stockholders of the Tejon Ranch Company, October 11, 1971.

29. *Sacramento Bee*, June 17, 1857; *Sacramento Guide Book* (no date, no place), 186; Thompson & West, *History of Sacramento County* (Oakland, reprinted in 1960 by Howell-North), 213; *Sacramento County and Its Resources* (1894), 74–76.

For records of these transactions, see the following: *Sacramento Union*, August 28, 1860; *History of Sacramento County*, 213; *San Francisco Examiner*, June 27, 1897. See document in the court sale of a portion of San Buenaventura—possibly 21,250 acres—to Haggin, Reading Papers, State Library, Sacramento. *Santa Barbara Press*, July 2, 1883, clipping in 23 California Scrapbooks, State Library, p. 13; Thompson & West, *History of San Luis Obispo County*, pp. 232-233, shows Haggin owning in 1883 16,472 acres and Haggin and Cebrian owning 11,236 acres in the county and elsewhere (p. 216). Haggin and Tevis are also shown the owners of Whim rancho (30,000 acres) which had been acquired from the government.

30. Genevieve K. Magruder, *The Upper San Joaquin Valley, 1772-1870* (Kern County Historical Society, Bakersfield), p. 91: Margaret A. Cooper, "Land, Water and Settlement in Kern County, California, 1850-1890," M.A. thesis, University of California, Berkeley, 1954, p. 57 *passim*.

31. Edward F. Threadwell, *The Cattle King* (Boston, 1950), pp. 58, 179 and elsewhere. The end papers show the location of the ranches of Miller & Lux in California, Nevada, and Oregon. Here and throughout this paper the data on land acquisitions of the United States have been compiled from the abstracts of entries of the various land offices and the data on the purchase of state land came from the volumes of abstracts of entries and the patent books in the State Land Office in Sacramento. Richard G. Lillard, *Desert Challenge* (New York, 1942), 18—19, has information on Miller's control of water sites and extensive ranches in that state.

32. *Congressional Record*, 44th Cong., 2nd Sess., February 27, 1877, pp. 1964–74.

33. *History of San Luis Obispo County* (Oakland, 1883), p. 216; Margaret A. Cooper, "Land, Water and Settlement in Kern County, California, 1850-1890," M.A. thesis, University of California, 1954, pp. 160 ff.; Gerald D. Nash, "The California State Land Office, 1858–1898," 354.

34. The 282 farms seems to have meant that 282 persons owned farms, large or small.

35. Virginia E. Thickens, "Pioneer Agricultural Colonies of Fresno County," *California Historical Society Quarterly*, XXV (March and June 1946), 17–38 and 169–77; Gerald D. Nash, "Henry George Reexamined: William S.

Chapman's Views on Land Speculation in Nineteenth Century California," *Agricultural History,* XXXIII (July 1959), 133–37.

36. Quoted in the *Visalia Delta* of March 25, 1887 and clipped in the Kern County Scrapbook, p. 39, California State Library.

37. The *Echo* referred particularly to the suspended desert land entries which were still held by the parties for whom they had been entered. Kern County Scrapbook, p. 54.

38. "Violations of Free Speech and Rights of Labor," *Hearings of Subcommittee of Senate Committee on Education and Labor* (LaFollette Committee), 66th Cong., 3rd Sess., 1940, part 62, pp. 22796–98.

39. *New York Times,* July 17, 1966. Kern County Land Company, *Annual Report,* 1971. In 1970 the acreage owned had diminished to 967,002 and the acreage leased to 520,273, all in California and Arizona.

40. *Annual Reports,* 1965-1968. The J. I. Case Company which was controlled by the Kern County Land Company had an "experimental farm" in British Honduras.

41. *New York Times,* January 17, 1970. In 1964 the Kern County Land Company sold 10,000 acres of improved farm land but whether they were scattered tracts does not appear.

CHAPTER 9

THE TAMING OF THE WEST:
Military Archives as a Source for the Social History of the Trans-Mississippi Region to 1900

James B. Rhoads

James Berton Rhoads first knew Everett Dick as an undergraduate student at Union College in 1947–1948; a few years later he served as Professor Dick's reader when the latter spent a term on the Berkeley campus. Neither realized then that this capable young student would ascend to the highest pinnacle of the archival profession. Long before completing his doctorate at the American University in 1965, Bert Rhoads entered the service of the National Archives, serving in various capacities before rising to Associate Archivist for Civil Affairs in 1965, Deputy Archivist of the United States in 1966, and Archivist of the United States in 1968. Scholars familiar with his many books and articles will be interested in the essay he has prepared for this volume, an essay that reveals the undreamed-of riches awaiting social historians of the West in the National Archives.

The settlement and development of the American West in the nineteenth century was an amalgam of public and private enterprise.* The interrelationships between these two powerful and motivating forces are nowhere more fully revealed than in the archives of the federal government. Although there are numerous and important non-federal sources for the study of the peopling of the West, none can claim to represent so fully the entire sweep of settlement, either chronologically, geographically, or topically. An overview of the totality of original source material will quite certainly lead one to conclude that, both individually and collectively, non-federal sources are supplementary and complimentary to the great backbone of federal archives.

That this is so is due not so much to considerations of volume or mass, or to the fact that federal archives are largely centralized and that other manuscript resources are widely scattered, as to the basic, central, and pivotal role played by the national government in the opening and taming of the vast trans-Mississippi region during the nineteenth century.

It may also be argued that no instrumentality of federal power was as important in this grand endeavor as the military. The army played a significant role in basic exploration of the region, fought to win parts of it from Mexico, and conducted an intermittent war of attrition for nearly a century to pacify it. Without the army's assistance in extinguishing Indian land titles, in guarding railroad construction, and in protecting frontier settlements, it is difficult to see how the West could have been populated to more than a very marginal extent. Even after the threat of Indian hostilities was much abated, the military often provided the only meaningful, if rudimentary, government for the civilian populace.

Every element of the military forces produced records, and many of them survive today in the National Archives. Some,

*The author is indebted to many members of the National Archives' staff for assistance in locating pertinent sources for this chapter, particularly Dr. Mabel E. Deutrich, Director, Military Archives Division, and the staff of the Old Military Branch.

of course, provide little insight into the social history of the West. But a great many do. The survey that follows will identify some of those that relate to the social history of the military forces. Because it is not possible in a few pages to deal comprehensively with so vast a topic, reference will be made to materials that illustrate available sources and suggest fruitful lines of deeper inquiry. The great difficulty is not in locating appropriately illustrative sources—they are overwhelming in volume—but in defining the scope of the survey and the internal organization of the material to be presented.

This essay is based on the assumption that there were three basic population groups in the trans-Mississippi West, all of them constantly interacting: the Indians, the military, and the non-aboriginal civilian population. The focus is on the military, but because soldiers were inextricably involved with both Indians and settlers, it is not possible to deal with the military *in vacuo*. Studies might also be undertaken, for example, on military archives as sources for the social history of Indians or settlers, both of which would also have to involve the other two population groups.

Selection of material to be cited, therefore, involves a judgment as to whether the emphases of given documentary sources lie with the military or the other population groups. It must be confessed that occasionally rather arbitrary decisions have been made as to *what* should be included or excluded, and as to *where* materials best fit within the framework, for little of the documentation lends itself to a mutually exclusive form of internal organization.

The source materials dealt with here reflect life in the military service in three major kinds of situations: on exploratory missions, on campaigns and in battle, and on military posts; there is, in addition, much to be found relating to more or less peaceful military relationships with the Indians, and to relationships with the rest of the population. The subdivisions therefore, reflect these five aspects of military life in the West.[1]

On Explorations

Although not all governmental explorations in the West were sponsored by the military, those of the Geological Survey being a major exception, the army played a most important role in searching out the land, and in acquiring precise and authentic information about the topography, flora, fauna, and aboriginal inhabitants of the West. Not infrequently the civilian explorations included military men in scientific rather than protective roles.

The Office of the Quartermaster General, charged with supplying the army, produced and accumulated records of value to an understanding of western social history as they indicate the kinds and amounts of stores provided for a particular station or expedition, the cost of such commodities, whether or not they were supplied locally or from long distances, and the manner in which payment for them was made.[2]

Of particular interest are the records of Brigadier General Thomas S. Jesup, Quartermaster General, including letters and reports concerning the Yellowstone or Western expedition of 1819 which employed steamboats to transport men and supplies up the Mississippi and Missouri rivers. Jesup participated personally in the expedition, and his firsthand observations relate the progress of the endeavor, problems encountered, the condition of the rivers, and the feasibility of steamboat navigation on those waters. Jesup's files also include a lengthy statement prepared in 1820 for a board of arbitrators that was investigating claims against the Quartermaster Department filed by Colonel James Johnson, the contractor who furnished steamboats for the expedition. It contains material relating to the boats and their operation, the navigation conditions experienced, the comparative costs of utilizing steamboats or keelboats, and the costs of transporting various types of supplies from one point to another along the Mississippi—Missouri system.

During the major part of the nineteenth century, the immediate military control of the army was vested in the Commanding General. In the Trans-Mississippi West that official was

The Taming of the West

particularly concerned with campaigns against Indians; the inspection, supply, and movements of soldiers at military posts; the construction of military roads; expeditions; and the maintenance of order in towns, Indian reservations, and frontier settlements. Both the letters sent and received by his office, therefore, contain much of value to the social historian.

Of particular interest (in the letters received) is a journal-type description of the land and the people from an 1831 expedition "for the purpose of exploring that part of the country comprised between the Eastern line of the Osage Reservation and the Arkansas River."[3]

The Congress frequently requested special reports from the Secretary of War on matters of interest to it, and a set of these reports covering the period 1803-1870 was retained in the secretary's office. Among these is a thirty-eight-page "Extract from a journal of an expedition from San Diego, California, to the Rio Colorado from September 11 to December 11, 1849, by A. W. Whipple, Lieut., U.S. Topographical Engineers." This report describes Indian life in detail, including their crops, living conditions, foods, and dress; relates encounters with Christian Indians; and lists Indian language equivalents of common English words—including Yuma equivalents of 250 common English expressions.[4]

A great deal of the military exploration and surveying of the West was done by either the Topographical Engineers or the regular Corps of Engineers, and the records of the two organizations contain much of historical value. They are especially useful to those studying transportation before the arrival of the railroads, but they also contain a wealth of material relating to other aspects of social history.

Among the letters received by the headquarters of the Topographical Bureau is a document by Philip Tyson dated March 1850 and entitled "Report of geological researches in upper California during the year 1848 and a brief sketch of the mineral and agricultural resources of the country." It describes in great detail the agricultural and commercial opportunities available, with particular emphasis on mining and the dangers of an economy based entirely on gold.[5] In addition there are two reports dated August 1849, and April 1850, from Lieutenant James H. Simpson that contain descriptions of the Navahoes in Chelly Canyon, the pueblo ruins at Canyon Bonito and Chaco Canyon, life in an immigrant wagon camp, and a peace talk with the Comanche. The reports also include suggestions for future Indian—white relations; a survey of the Indians in New Mexico Territory, including a comparative vocabulary of six different linguistic groups; and descriptions of existing trails, with evaluations of their suitability for future immigrant travel.[6]

Most of the regular Corps of Engineers records relate to rivers, harbors, roads, and other public works, but the correspondence of the Office of Explorations and Survey, 1857–1861, does contain significant materials of interest to the social historian. Among them are reports from survey expeditions that discuss the effect of military roads on settlement, relations between survey parties and Indians, and the desirability of the land for future settlement.

By the late 1860s a photographer was often an important member of the expeditions that explored the West. The photographic processes used were cumbersome, requiring a large camera and the wet plate or collodion negative. The photographs that survive are of considerable historical significance and are often of better quality than those created with relative ease in later years, when picture taking became much simpler.

Among the records of the Office of the Chief of Engineers are the photographic records of two important army surveys in the West. The first of these documents the Geological Exploration of the Fortieth Parallel of the United States, conducted by Clarence King, 1867–1869. There are approximately 150 glass collodion negatives, and some prints for which there are no negatives, made by Timothy H. O'Sullivan. These include views of mines and mining towns in Nevada, the photographs of work in the interior of the Comstock Mine at Virginia City being of special interest.

A group of photographs made by O'Sullivan and William Bell, 1871–1874, when they served as members of the United States Geographical Surveys West of the 100th Meridian, under the leadership of Lieutenant George M. Wheeler includes views of forts in California, Nevada, and Arizona Territory, and of Indians in the territories of Arizona and New Mexico.

Photography is an important and frequently overlooked source for research in the social history of the American West. Textual records all too often record the unique, the exception, or the culmination of events. Records of a military post, for example, might show who deserted or how many were on sick call, but rarely do they tell how many sat down to a meal together or how the meal was served. Photographs allow a town to grow before one's eyes in a way that manuscripts can hardly convey, and they are of importance to social history just because they show the routine—the day-to-day life of the homesteader or of a soldier's family in the field.

Maps are rarely primary sources for social history, but they do provide another kind of graphic aid to a fuller understanding of the textual and pictorial sources. For many of the major bodies of textual records cited in this chapter there are extensive cartographic counterparts in the National Archives.

On Campaigns and in Battle

Although a number of important engagements and campaigns were fought west of the Mississippi during the Civil War and the war with Mexico, the main focus of this section will be on military activity directed against Indians, irregular forces in Kansas and Missouri before and during the Civil War, and disturbers of peace along the Mexican border during the last third of the nineteenth century.

The Adjutant General's Office was the administrative and recordkeeping agency of the War Department. It was charged with responsibilities pertaining to the command, discipline, and administration of the military establishment, which included such duties as recording, authenticating, and communicating to troops and individuals in the military service the orders, instructions, and regulations issued by the Secretary of War. In its recordkeeping capacity it acquired custody of many War Department documents, including correspondence and reports submitted by army officers. The correspondence files of the Adjutant General's Office provide perhaps the richest single source among records of the department for information relating to the social history of the West, and the researcher would be well-advised to consult these materials before searching other military archives. The correspondence files contain material in the most convenient form for use, as related documents were frequently placed in consolidated files. Although information on a subject relating to western social history is often duplicated in lower-level command records, a great deal more effort at compilation is likely to be required. In addition, the Adjutant General's Office files often provide the best opportunity to obtain a comprehensive view of all levels of army participation in a given situation. As the final referral point for reports and correspondence, material produced at all command levels was received in the Adjutant General's Office—from regimental and post commanders in the field to departmental and district commanders and higher War Department officials.[7]

A great number of the consolidated correspondence files contain information on the life of soldiers campaigning against the Indians and in battle with them. Examples include: reports of Colonel Henry Leavenworth's expedition against the Arikara in the upper Missouri River area, 1824[8]; papers relating to the Sioux uprising in Minnesota, 1862[9]; papers describing the war with the Modoc Indians in northern California, 1871–1873[10]; papers relating to the campaign against Arapaho, Cheyenne, Comanche, and Kiowa bands in Indian territory (the Red River War), 1874–1875[11]; documents on the defeat of General George A. Custer and the Seventh U.S. Cavalry Regiment at the Battle of the Little Big Horn, 1876[12]; correspondence relating to the war with the Bannock Indians and their associated tribes, the Paiute, Klamath, and Umatilla, 1877–1879[13]; papers on the Ute uprising at the White River Agency, Arizona, and subsequent military operations and reprisals against them, 1879—1883[14]; papers relating to military operations against Chief Victorio's band of Mescalero Apache in southern New Mexico, 1879—1881[15]; papers relating to the uprising of the Chiricahua Apache under Geronimo, Chatto, and Natchez, and to their subsequent imprisonment in the East, 1884—1906.[16]

Additional information about military life on campaigns may be found among the records of individual cavalry and infantry regiments (Records of United States Regular Army Mobile Units).[17] To illustrate, in 1878 a battalion of the First Cavalry under Major George B. Sanford was involved in the Bannock Indian campaign; in his letters Sanford tells how civilian volunteers from the Grande Rancho Valley provided valuable assistance to his troops by supplying information on the daily movement of Indians in the area.

A generation earlier the cavalry had seen action against a different enemy and under quite dissimilar circumstances. In August 1856, the Second Dragoons were ordered into Kansas to end rioting between slavery and antislavery factions. The letters sent by their commander, Lieutenant Colonel P. St. George Cooke, provide information on the movement of the dragoons, the role of the Missouri militia, and the views of many Kansas officials.

Records emanating from a higher level military echelon (Records of United States Army Continental Commands) also deal with life in the army in the chaotic Kansas—Missouri area. During most of the nineteenth century the United States field forces were organized into commands designated as geographical divisions and departments (and under certain conditions the departments were organized partially into districts).[18] One of these, the District of Central Missouri, was occupied during much of the period 1862—1865 in fighting rebels and guerrillas, chasing gangs of thieves, answering complaints that Kansas troops were robbing Missouri citizens under the cloak of freeing Negroes, and trying civilian brigands by military commissioners. The letters sent by the district refer to the problems facing farmers called from their crops to serve as irregulars in fighting the Confederates, and to the difficulties arising when families of Confederate soldiers residing in Union areas aided the enemy by sheltering vagabonds and guerrillas. They also describe the losses sustained by local citizens at the hands of Union troops during raids. In a volume of battle and scout reports received by the district are reports of bushwackers and house robbers, and attempts of citizens to resist them by fortifying their settlements with railroad ties and bales of hay.

Records of another army command, the District of the Rio Grande, document the unsettled conditions along the Mexican border during the years 1873-1881. The correspondence refers to stolen cattle being taken across the river, the invasion of Mexican soil by United States troops, armed bands organizing for an invasion of Mexico, Mexicans shooting across the river and wounding American citizens, and the suppression of marauders on the frontier.

A few years later the turbulence of this same border area is reflected in records of the Department of Texas. Especially rich as a source of social history is a special collection of letters and reports accumulated by the department relating to the Garza Revolution, 1891-1893. These communications, mostly from Fort McIntosh and Fort Ringgold, reveal graphically the confused situation in the area. Catarino Garza was recruiting on both sides of the Rio Grande for his rebellion against Porfirio Diaz. It was nearly impossible to separate the true Garza revolutionaries from members of a gang calling themselves Garzistos, who were horse and cattle thieves—outlaws and outcasts of the worst sort—but who posed as sheep shearers and the like. Because of the confused political situation in Mexico, this division created untold confusion and the correspondence includes complaints and grand jury reports relating to depredations of American soldiers upon Texans while in search of Garza, reports and investigations of bandit attacks, reports of scouts, accounts of meetings with Mexican officers and their reports of bandit attacks, and documentation on the capture of bandits and revolutionaries and of unsuccessful efforts to apprehend Garza himself.

On the Post

Among the records of the U.S. Army Continental Commands are the records of individual military posts. As the army's basic field installation, the military post played an integral part in the development of the West. A garrison situated in a sparsely settled area frequently came into contact with the civilian population of the region, while the post itself often became the center of a developing frontier society. Establishment of a military post served not only to protect existing transportation routes and population centers, but stimulated the development of new routes, new towns, and new commercial enterprises. An army fort was also a place where settlers, travelers, and immigrants might seek protection and aid in times of adversity.

When local civilian authorities could not cope with natural calamities or civil disturbances, they called upon the garrison of a nearby fort for assistance. At such times, or during Indian uprisings, the army post was a place to concentrate troops and supplies and served as a point from which scouts, patrols, or expeditions could be dispatched to render assistance, restore order, or deal with the Indians. Sometimes the personnel came into direct contact with civilians because the garrison was the only local instrument of the federal government and almost by default became responsible for the execution of federal policies. This was the case, for example, in the South following the Civil War when numerous posts were established to enforce federal reconstruction policies.

Thus the records of United States military posts can be rich sources of information on the society of the West. These usually consist of headquarters files and the records of one or more staff officers such as a quartermaster, commissary officer, ordnance officer, or post surgeon.

As railroad construction pressed westward following the Civil War, the presence of hostile Indians required that construction crews be protected, and troops from military posts located along rights-of-way provided that service. Cantonment Bad Lands, Dakota Territory, for example, was established to prevent Indians from harassing the crews of the Northern Pacific Railroad who were working in the vicinity of the Little Missouri River. The records of this post include letters and reports referring to activities of the railroad workers, the movements of bands of Indians, and descriptions of the terrain and natural resources. There is also information on the influx of settlers, and among the letters received by the post commander are several requests from private individuals for permission to mine coal in the surrounding area.

Fort Fred Steele, Wyoming Territory, was built to protect the Union Pacific Railroad line from Rock Creek to the North Platte River. Its records provide information on Indian activities that hindered the movement of trains, difficulties between military personnel and local railroad officials, and explorations into other parts of the territory in search of gold and silver.

In addition to the military post records, valuable information about life on Army posts in the West is to be found among the records of the Office of the Quartermaster General. Quartermasters stationed at various commands or attached to units in the field were required to submit reports to the Quartermaster General concerning their activities and the operation of their offices. Generally these reports were made annually but special duties or extraordinary circumstances sometimes necessitated special reports.[19] A typical report might include one or more of the following: 1) a personal narrative by the quartermaster stating his duties and listing stations to which he was assigned, a description of any hostilities in which he had been involved, and suggestions relating to the procurement, construction, or use of military property or equipment; 2) a statement concerning the number and kind of buildings constructed or sold under his supervision; 3) comments on the resources of the post or posts at which he served, the distances and routes to other military installations or important population centers, and a description of the types of public conveyances available for passenger and freight service, and their rates and schedules; and 4) a statement of funds expended. The reports also contain references to the prices of goods and services, and comments on the variation of prices because of seasonal conditions.

In order to supply the army, the Quartermaster Department, through its field quartermasters, contracted with individuals and business concerns for supplies and services. The files of contracts and proposals and related correspondence concern every facet of the supply operation, including subsistence stores, forage, fuel, furniture, clothing, building materials, horses, wagons, and other materials and services necessary to the maintenance of troops in the field and in permanent garrisons. Contracts were also let for rail, water, and overland transportation of personnel and supplies. In addition, the Quartermaster Department made arrangements for leasing land, buildings, and even individual rooms needed to accommodate military personnel.

Another of the functions assigned to the Quartermaster Department was that of processing, investigating, and making recommendations for settlement of claims arising from military operations or from contracts with civilians. These claims records are arranged in three major categories: 1) Regular, 1848–1890, pertaining to barracks, quarters, horses, forage, fuel, and other supplies regularly needed by the Army; 2) Transportation, 1848–1886, relating to rail, water, and overland movements of troops, prisoners, and supplies; and 3) Miscellaneous, 1848–1890, which includes all other claims, such as those associated with national cemeteries, extra duty, mileage, and personal services and allowances.

Functions closely related to those of the Quartermaster General were carried out by the Office of the Commissary General of Subsistence.[20] Its records relate primarily to the acquisition of subsistence provisions (basically food) for the army. They include information concerning bids, contracts, prices, kinds and quantities of goods needed and provided; transportation of goods; and tests of products. Many of the provisions were produced locally, and in many instances records relating to individual military posts can be identified. For example, there are segregated files concerning farm culture at military posts, 1851–1855.

Much earlier information on farming by the military may be found in records of the Sixth Infantry Regiment, which are included in the records of the U.S. Regular Army Mobile Units. While stationed at Fort Atkinson, under the command of Colonel Henry Leavenworth in 1822 and 1823, the regiment engaged in extensive farming. The letters sent by Leavenworth describe farming techniques, explain crop failures, and report the results of harvests. They also complain of Indians rustling government cattle from the military reservation.

The records of the Surgeon General include a limited amount of documentation of considerable value for an understanding of living conditions on western military posts.[21] Among them are inspection reports on medical facilities and sanitary conditions at army posts, 1890–1894, which describe weather conditions; living quarters, including the sizes of rooms, number of men per room, ventilation, and bedding; water supply; heating and sewerage systems; food, including menus, methods of preparation, and quality; morale and morals of soldiers; and prevalent diseases, incidence and treatment thereof, and the number of births and deaths. For Fort Sill, Fort Spokane, and Vancouver Barracks there are special sanitary reports for June 30, 1893, which contain additional information on the history of the posts plus a summary of the geology and botany of the surrounding country. In addition there are reports of epidemics, rare diseases, and vaccinations for the period 1888–1917. For some posts these reports include histories of epidemics and diseases, information on treatment, and statistics on the ill and the dead. Vaccination reports describe unusual reactions and innovations in the administration of vaccine.

Beginning in 1868 army surgeons were required by the Surgeon General to maintain medical histories of their posts. These documents frequently contain data relative to the geology,

The Taming of the West

botany, zoology, ethnology, and water supply of the surrounding area. These are now a part of the records of the Adjutant General's Office.

The Confederate War Department included a medical department, which was responsible for operating hospitals and caring for sick and wounded soldiers. Fragmentary records have survived for several hospitals located west of the Mississippi.[22] For example, there is a prescription book used at the hospitals at Fort Fillmore, New Mexico Territory, and Dona Anna, Arizona Territory, giving the names of patients, diagnoses of their ailments, and medicines prescribed. The registers of patients at hospitals in Little Rock, Arkansas, and Franklin, El Paso, Galveston, and Houston, Texas, usually contain information on the nature of each illness, its treatment, the length of confinement, and the disposition of the case. A record book of the general hospitals at Galveston and Houston enumerates requisitions and returns of medical equipment, drugs, and hospital supplies, and provides statistics and reports on the sick and wounded.

One final aspect of life on army posts may be mentioned—education. The records of the Division of the Missouri (in the records of the U.S. Army Continental Commands) include a series of annual reports of operations received from the various department commanders, 1871–1887. The sections relating to post schools, barracks, and quarters are of particular interest as they give the numbers of children over five years of age, and the numbers of children in post schools whose fathers were officers, enlisted men, and civilians. The reports frequently contain remarks that shed light on various aspects of the post school system.

Relations with the Indians

Involvement of the army on the frontier with Indians was not limited to times of open hostilities. The army often was responsible for major operations, such as moving large groups of Indians to a reservation, or their transfer from one reservation to another. Some involved combat, others did not. The army often found itself in charge of providing substantial quantities of food and supplies to the Indians, not infrequently surmounting major logistical problems in the process.[23] On a smaller scale, when destitute Indians visited a military post, or when an Indian agent requested assistance, the commander might supply food, clothing, tools, and other supplies. The records of military posts frequently contain evidence of such occurrences.[24]

Once again, however, the records of the Adjutant General's Office, particularly the consolidated correspondence files, are the best source for information about the interactions between military forces and Indians. Examples of such files that relate to moving Indians to reservations and administration of the reservations are correspondence regarding efforts to force the Utah Indians to go onto the Uintah Valley Reservation, 1872,[25] correspondence relating to the removal of nearly one thousand Winnebago Indians from Wisconsin to Nebraska, 1873–1874,[26] correspondence relating to a request from the Department of the Interior that the War Department provide transportation for supplies and assistance in moving Little Chief and members of his band of Northern Cheyenne from the Cheyenne and Arapaho Agency, Indian Territory, to the Pine Ridge Agency, Dakota Territory, 1881—1883,[27] reports, recommendations, and other papers regarding efforts by the army and the Interior Department to return Jicarilla Apache encamped near Espanola, New Mexico, to the Mescalero Reservation, and to adjust their grievances, 1886–1888.[28]

Examples of consolidated files relating to the issuance of food and other supplies to Indians are correspondence relating to the provision of food and ammunition for hunting to nearly three thousand starving Arapaho, Cheyenne, and Sioux under Chief Red Cloud at Fort Laramie, Wyoming, 1871–1872[29]; correspondence on a planned reduction of beef rations for the Arapaho, Cheyenne, Comanche, and Kiowa Agencies, fears among army officers that this could result in an outbreak of violence, and efforts of some officers to avoid a general uprising by obtaining adequate beef rations, 1882[30]; papers concerning threatened starvation on the Mescalero Apache Reservation, New Mexico, after Congress failed to appropriate funds for rations, and subsequent efforts by army officers and the Interior Department to obtain rations, 1882–1884.[31]

Among the other sources dealing with relations between the military and Indians are the records of cavalry and infantry regiments stationed in the West (Records of the U.S. Regular Army Mobile Units). Illustrative is a series of letters sent by a detachment of the First Dragoon Regiment (later the First Cavalry) stationed in Iowa from 1834 to 1837 and from 1841 to 1843. These describe the role of the dragoons in maintaining peace between settlers and Indians, and document repeated efforts to prevent traders from cheating and selling liquor to the Sac and Fox.

Letters sent by a field detachment of the Eighth Cavalry stationed near the Cheyenne River Indian Agency, 1890–1891, provide an almost daily account of affairs in that part of South Dakota. Much attention is given to the Battle of Wounded Knee, but there is considerable information about Indian—white relations in the area and about settlers' attitudes toward the Indians prior to the battle.

Relations with the Settlers

On the western frontier, where the army post was the center of society, troops were closely involved in the daily life of the civilian population. Contacts were multiplied during unsettled times—during Reconstruction Era, during strikes, during floods and pestilences—when the local civilian government was unable to protect people and their property. The records of all military posts contained in the U.S. Army Continental Commands records are a valuable source of information about the relationships between the army and settlers, but the records accumulated by the Adjutant General's Office are especially full and revelatory.

Among them are the letterbooks containing copies of the letters sent by the Military Governors of California, 1847–1848.

Addressed to federal and local officials, army and navy officers, and private persons, they reflect almost every conceivable aspect of life in an emerging community.[32] A complement to the letterbooks is a major consolidated file of letters received by the Adjutant General's Office relating to the activities of Brigadier General Stephen W. Kearney and the Army of the West in New Mexico and California.[33] Included are a copy of the legal code for New Mexico, drafted by Colonel Alexander W. Doniphan, and papers relating to Kearney's civil appointments in New Mexico. Reports from Kearney describe the attitudes of native Californians, their troubled relations with recent American immigrants, and the nature of settlement in various parts of California.

Contemporary with these records are those maintained by the Tenth Military Department, then comprising Oregon Territory and California. Reports to the department from commanders of military districts, found in the Records of the U.S. Army Continental Commands, describe the hostility of Californians to the government, and officers' investigations of civilian complaints of all sorts. Other documentation describes the Catholic missions, their state of decay, their occupants, and their treatment of visitors, as well as the seizure of some of the missions by American citizens.

Reports by the Tenth Military Department to the Adjutant General's Office conveyed much information about prevailing conditions during the gold rush of 1849. In them Lt. Col. Bennet Riley, the department commander, discussed the possibility of Indian attacks upon exposed groups of miners, ill feelings between American and foreign miners, and general conditions in the gold fields. On August 30, 1849, Riley reported on his recent visit to the mining area, noting that the old diggings were still productive and that new strikes were being made daily. He found reports of conflict between miners to be greatly exaggerated, but noted that Americans and Europeans did tend to side against Mexicans and South Americans.[34]

Additional information on the California gold rush is found

in a consolidated file pertaining to assistance rendered by the military to overland immigrants late in 1849. Here a number of reports deal with conditions among the immigrants and document the amounts and kinds of food and other supplies issued to them.[35]

The nominal existence of civil authority was no guarantee that the army would not be needed to keep the peace. A large consolidated file of the Adjutant General's Office pertains to an attack upon Brownsville, Texas, in 1859 by a group of Mexican bandits led by Juan Nepomuceno Cortinas, and to subsequent efforts by the army to apprehend him and to restore law and order. It contains reports from Lieutenant Colonel Robert E. Lee dealing with border conditions, in one of which he notes, "Most of the Ranchos on the River . . . have been abandoned or destroyed. Those spared by Cortinas have been burned by the Texans. The occupants have generally taken refuge in Mexico. . . ."[36]

Other consolidated files on civil disturbances that resulted in surveillance or intervention by the army include those pertaining to the activities of the Irish-American Fenian Brotherhood in Dakota Territory along the Canadian Border, 1868–1871[37]; riots and murders caused by cattle herders and Indians in Lincoln County, New Mexico, 1874–1881[38]; lawlessness in the Texas panhandle region, during which Philip J. Goodfellow, a British subject and a Texas rancher, was hanged by vigilantes, 1877[39]; and violations of the rights of Chinese, including an attack on Chinese workers on the Union Pacific Railroad at Rock Springs, Wyoming, 1885–1897.[40]

Toward the end of the nineteenth century, the army was increasingly involved in dealing with labor unrest in the West. Miners and railroad workers most often were the targets of this intervention. For example, in 1892 members of the Miner's Union in the Coeur d'Alene region of northern Idaho rioted, destroyed property, and drove nonunion men from the mines. There was some loss of life. At the request of the Governor of Idaho the President dispatched federal troops to the area. Reports from troop commanders in the field to the Adjutant General's Office describe the destruction and chaos they encountered and the steps taken to restore order.[41] The records of the U.S. Army Continental Commands concerning the Department of Colorado also extensively document military intervention in labor disputes.

Occasionally inspection reports of a military command refer to relations between the military and civilian populations. An outstanding example, though not typical, is the report of October 5, 1866, by Colonel Orville E. Babcock, pertaining to an inspection of the Military Division of the Missouri and a visit to the Mormon community in Utah, including an assessment of possible difficulties that could arise between it and the United States government.[42] Babcock visited Salt Lake City in June and July 1866, conferred with Brigham Young and other leaders, and incorporated an account of his experiences in his report. He advised against coercive policies, believing that the Mormons could be shown the "error of their ways" by the "enlightened example" of carefully selected civil and military officers.

Another pertinent inspection report is that of Colonel N. H. Davis, March 15, 1869, in which he recommended issuance of food and supplies to settlers in the Solomon, Saline, and Republican valleys of Kansas, who had suffered from Indian depredations. He included an enumeration of the males, females, and children in each stricken family, a statement of losses sustained, and estimates of the cost of rations needed to relieve the destitution.[43]

During the 1870s and 1880s the army was heavily involved with the white population in another form of peacekeeping—keeping intruders off Indian reservations. Selected consolidated files of the Adjutant General's Office describing these efforts include papers relating to the removal of trespassers on the Miami Indian Reservation, Kansas, 1870[44]; correspondence relating to reports that miners had been working in the Black Hills country of the Sioux Indians Reservation, 1874–1875[45]; correspondence regarding the intrusion of miners and ranchers on Chief Moses' Reservation, Washington Territory, 1881–1884[46]; papers relating to the protection of the Klamath Indian Reservation, Oregon, against poachers, cattlemen, and settlers, 1887–1888.[47]

The problem of keeping white settlers out of Indian Territory was superseded by others when Oklahoma was opened to settlement in 1889. The records of the two military posts most heavily involved, Camp Oklahoma and Camp Guthrie, are especially informative. Here are letters and reports on the conflicts between homesteaders and townsite parties, claim jumping, and illegal liquor traffic. The records of Camp Oklahoma are rich with information on conditions and activities in Oklahoma City. Captain D. F. Stiles, commanding officer of this post, reported on October 17, 1889, that the city authorities were "powerless to maintain peace and good order without the moral support of the military . . . "[48] Other correspondence reports on corruption in city politics, bogus elections, the rumored assassination of the mayor, attempted murders of city marshals, the closing of gambling houses, and the elimination of "dance houses of low character." On several occasions troops were sent into the city to maintain order when claimants to tracts of land, who sometimes numbered as many as twelve for a single piece of property, attempted to remove their competitors.

When five military districts were established in the South pursuant to the Reconstruction Acts of March 1867, the powers of their commanding generals were both civil and military. Accordingly, in each district an office of civil affairs was established. Thus, in still another context did the military interrelate with the civilian population. Two military districts, the fourth and the fifth, were, in part, west of the Mississippi.

Records of the Office of Civil Affairs of the Fifth Military District, which included Texas, will illustrate the nature of the army's involvement. Letters received by this office refer, all too frequently, to gangs of marauding murderers and their crimes, such as the party that killed " . . . two soldiers of Captain Lancasters *(sic)* companys *(sic)*, about 6 or 7 Negroes and a

Mrs. Roach, and an Irishman. . . ."[49] They contain complaints that arrested men were let loose before being brought to trial, and local law officers' reports about their unsuccessful attempts to catch desperadoes, as well as reports on tax collection, requests for aid after tornadoes, and sundry complaints of a political nature. Substantial amounts of material deal with the administration of justice, voter registration, and elections.

Military involvement with the civilian population during Reconstruction included the activities of the Bureau of Refugees, Freedmen, and Abandoned Lands, an agency of the War Department. The bureau not only supervised all affairs relating to refugees and freedmen, but had custody of abandoned or confiscated lands and property. It issued rations, clothing, and sometimes free transportation to destitute refugees and freedmen, and supervised the writing of labor contracts and terms of indenture involving freedmen. The Bureau was most active between 1865 and 1869, but the correspondence and reports received by its headquarters from its officials in the field portray in detail the nature and extent of its far-flung relief activities.[50]

The military maintained a strong interest in civil affairs in the Far West both during and after the Civil War. Among the communications received by the District of Southern California, 1861–1866, are references to secessionist sympathizers, Confederate spies, and disloyalty in general, as well as reports of detachment commanders sent "to silence those opposed to our government and to restore confidence to the union element. . . ."[51], and reports on bands of thieves menacing the county of San Diego and horse thieves in the mountains. A report by Lieutenant Colonel George S. Evans in April 1862 describes the living conditions of both Indians and whites in Owen's River Valley.[52] After the Confederates had been swept from Arizona in the spring of 1862, a military government was established. One may find in the records of the District of Arizona, 1862–1870, a good deal of material relating to civil affairs: the discovery of silver; the need for troops to preserve order; the licensing of gamblers, liquor sellers, and other

The Taming of the West

businessmen; the removal of secessionist alcaldes and the appointment of new ones; and the flight and apprehension of secessionists.

The Provost Marshal General's Bureau, created by law in 1863, was responsible for enrollment for the draft and for the detection and arrest of deserters. Among its records is a series of reports, submitted in 1865, summarizing the work done by the state and local provost marshals.[53] These usually include explanations of how the enrollment process was carried out in a particular state or district. Some, however, discuss particular problems, such as means of reducing the desertion rate, methods of spying on and infiltrating anti-draft leagues, and means of inducing men to volunteer. Others describe in detail the attitudes toward the draft of specific groups, such as urban dwellers, miners, farmers, and aliens.

A provost marshal system was also adopted by the military departments, and records reflecting these activities are among those of the individual commands found in the records of the U.S. Army Continental Commands. Provost marshals were responsible for both the military policing of soldiers and military control over civilians in sparsely settled or once rebellious areas. Thus they were concerned with suppressing gambling houses, barrooms, brothels, and brawls beyond the limits of military camps; and with resolving complaints of citizens as to the conduct of soldiers. They also issued travel passes and trade permits, and determined eligibility for government food and supplies. The proceedings of the provost court of the Department of Arkansas, 1865-1866, are informative both as to the types of crimes brought before it—inhumane treatment of animals, larceny, drunkenness, maltreatment of wives, disorderly conduct, gambling, and vagrancy—and the sentences meted out for these offenses.

Yet another instance of military administration of civil justice is to be found among the records of the Office of the Judge Advocate General.[54] The primary function of this office was the administration of military justice, but during the Civil War and

Reconstruction many civilians were brought before military courts and commissions in federally occupied areas such as Missouri, Arkansas, Texas, Kansas, and New Mexico. Many were tried for participating in rebellion against the United States, treason, and harassment or murder of pro-Union citizens. A typical case was that of James H. Holmes, proprietor, editor, and publisher of the *Santa Fe Republican,* who was tried by a military commission in 1862. He was charged with giving intelligence, aid, and comfort to the enemy by publishing information about the federal installation at Fort Union, New Mexico.[55]

Some trials resulted from the policies pursued by Union officers in administering occupied areas. A court of inquiry, headed by Major General Irvin McDowell, was convened at St. Louis in 1863 to investigate the extent to which Union officers had participated in the Arkansas cotton trade and in granting trade licenses to civilians. In the course of the investigation it was revealed that Major General Samuel R. Curtis, commanding Union forces at Helena, Arkansas, had confiscated cotton from the plantation of Confederate General Gideon Pillow, which he turned over to the plantation slaves to sell. Curtis contended that it was necessary to allow the Negroes to sell the cotton, and also some cattle, because his own troops in stripping the plantation had left the slaves in a starving condition.[56]

The Quartermaster Department came into contact with civilian society on practically a daily basis. The records of its business transactions—contracting for supplies, transportation, and construction; hiring civilian employees; seeking to acquire better and cheaper supplies and equipment—provide significant information about the nature of the society. Like the civilians who crossed the Mississippi, the army encountered new challenges and new problems in constructing shelter, acquiring food, transporting materials, and achieving a modicum of comfort and safety. The manner in which these challenges were met, as well as the interaction of the civilian population and the army as both moved westward, is amply documented in the Records of the Office of the Quartermaster General.

This is best illustrated in the monthly reports submitted to the Quartermaster General by quartermasters assigned to military commands or installations. These list the names of civilians employed, their occupations and the nature of their duties, the inclusive dates of their employment, the rates of compensation, the dates of the contracts under which they were employed, the amounts paid for their services, and the money still owed to them. The reports provide information on a wide range of occupations of the civilian personnel hired by the army: teamsters, interpreters, wagon masters, storekeepers, engineers, blacksmiths, carpenters, and scouts. When a quartermaster hired horses, wagons, or machinery he entered in his report the type of article hired and the name of the owner or consigner, along with information as to the length of time the article was in the public service and the amount of money paid or owed to the owner. These reports reveal a great deal about civilian participation during expeditions or at military installations.

Information about life on and around military posts is also reflected in the military reservation file maintained by the Military Reservation Division of the Adjutant General's Office.[57] This division was charged with handling all correspondence relating to the establishment, occupation, maintenance, and abandonment of military posts. In addition much of the documentation illustrates the interaction between the posts and surrounding communities. In the file for the San Carlos Agency, Arizona, for example, is a memorial to Congress from the Arizona Legislative Assembly requesting a new post near Gibson's Well as an additional safeguard against Indian depredations.[58] Similarly, the Camp Stambaugh, Wyoming, file includes a petition from Sweetwater County, dated April 1870, requesting a cavalry force to deal with Indians who had been interfering with settlers' mining operations.[59] The Fort Bidwell, California file includes a great deal of information relative to conditions on the nearby Paiute Indian Reservation at Pyramid Lake, and in white settlements in the area. Of particular interest is an 1890 report by Captain J. M. Lee on the possible abandonment of the post. The report discusses the character and extent of surrounding settlements, both Indian and white, and the disposition of the former toward the latter. Lee also solicited statements from Indians and whites, which he included in the report, relative to their attitudes toward the military in general and the abandonment of the post in particular.[60]

Finally, an understanding of the relationships of the military on the frontier with the civilian world can be much enhanced by photographs. The best source of this kind in federal archives will be found in the photographic records of the Office of the Chief Signal Officer.[61] The Army Signal Corps engaged in special photographic activities from the time of its organization in 1863. The approximately twenty-five hundred items relating to the army's guardian function in the West between 1865 and 1895 illustrate vividly not only soldiering as it was done on and off the post, but much about the civilians who interacted in a variety of ways with the soldiers.

Military archives have been used extensively since the establishment of the National Archives in 1934 by students of military history, by those interested in the development of Indian policy, and by researchers delving into other aspects of American history in which the armed forces had some involvement. They have also been used to a degree by social historians; but when one considers their extent, variety, and richness it must be concluded that such use has been marginal. The military archives of the nation are a largely unexplored and unexploited resource that beckons compellingly to the social historian.

NOTES

1. A note on the interrelationships between sections of this chapter. "On Explorations." There are important similarities between exploratory expeditions and military campaigns, but they had quite different objectives. One was essentially peaceful in intent, the other hostile. Hence the decision for separate sections. In this section more is said about what the soldiers observed than about what they did. To observe and report was, after all, the objective of the mission. But the records also shed light on the activities of the members of the expeditions. "On Campaigns and in Battle" includes information on relationships with

The Taming of the West

Indians and settlers, the primary subjects of the final two sections. "On the Post" includes information on relations with Indians, and much about relations with settlers, but the emphasis is on the life of the *military* on the *post*. "Relations with the Indians" deals primarily with the relatively peaceful contacts that the military had with the Indians, hence the distinction between this section and that on campaigns and battles. Some of the peaceful contacts, however, are documented in the section on explorations. Finally, this section also deals to some extent with relations between settlers and Indians. Much of the information in "Relations with the Settlers" has to do with life on the military post. The major distinction between this section and "On the Post" is that this one focuses on military relations with the civilian community, and the other concentrates on the life of the soldiers on the post.

2. Records of the Office of the Quartermaster General, RG 92, National Archives Building, Washington, D. C. (Hereafter, unless otherwise indicated, all records are in the National Archives Building, Washington, D.C.) Many of the records discussed or cited in this chapter are available as National Archives microfilm publications. For further information see *Catalog of National Archives Microfilm Publications* (Washington, D.C. 1972).

3. Captain E. S. Hawkins to Maj. Gen. Alexander Macomb, August 24, 1831, Letters Received Relating to Military Discipline and Control. Records of the Headquarters of the Army, RG 108.

4. Extract from journal by Lt. A. W. Whipple, U.S. Topographical Engineers, Vol. 6, pp. 370-408, Reports to Congress. Records of the Office of the Secretary of War, RG 107.

5. Philip Tyson to Topographical Bureau, March 1850, File T-255-1850, Letters Received, 1832−1865, Topographical Bureau. Records of the Office of the Chief of Engineers, RG 77.

6. Lt. James H. Simpson to Topographical Bureau, March 1849, File S−674−1849, and April 1850, File S−542−1850, Letters Received, 1832−65, Topographical Bureau, RG 77.

7. Records of the Adjutant General's Office, RG 94.

8. Letters Received, File S−14−1824, RG 94.

9. Letters Received, File 5−1−1866, RG 94.

10. Letters Received, File 2418 AGO 1871, RG 94.

11. Letters Received, File 2815 AGO 1874, RG 94.

12. Letters Received, File 3770 AGO 1876, RG 94.

13. Letters Received, File 7316 AGO 1877, RG 94.

14. Letters Received, File 4278 AGO 1879, RG 94.

15. Letters Received, File 6058 AGO 1879, RG 94.

16. Letters Received, File 1066 AGO 1883, RG 94.

17. Records of United States Regular Army Mobile Units, 1821−1942, RG 391.

18. Records of United States Army Continental Commands, 1821−1920, RG 393.

19. There are files of quartermaster reports for the years 1863–1870; 1872–1880; and 1882–1886.

20. Records of the Office of the Commissary General of Subsistence, RG 192, Washington National Records Center, Suitland, Maryland.

21. Records of the Office of the Surgeon General (Army), RG 112.

22. War Department Collection of Confederate Records, RG 109.

23. In these activities the army cooperated closely with the Bureau of Indian Affairs. It will be recalled that until 1849, primary responsibility for Indian affairs had been in the Department of War. When this responsibility was transferred to the new Interior Department, most of the related records were transferred also.

24. RG 393.

25. Letters Received, File 2770 AGO 1872, RG 94.

26. Letters Received, File 4746 AGO 1873, RG 94.

27. Letters Received, File 5200 AGO 1881, RG 94.

28. Letters Received, File 5939 AGO 1886, RG 94.

29. Letters Received, File 113 AGO 1871, RG 94.

30. Letters Received, File 1280 AGO 1882, RG 94.

31. Letters Received, File 2180 AGO 1882, RG 94.

32. Letters Sent by Military Governors of California, 1847–1848, RG 94.

33. Letters Received, File 209–K–1846, RG 94.

34. Letters Received, File 244–R–1849, RG 94.

35. Letters Received, File 120–S–1850, RG 94.

36. Letters Received, File 198–T–1859, RG 94.

37. Letters Received, File 257–A–1868 and 370–A–1870, RG 94.

38. Letters Received, Files 554 AGO 1874 and 1405 AGO 1878, RG 94.

39. Letters Received, File 2675 AGO 1877, RG 94.

40. Letters Received, File 5820 AGO 1885, RG 94.

41. General Correspondence, File 34728 PRD 1892, RG 94.

42. Letters Received, File 19–B–1866, Records of the Office of the Inspector General, RG 159.

43. Letters Received, File 19–M–1869, RG 159.

44. Letters Received, File 186–I–1870, RG 94.

45. Letters Received, File 5009 AGO 1874, RG 94.

46. Letters Received, File 5517 AGO 1881, RG 94.

47. Letters Received, File 477 AGO 1887, RG 94.

48. Capt. D. F. Stiles to the Assistant Adjutant General, Department of the Missouri, October 17, 1889, Letters Sent, Camp Oklahoma, Indian Territory, RG 393.

49. Fritz Palm to Gen. J. J. Reynolds, undated, File P127 V^2 5MD '69, filed with Lt. J. Whitney to Capt. James Biddle, June 9, 1869, File B (Vol. 2) 65, C. B., 5MD '69, Letters Received, Office of Civil Affairs, Fifth Military District, RG 393.

50. Records of the Bureau of Refugees, Freedmen, and Abandoned Lands, RG 105.

51. Capt. James M. Roper to Lt. Thomas Barker, December 13, 1863, enclosed in Roper to District of Southern California, December 21, 1863, Letters Received, District of Southern California, RG 393.

52. Lt. Col. George S. Evans to District of Southern California, April 29, 1862, Letters Received, District of Southern California, RG 393.

53. Records of the Provost Marshal General's Bureau (Civil War), RG 110.

54. Records of the Office of the Judge Advocate General (Army), RG 153.

55. File KK−96, Court-Martial Case Files, RG 153.

56. File KK−885, Court-Martial Case Files, RG 153.

57. Although this division existed only from 1882 to 1890, many records in the reservation file predate and postdate this period.

58. The memorial is undated, but was probably prepared in March 1889. San Carlos File, Military Reservation Division, RG 94.

59. Camp Stambaugh File, Military Reservation Division, RG 94.

60. Fort Bidwell File, Military Reservation Division, RG 94.

61. Records of the Office of the Chief Signal Officer, RG 111.

APPENDIX:
The Writings of Everett Dick

Every historian of the West is familiar with the books that have won Everett Dick the respect of the profession: <u>The Sod-House Frontier, Vanguards of the Frontier, The Dixie Frontier, and The Lure of the Land</u>. These deserve to be, and are, ranked among the truly significant contributions of our generation. Few historians, however, realize that these volumes and the many historical articles supplementing them form only a part of Everett Dick's writings. They are matched by an equally distinguished series of books and articles from his pen dealing with his Adventist faith. The impressive list of works that follows was kindly supplied by Mrs. Everett Dick.

BOOKS

The Sod-House Frontier 1854-1890, A Social History of the Northern Plains from the Creation of Kansas and Nebraska to the Admission of the Dakotas. New York, 1937.

Founders of the Message. Washington, 1938.

Vanguards of the Frontier, A Social History of the Northern Plains and Rocky Mountains from the Earliest White Contacts to the Coming of the Homemaker. New York, 1941.

Union College, Fifty Years of Service (Co-authored with D. D. Rees). Lincoln, Nebraska, 1941.

Life in the West before the Sod-House Frontier. Lincoln, Nebraska, 1947.

The Dixie Frontier, A Social History of the Southern Frontier from the First Transmontane Beginnings to the Civil War. New York, 1948.

Medical Cadet Corps Training Manual. Lincoln, Nebraska, 1955.

Tales of the Frontier, from Lewis and Clark to the Last Roundup. Lincoln, Nebraska, 1963.

Union—College of the Golden Cords. Lincoln, Nebraska, 1967.

The Lure of the Land, A Social History of the Public Lands from the Articles of Confederation to the New Deal. Lincoln, Nebraska, 1970.
The Great American Desert: Nebraska. Lincoln, Nebraska, in press.

CONTRIBUTIONS TO REFERENCE WORKS

Articles in *The Dictionary of American Biography.* Published under the auspices of the American Council of Learned Societies, Allen Johnson, ed. 20 vols. New York, 1928–1936.
    Joshua V. Himes
    William Miller
    Uriah Smith
    Henry Dana Ward
    Ellen G. White
    James White

Articles in *The Dictionary of American History.* James Truslow Adams, ed. 5 vols. New York, 1940.
    Adobe
    Cabanne's Trading Post
    Dugout
    The Frontier Family
    Prairie Fires
    The Prairies
    Sod House
    and others

Articles in *The Seventh-day Adventist Encyclopedia.* Washington, D.C., 1966.
    Boulder Memorial Hospital
    Christian Record Braille Foundation, Inc.
    Clinton Theological Seminary.
    Colorado Conference
    Hutchinson Theological Seminary
    Iowa Sanitarium
    Kansas Sanitarium
    Nebraska Sanitarium (Hastings, Nebraska)
    Nebraska Sanitarium (Lincoln, Nebraska)
    Porter Memorial Hospital
    Union College
    Wyoming Conference

PAPERS AND ADDRESSES PUBLISHED

"The Long Drive" (Master's thesis, University of Nebraska, 1925), Kansas State Historical Society *Collections,* XVII (Topeka: Kansas State Historical Society, 1928), 27–97.

"Ed. Howe, A Notable Figure on the Sod House Frontier," *Nebraska History,* XVIII (April-June, 1937), 138−143.

"The Forgotten Man," *Report of the Blue Ridge Educational Convention, August 17-25, 1937* (Washington, D.C.: Washington Missionary College Press, 1937), pp. 179 0−185.

"Beyond the Ninety-fifth Meridian." *Agricultural History,* XVII (April, 1943), 105−112.

"Problems of the Post-Frontier Prairie City as Portrayed by Lincoln, Nebraska, 1880−1890," *Nebraska History,* XXVIII (April-June, 1947), 132−143.

"Free Homes for the Millions," *Nebraska History,* XLIII (December, 1962), 211−227.

"Sunbonnet and Calico, the Homesteader's Consort," *Nebraska History,* XLVII (March, 1966), 3−13.

"Water, a Frontier Problem," *Nebraska History,* XLIX (Autumn, 1968), 215−245.

"Some Aspects of Private Use of Public Lands," *Journal of the West,* IX (January, 1970), 24−32.

BOOK REVIEWS

Appearing in—
  a. *American Historical Review,* Washington, D.C.
      Sandoz, Mari, *Crazy Horse The Strange Man of the Oglalas* (Washington, 1942), *American Historical Review,* XLVIII (July, 1943), 877−878.

      Nelson, Bruce, *Land of the Dacotahs* (Minneapolis, 1946), *American Historical Review,* LIII (October, 1947), 126−127.

      Tilghman, Zoe A., *Marshal of the Last Frontier William Matthew (Bill) Tilghman* (Glendale, Calif., 1949), *American Historical Review,* LV (October, 1949), 243.
  b. *Journal of Southern History,* Baton Rouge, Louisiana
      Rister, Carl Coke, *Land Hunger: David L. Payne and the Oklahoma Boomers* (Norman, 1942), *Journal of Southern History,* IX (May, 1943), 277−278.

      Gard, Wayne, *Frontier Justice* (Norman, 1949), *Journal of Southern History,* XVI (May, 1950), 255−226.

      Dale, Edward Everett, *Frontier Ways: Sketches of Life in the Old West* (Austin, 1959), *Journal of Southern History,* XXVI (August, 1960), 412−413.
  c. *Mississippi Valley Historical Review,* Lincoln, Nebraska
      Giles, Dorothy, *Singing Valleys: The Story of Corn* (New York, 1940), *Mississippi Valley Historical Review,* XXVIII (September, 1941), 312−313.

Peterson, William J., *Iowa The Rivers of Her Valleys* (Iowa City, 1941), *Mississippi Valley Historical Review,* XXVIII (December, 1941), 445-447.

Dale, Edward Everett, *Cow Country* (Norman, 1942), *Mississippi Valley Historical Review,* XXIX (September, 1942), 260—270.

Kraenzel, Carl F., Thomas Watson and Glenn H. Craig, with the collaboration of E. A. Corbett, O. A. Parsons, and Stanley Rands, *The Northern Plains in a World of Change* (N. P., 1942), *Mississippi Valley Historical Review,* XXX (January, 1944), 461-462.

Paden, Irene D., *The Wake of the Prairie Schooner* (New York, 1943), *Mississippi Valley Historical Review,* XXX (March, 1944), 610-611.

Boatright, Mody C. and Donald Day, eds., *From Hell to Breakfast* (Austin, 1944), *Mississippi Valley Historical Review,* XXXII (June, 1945), 147-148.

Price, Conn, *Trails I Rode* (Pasadena, Calif., 1947), *Mississippi Valley Historical Review,* XXIV (September, 1947), 312.

Thomas, Sister M. Evangeline, *Footprints on the Frontier: A History of the Sisters of Saint Joseph, Concordia, Kansas* (Westminster, Maryland, 1948), *Mississippi Valley Historical Review,* XXXVI (June, 1949), 153-154.

Atherton, Lewis E., *The Southern Country Store, 1800-1860* (Baton Rouge, 1949), *Mississippi Valley Historical Review,* XXXVII (June, 1950), 123.

A Merry Briton in Pioneer Wisconsin: A Contemporary Narrative Reprinted from Life in the West: Back-wood Leaves and Prairie Flowers. Rough Sketches on the Borders of the Picturesque, the Sublime, and Ridiculous. . . (Madison, 1953), *Mississippi Valley Historical Review,* XXXVIII (September, 1950), 320-321.

Power, Richard Lyle, *Planting Corn Belt Culture* (Indianapolis, 1953), *Mississippi Valley Historical Review,* XLI (June, 1954), 118-119.

Kraenzel, Carl Frederick, *The Great Plains in Transition* (Norman, 1955), *Mississippi Valley Historical Review,* XLIII (September, 1956), 329-330.

Richardson, Rupert Norval, *The Frontier of Northwest Texas 1846 to 1876: Advance and the Defense by Pioneer Settlers of the Cross Timbers and Prairies* (Glendale, Calif., 1963), *Mississippi Valley Historical Review,* L (March, 1964), 706.

d. *Nebraska History,* Lincoln, Nebraska.

Pickard, Madge E. and R. Carlyle Buley, *The Midwest Pioneer His Ills, Cures, and Doctors* (New York, 1946), *Nebraska History,* XXVIII (July-September, 1927), 202-204.

Billington, Ray Allen, ed., *The Frontier Thesis—Valid Interpretation of American History?* (New York, 1966), *Nebraska History,* XLVIII (Summer, 1967), 200–203.

Welsch, Roger L., *Sod Walls, The Story of the Nebraska Sod House* (Broken Bow, Nebraska, 1968), *Nebraska History* (Autumn, 1968), 325–327.

Linderman, Frank B., *Montana Adventure, The Recollections of Frank B. Linderman* (Lincoln, 1968), *Nebraska History* XL (Winter, 1968), 448–449.

Drache, Hiram M., *The Challenge of the Prairie, Life and Times of Red River Pioneers* (Fargo, 1970), *Nebraska History,* LII (Spring, 1971), 106–107.

e. Miscellaneous Journals

Peattic, Donald Culross, *A Prairie Grove* (New York, 1938), *Yale Review,* XXVII (June, 1938), 829–830.

Clark, Thomas D., *The Rampaging Frontier* (Indianapolis, 1939), *Saturday Review of Literature,* XX (June 3, 1939), 6.

Woestermeyer, Faye Ina and J. Montgomery Gambrill, eds., *The Westward Movement* (New York, 1939), *Saturday Review of Literature,* XX (July 22, 1939), 17.

Burlingame, Merrill G., *The Montana Frontier* (Helena, 1942), *Minnesota History,* XXIV (June, 1943), 158–159.

Mirsky, Jeannette, *The Westward Crossings* (New York, 1946), *Minnesota History,* XXVIII (March, 1947), 57–58.

Athearn, Robert G., *Westward the Briton* (New York, 1953), *Indiana Magazine of History,* L (March, 1954), 69–70.

Emmett, Chris, *Shanghai Pierce, A Fair Likeness* (Norman, 1953), *Pacific Historical Review,* XXIII (May, 1954), 174–175.

Drago, Harry Sinclair, *Outlaws on Horseback* (New York, 1964), *Journal of the Illinois State Historical Society,* LVII (Autumn, 1964), 303—305.

Lass, William E., *A History of Steamboating on the Upper Missouri River* (Lincoln, 1962), *Arizona and the West,* VI (Autumn, 1964), 246–247.

Kennedy, Michael S., ed., *Cowboys and Cattlemen, A Roundup from Montana, The Magazine of Western History* (New York, 1964), *Southern California Quarterly,* XLVII (March, 1965), 122–123.

Jacobs, Wilbur R., John W. Caughey and Joe B. Franz, *Turner, Bolton, and Webb: Three Historians of the American Frontier* (Seattle, 1965), *Southern California Quarterly,* XLVIII (September, 1966), 321–323.

Cook, Harold J., *Tales of the 04 Ranch, Recollections of Harold J. Cook* (Lincoln, 1968), *Arizona and the West,* XII (Spring, 1970), 99–100.

Kemp, Ben W., *Cow Dust and Saddle Leather* (Norman, 1968), *Arizona and the West*, XII (Spring, 1970), 99–100.

Emmons, David M., *Garden in the Grasslands: Boomer Literature of the Central Great Plains* (Lincoln, 1971), *Colorado History*, XLIX (Winter, 1972), 79–80.

ARTICLES IN CHURCH PERIODICALS

a. *Review and Herald*, Washington, D.C.

"Behold He Cometh, The One Hundredth Anniversary of the Birth of the Advent Message in America," *Review and Herald*, CVIII (November 12, 1931), 4–5.

"The Great Awakening," *Review and Herald*, CVIII (November 19, 1931), 7, 8.

"The Origin of Camp Meetings," *Review and Herald*, CVIII (November 26, 1931), 4, 5.

"Organization of the Movement," *Review and Herald*, CVIII (December 3, 1931), 7, 8.

"Origin of the Adventist Publishing Work," *Review and Herald*, CVIII (December 10, 1931), 7, 8.

"The Year 1843," *Review and Herald*, CVIII (December 17, 1931), 7, 8.

"The Passing of the Time," *Review and Herald*, CVIII (December 24, 1931), 5, 6, 7.

"The True Midnight Cry," *Review and Herald*, CVIII (December 31, 1931), 5, 6.

"Our Adventist Service Men in Korea," *Review and Herald*, CXXX (April 30, 1953), 14, 15.

"The Work of the Army Chaplains," *Review and Herald*, CXXX (June 25, 1953), 15-16.

"Medical Cadet Corps Training," *Review and Herald*, CXXX (December 10, 1953), 17.

"Seventieth Anniversary of Union College," *Review and Herald*, CXXXVII (April 7, 1960), 22, 23.

b. *The Youth's Instructor*, Washington, D.C.

"Rolling Post Offices," *Youth's Instructor*, LXXI (August 14, 1923), 7, 14.

"William Miller, Preacher of the Advent Hope," *Youth's Instructor*, XCII (January 4, 1944), 4, 13.

"Joshua Vaughn Himes," *Youth's Instructor*, XCII (February 22, 1944), 4, 12.

"Joseph Bates, Pioneer of Pioneers among Seventh-day Adventists," *Youth's Instructor*, XCII (March 21, 1944), 4, 5, 14, 15.

"James White, Founder of the Publishing Work," *Youth's Instructor*, XCII (April 18, 1944), 7, 13.

"Ellen G. White, Messenger of God," *Youth's Instructor*, XCII (May 9, 1944), 7, 12.

"John Nevins Andrews, First Overseas Worker," *Youth's Instructor*, XCII (June 13, 1944), 4, 12.

"Uriah Smith," *Youth's Instructor*, XCII (July 18, 1944), 6, 13.

"Chronicler of Pioneer Days J.N. Loughborough," *Youth's Instructor*, XCII (August 8, 1944), 4, 13.

"William Warren Prescott—Educator," *Youth's Instructor*, XCII (September 5, 1944), 5, 13.

"Arthur G. Daniells, Organizer," *Youth's Instructor*, XCII (October 24, 1944), 4, 12, 13.

"W. A. Spicer, Kindly Optimist," *Youth's Instructor*, XCII (September 14, 1944), 4, 13.

"In Line of Duty," *Youth's Instructor*, C (July 8, 1952), 1, 18.

"We Meet in Korea," *Youth's Instructor*, CI (September 1, 1953), 13, 20, 22.

"Twentieth Anniversary of Medical Military Training among Seventh-day Adventists," *Youth's Instructor*, CII (May 4, 1954), 10, 24.

"I Was There, the Story of Byron Moe," *Youth's Instructor*, CIII, (April 12, 1955), 5, 6, 23: (April 19, 1955), 9, 10, 21, 23.

"Faithful Unto Death," *Youth's Instructor*, CIII (June 7, 1955), 9, 21, 23, 25.

"Idle Words and the FBI," *Youth's Instructor*, CIV (May 1, 1956), 9, 20, 21, 22.

"Continue the Program," *Youth's Instructor*, CIV (May 15, 1956), 11.

"Commendation from the CO," *Youth's Instructor*, CIV (June 12, 1956), 6.

"Ammunition for the Sergeant," *Youth's Instructor*, CVI (April 29, 1958), 3, 19.

c. Miscellaneous Articles

"The Marvels of the 1833 Star Shower," *Signs of the Times* (Mountain View, California), LX (November 7, 1933), 8, 9, 15.

"Europe on the Brink of War—Why," *Signs of the Times*, LXII (October 8, 1935), 1, 5, 14.

"Caesar Sends Forth His Legions," *Signs of the Times*, LXII (November 5, 1935), 8, 9.

"Mars in Africa," *Signs of the Times*, LXII (November 19, 1935), 1, 5.

"What Next in Europe," *Signs of the Times*, LXIII (January 14, 1936), 1, 2.

"The Passing of the Frontier—Shall Its Ideals PassWith It," *Watchman Magazine* (Nashville, Tennessee), XXXIV (July, 1925), 21, 24.

"The Castle," *Educational Messenger* (College View, Nebraska), XXII (May, 1926), 8, 25.

"Beware of Rash Forecasting," *The Ministry* (Washington, D.C.), XIII (February, 1940), 19.

"W.W. Prescott, Father of Adventist Colleges," *Journal of True Education* (Washington, D.C.), VI (October, 1944), 7.

"John Fitzgerald Kennedy 1917–1963" (A memorial address at a teacher's convention in session at the time of the President's death), *Journal of True Education*, XXVI (January-February, 1964), 32.

"In Memoriam—Pearl Reese," *Journal of True Education*, XXVIII (April-May, 1966), 32.

"Our Church Schools," *Central Union Outlook* (Lincoln, Nebraska), XIV (October 13, 1935), 2.

"Whosoever Will," *Central Union Outlook*, XV (February 9, 1926), 5.

"A Mighty Army," *Central Union Outlook*, XV (March 30, 1926), 1.

"Missionary Volunteers," *Central Union Outlook*, XV (April 27, 1926), 1.

"Starving the Lambs," *Central Union Outlook*, XV (April 27, 1926), 1.

"Medical Corps Camp," *Northern Union Outlook* (Nevada, Iowa), II (May 16, 1939), 1.

"Union College Medical Corps Camp," *The Record* (Keene, Texas), XXXIX (March 27, 1940), 5, 6.

"Notice to Men of Draft Age," *Southern Tidings* (Collegedale, Tennessee), XLV (April 25, 1951), 1.

"Young Men Attention, National Medical Cadet Camp," *Pacific Union Recorder* (Angwin, California), LI (June 16, 1952), 1.

"Parents, Is Your Boy Ready?" *North Pacific Union Gleaner* (College Place, Washington), XLVII (July 7, 1952), 2.

"Our Boys and the United States," *Southern Tidings*, XLVI (July 23, 1952), 3.

"Iowa a Hundred Years Ago," *Northern Union Outlook*, XXVII (Special Iowa Conference Centennial number 1863–1963, June 11, 1963), 3–5.

ARTICLES IN NEWSPAPERS

a. *The Clock Tower*, Lincoln, Nebraska

"Fleeting Treasures," October 30, 1930.

"Union is Less Expensive than the Average University," July 29, 1931.

"Diplomas a Result of Whittling," August, 1932.

"Small School Praised by Authorities," Summer Issue, 1932.

"Knights of Old No Longer Bold in Stronghold," December 8, 1932.

"History Teaching at Union College," January 19, 1933.

"Employment Bureau Recommands Graduates," August 11, 1934.
"Summer School Offers Work and Study Plan," August 16, 1934.
"The Real College," October 8, 1943.
"In Honor of Union's First President," March 15, 1944.
"Lengthen the Tether," September 15, 1949.
"Tribute to D. D. Rees," October 14, 1949.

b. *Lincoln State Journal,* Lincoln, Nebraska
"Union College Celebrates Fortieth Anniversary," September 20, 1931.

c. *Lincoln Sunday Journal and Star,* Lincoln, Nebraska
"Union College Represents Big Victory for Lincoln 74 Years Ago," April 5, 1964.

d. *Southeast Shopper* (a semi-monthly), Lincoln, Nebraska
"Way Back When" (a column on the social history of College View, a suburb of Lincoln, Nebraska). It contained the following articles:
"Way Back When," September 22, 1957.
"Early Business Houses in College View," September 29, 1957.
"U. C. Power House Burned," October 6, 1957.
"College View Was Young," October 20, 1957, November 17, 1957.
"Life in Southeast Lincoln in the 90's," November 3, 1957.
"Town Government was Formed," December 15, 29, 1957.
"College View Streets were a Problem," January 12, 1958.
"Crude Fire Fighting Methods," January 26, 1958.
"Water Came from Wells," February 9, 1958.
"Kerosene Lights Burned," February 23, 1958.
"Weiss Sold Peanuts," March 9, 1958.
"College View Had a Jail," March 23, April 6, 1958.
"Horse and Buggy Flourished," April 20, 1958.
"When the Library was Started," May 4, June 1, 1958.
"Numbering the Streets," June 16, 1958.
"The Sanitarium Started," June 29, 1958.
"Indians Roamed Southeast Lincoln," August 10, 1958.
"Salt Was Boiled in Lincoln," August 24, September 7, 1958.
"First Settlement of Lincoln," September 7, October 5, 1958.
"Lincoln Becomes the State Capital," October 19, November 16, 1958.
"Lincoln Sought Another College," January 25, 1959.
"Union College Was Located," February 8, 1959.
"The U. S. Government Bought the Land," February 22, 1959.
"The Burlington Railroad Owned Lincoln," March 8, 1959.
"College View was Plotted," March 22, 1959.
"48th Street Got its Jog," April 12, 1959.
"The Railroad Came to College View," April 26, May 10, 1959.
"Lincoln Citizens Celebrate Railroad's Coming," June 28, 1959.
"Lincoln Tries for Another College," July 19, 1959.

"Well Back in '02," August 25, 1957.
"Who is Hoo Hoo," September 22, 1957.
"Gotfredson is Earliest Businessman," November 3, 1957.
"Frank Hornung Here 41 Years," December 1, 1957.
"Morse Oldest Businessman," September 21, 1958.

INDEX

Abbott, Lyman, as Indian reformer, 123; attacks contract schools, 140-141; urges Indian assimilation, 134; urges Indian education, 135

Abilene, Kansas, "Wild Bill" Hickok in, 87-88; Hickok, marshal at, 112

Abourezk, James, investigates corporate farms, 154

Adams, James Truslow, 86

Adjutant General, historical sources in office of, 181-182, 190-192, 194, 199-200

Agricultural Adjustment Administration, program of, 147

Agricultural Stabilization and Conservation Program, effect of on farming, 147-148

Agriculture, see Farming

Alamosa, Colorado, crime in, 114-115

Amana Society, receives benefits, 149

American Farm Bureau, defends corporate farming, 155

American Protective Association, as nativistic society, 138

Americanism, as function of Protestantism, 131-133; as means of Indian assimilation, 133-135; to be spread by schools, 134-138

Andreasen, M. L., as Adventist leader, 16

Andrews University, awards Everett Dick honorary degree, 19

Apache Indians, sources for study of, 182-183, 190-191

Arizona, farming in, 167; Indian uprising in, 182-183; sources for study of, 189, 186-197, 199

Arkansas, sources for study of, 197-198

Armstrong, Major-General George, aids Medical Cadet Corps, 17

Army, role of in West, 176; sources for study of, 177-200

Army Continental Command, records of, 197

Army of the West, sources on, 192

Army Signal Corps, use of records of, 200

Asbury, Francis, on frontier violence, 26-27

Assimilation, as goal of Indian reformers, 131

Atherton, Lewis A., quoted, 84

Austin, Mary, quoted, 160

Babcock, Orville E., sources for study of, 194

Baltimore, police force in, 116

Bancroft, Hubert Howe, quoted, 80, 99

Bannock Indian War, reports from, 182; sources for study of, 183

Baptists, in Indian reform movement, 122-123; on early frontiers, 27-28; on Kentucky frontier, 27

Beale, Edward F., attacks on as land holder, 166; forms Tejon Ranch Company, 159-160; plans Indian reservation, 159

Beale, Truxton, operates Tejon Ranch, 160-161

Beard, Joseph, death of as marshal, 113

Beatrice, Nebraska, use of marshals in, 116

215

Bell, William, as frontier photographer, 181
Billy the Kid, as frontier criminal, 87-88; praised, 113
Black Hills Reservation, protection of by army, 194-195
Board of Indian Commissioners, formed, 122; urges schools for Indians, 135
Bonney, William, see Billy the Kid
Boone, Daniel, as trail blazer, 23-24; westward migration of family of, 24-26
Boston, as center for Indian reformers, 121
Boston Indian Citizenship Committee, formed, 121
Boston Ranch Company, receives government payments, 149
Boswell, J. G., accepts benefits, 148-149
Bowles Farming Company, receives government benefits, 148
Bradford, John, as frontier editor, 35-36
Brown, Dee, writes on Indians, 95
Bryant, Edwin, quoted, 30, 31, 34, 36
Bryce, James, quoted, 132
Buchanan, James, land policy of, 156-157
Buffalo, effect of extermination of, 65-66
Bureau of Refugees, Freedmen and Abandoned Lands, records of, 196
Burgher, Emil H., aids in establishing Medical Cadet Corps, 16
Butterfield Overland Stage, escapes Indian attacks, 98
Butz, Earl L., as Secretary of Agriculture, 152-153

California, corporate farming in, 148-169; geological exploration of, 179-180; operation of land laws in, 158; sources for study of, 191-192, 196, 199-200; treatment of Indians in, 93-94, 179, 182
California Trail, need for research on, 44-61
California Water Project, aids corporate farmers, 169; effect of on Tejon Ranch, 161-162
Cantonment Bad Lands, sources for history of, 186
Carpenter, Helen, as author of trail journal, 59
Carr, William B., as land speculator, 164; land holdings of, 163
Carson, Lindsey, as pioneer, 24-25
Cartwright, Peter, on frontier society, 26-27
Catholics, attacks on, 137-138; attacks on Indian schools of, 138-141; on frontier, 75
Cattle towns, lack of crime in, 98-99
Chapman, William S., as land holder, 164
Charless, Joseph, as frontier editor, 35-36
Chief of Engineers, documents of on exploration, 180-181
Chileans, mistreatment of, 92
Chinese, persecution of in mining camps, 77-78; sources for study of, 193; subjected to frontier violence, 88-90
Claims Clubs, methods used by, 65
Clark, George Rogers, purchases handcuffs, 172
Clark, Thomas D., sketch of, 21; essay by, 21-44
Coe, Phil, shooting of by Hickok, 112
Coeur d'Alene, labor troubles in, 193-194
Colleges, on frontier, 38
Colorado, large-scale mining in, 154
Commanding General of the Army, importance of records of, 179
Commissary General of Subsistence, importance of records of,

187-188

Comstock Lode, early photographs of, 180; returns on investments in, 163; rush to, 64

Conestoga wagons, use of by freighters, 53

Confederate War Department, importance of records of, 189

Continuity, on mining frontier, 81-82

Contract schools, attacks on, 138-139; end of support for, 139-140

Cook, Joseph, quoted on Indian policy, 123

Cooke, Lucy, keeps overland trail journal, 59

Cooke, Philip St. George, military operations of in Kansas, 183

Coomes, Mary, as frontier teacher, 37

Cooper, James Fenimore, attitude of toward Indians, 95

Cooperation, on Great Plains frontier, 76; on mining frontier, 82-83; on overland trails, 53-54, 56; practiced on frontier, 31, 98

Cornish, in mining camps, 77

Cornwall, Joseph A., as frontier minister, 28

Corporation farming, rapid growth of, 147; use of in California, 147-169

Corps of Engineers, records of explorations of, 179-180

Cortinas, Juan N., sources for study of, 193

Cotton, increase in production of, 151

Council Bluffs, as center for overland-trail travel, 47-48

Craig, Elijah and Lewis, as frontier Baptist leaders, 27

Crime, effect of vagrants on, 109-111, 117; exaggerated accounts of in West, 98-99; in Texas, 195-196; nature of on frontier, 105-106; on Great Plains frontier, 78; on mining frontier, 78-79; on overland trails, 56-57; relations of to gambling, 107-109

Curry, George L., as frontier writer, 36

Curtis, Samuel R., sources for study of, 198

Custer, George A., sources for study of, 182

Dakota Territory, Indian raids on, 186; records of Indians in, 190; source materials on, 193

Davis, N. H., report by, 194

Dawes, Henry L., as Indian reformer, 126-127

Dawes Severalty Act, effect of on Indian schools, 135; seeks end of tribal ownership, 128

Defense, frontier techniques of, 30-31

Del Paso, as Mexican land grant, 163

Democracy, on mining frontier, 82

Denver, crime in, 112-113; gambling in, 108; Indian attacks on, 71

Denver University, Dick teaches in, 19

Department of Agriculture, attitude of toward small farmer, 153; criticisms of, 146-147; favors crop benefits, 150; programs of, 151; study of reported, 153-154

Department of the Interior, relations of to agriculture, 147

Desert Land Act, abuse of, 156-157; use of in acquiring land, 164-165

Des Moines, law enforcement in, 116

De Voto, Bernard, quoted, 83-84

Diaz, Porfirio, revolution against, 184

Dick, Arthur L., birth of, 10

Dick, Donald D., birth of, 10

Dick, Everett, as teacher, 8-11; as writer, 11-15; bibliography of writings of, 204-213; childhood of, 3-4; contributions of, 84; graduate training, 6-8; married, 6; publishes *The Sod-House Frontier,* 63-64; services of to Adventist Church, 15-19

Dick, Grandville G., as father of Everett Dick, 3-4

Dick, Lorle Ann, birth of, 10

Dixie Frontier, The, writing of, 13

Doctors, practice of on frontier, 73-74

Dodge City, Earp, marshal at, 112; lack of crime in, 98; Masterson, marshal at, 112

Dona Anna, sources of, 189

Doniphan, Alexander W., sources for study of, 192

Dorchester, Daniel, as superintendent of Indian schools, 138-139

Dubuque, treatment of vagrants in, 110

Dunleavy, James, as frontier minister, 28

Dykstra, Robert A., quoted, 84

Earp, Wyatt, as Dodge City marshal, 112

Eastland Plantations, receives government benefits, 149

Eastman, Charles, quoted, 66

Education, see Schools

Eisenhower, Dwight D., reads books on West, 87

Episcopalians, on frontier, 75

Estill, James R., as pioneer, 24

Evangelical Protestantism, influence of on Indian reform, 125-126; on Americanism, 131-133; seeks to retain Indian family unit, 130-131; stress on individualism in, 126-129; stress on work ethic, 129-130; urges Protestant schools for Indians, 134-141

Evans, George S., reports by, 196

Exploration, sources for study of by military, 177-181

Family, concept of by Indian reformers, 130; schools urged to strengthen, 137

Farming, at military posts, 188; attacks on large scale, 155; effect of railroads on, 71-72; hardships of on Great Plains, 67-68; introduction of large scale, 147-169; techniques of, 69-70

"Faro Harry," as frontier gambler, 107

Fellmeth, Robert C., prepares report on farming, 150, 169

Field, J. M., as frontier editor, 36

Fifty-Niners, rush of, 64

Findley, Paul, exposes corporate farms, 147-148, 152

Finley, John, as frontier revivalist, 28

Flint, Timothy, on religious influences, 28

Florida, large-scale farming in, 154

Food, on mining and farming frontiers, 70; on overland trails, 53; types of on frontier, 32-35

Ft. Atkinson, records for history of, 188

Ft. Bidwell, records for history of, 199

Ft. Filmore, records for history of, 189

Ft. Kearny, on Oregon Trail, 47-48, 50

Ft. Laramie, on overland trail, 49

Ft. Leavenworth, role of in migrations, 47

Ft. Madison, crime in, 106

Ft. Sill, records for history of, 188

Ft. Spokane, records for history of, 188

Ft. Steele, records for history of, 186

Ft. Union, records for history of, 198

Forty-Niners, nature of rush of, 64; on overland trails, 47-49; religion among, 28; sources for

Index

study of, 192-193; treatment of Indians by, 93-94; treatment of Mexicans by, 92-93; treatment of minorities by, 91-92

Franklin, John Hope, quoted, 97

Fremont, John C., sells California land, 160

French, in mining camps, 77

Frizzell, Lodisa, keeps overland trail journal, 59

Frontier, archival materials on, 176-200; as debtor area, 72-73; carries law westward, 102-117; early interest in, 5-6; effect of on education, 37-39; effect of on government, 39; effect of on religion, 26-29; epic quality of, 52; Everett Dick as product of, 3-4; exaggerated reports of lawlessness on, 98-100; influence of continuity on, 21-22, 24-29, 31-41, 74-75; influence of on violence, 86-87; legacy of, 70-84; reasons for violence on, 96-98; social life on, 75-77; studied by Dick, 7-9, 11-15; treatment of Indians on, 93-96; treatment of minorities on, 88-91; treatment of vagrants on, 109-111; violence on in mining camps, 91-93; urban developments on, 71-72

Gambling, lawlessness of, 106-107; prevalence of on frontier, 107-109; records for study of, 196-197

Garrett, Philip C., as Indian reformer, 131

Garza Revolution, sources on, 184

Gates, Merrill E., at Indian conferences, 123-125; attacks tribal organizations, 130; praises Dawes Severalty Act, 128; urges dissolving tribal relationships, 127; urges Indian missions, 140; urges work ethic on Indians, 129-130

Gates, Paul W., essay by, 146-174; sketch of, 146

General Land Office, use of by speculators, 157

Geographical Survey, sources on, 181

Germans, in mining camps, 77

Geronimo, Chief, sources on, 183

Giffen Incorporated, receives government benefits, 149

Goodfellow, Philip J., source materials on, 193

Government, as law enforcing agency, 103-104; demands for on frontier, 103; effect of frontier on, 39; reliance of frontiersmen on, 83

Grant, Ulysses S., peace policy of, 121

Great Platte River Road, contribution of, 46; deaths on, 57-58; effect of on emigrants, 55-57; sources for study of, 52-53; travel on, 53-55. See also Oregon Trail

Great Revival, in Kentucky, 27

Greeks, in mining camps, 77

Green, Thomas Jefferson, treatment of minorities by, 91-92

Grimes, Eliab, land holdings of, 163

Grimes, Hiram, inherits land holdings, 163

Guns, encourage violence, 97; use of by marshals, 112-113

Haggin, James Ben Ali, attacks on, 166; conveys land to company, 167; forms Kern County Land Company, 162-165

Hardin, Clifford, replaced as Secretary of Agriculture, 152

Hardin, John Wesley, as frontier criminal, 87

Harding, Warren G., quoted on Indians, 94

Harris, Fred P., attacks corporate farming, 154

Harrison, Benjamin, defeated for presidency, 139
Haun, Margaret, quoted, 35
Hawaii, large-scale farming in, 154
Hickok, James ("Wild Bill") B., as frontier criminal, 87-88, 112
Hicks, John D., as teacher of Everett Dick, 6-7; essay by, 3-20; sketch of, 3
History, Dick as teacher of, 7-10; Dick's interest in, 4-6; writing on by Dick, 10-14
Holliday, "Doc," as frontier criminal, 87
Hollon, W. Eugene, essay by, 86-100; sketch of, 86
Holmes, James H., sources on, 198
Hoyt, Henry L., as Portland marshal, 114
Hughes, Harold, attacks corporate farming, 154
Huntington Library, Everett Dick at, 19
Hutchinsin, Kansas, use of marshal in, 116
Hyatt, Marshal, as Colorado marshal, 114-115

Idaho, mining rush to, 64
Idaho City, bread riots in, 71
Immigrants, treatment of on mining frontier, 77-78
Independence, Missouri, on overland trails, 47
Indian Bureau, praised by reformers, 125
Indian Emancipation Act, adoption of, 128
Indian-Rights Association, formation of, 122; on legal rights of Indians, 128; religious influences on, 123; urges end of tribal land ownership, 128; views of, 126
Indians, assault on culture of, 65-66; attack overland emigrants, 51; California reservations planned for, 159; cut Denver supply lines, 71; defense against, 30-31; in Kentucky, 23-24; life of described, 179; materials for study of, 177; peace policy toward, 120-121; photographs of, 181; post-war policy toward, 121-141; protection of reservations of, 194-195; protection from asked, 199; records of military campaigns against, 181-185; records on life of, 196; relations of army with, 189-191; reports of visits to, 180; subjected to frontier violence, 88, 93-96; treatment of by miners, 65, 192
Individualism, in evangelical Protestantism, 126-129; on mining frontier, 82-83
Innovation, on mining frontier, 81-82
Irish, in mining camps, 77
Irish-American Fenian Brotherhood, sources on, 193
Irrigation, laws on revised, 168; on Tejon Ranch, 161-162; use of in large-scale farming, 151
Irvine Company, receives government benefits, 148-149; use of Mexican grants by, 155
Italians, in mining camps, 177

Jackson, W. Turrentine, essay by, 63-85; sketch of, 63
Japanese, treatment of on frontier, 90
Jeffersonian philosophy, effect of on frontier, 38-39
Jesup, Thomas S., source materials on, 178
Jews, treatment of on frontier, 96-97
J. I. Case Company, corporate ownership of, 167-168
Johnson, James, source materials on, 178
Johnson, Samuel, quoted, 94
Jordan, Philip D., essay by, 101-

Index

119; sketch of, 101
Judge Advocate General's Office, importance of records in, 197-198

Kansas, Everett Dick born in, 4; law enforcement in, 115; sources on campaigns in, 183-184; sources on history of, 194
Kansas City, on overland trails, 47
Kearney, Stephen W., sources for study of, 192
Keno, popularity of on frontier, 107-108
Kenton, Simon, as Kentucky pioneer, 23
Kentucke Gazette, as frontier newspaper, 35
Keokuk, law enforcement in, 116
Kern County, corporate farming in, 150-151, 162-169
Kern County Land Company, controls farm machinery company, 152; creation of, 162-166; incorporated, 166-167; operation of, 167-169; receives government benefits, 148-149; uses Mexican grants, 155, 160
Kern Echo, attacks large-scale farms, 166
Kern Gazette, attacks large-scale farms, 166
Ketchum, Rebecca, keeps overland trails journal, 59
King, Charles, sources for explorations of, 180
King, James M., attacks Catholic Indian schools, 139
Klamath Indian Reservation, protection of, 195
Knight, Amelia, keeps overland trails journal, 59
Korea, Medical Cadet Corps in, 17-18
Ku Klux Klan, violent acts of, 97

Labor unions, on mining frontier, 76; relations of army with, 193-194
La Harpe, Kansas, Everett Dick in, 4
Lake Mohonk Conferences, origins of, 122; religious influences on, 123-125; statements made at, 129, 131, 134, 139, 140; urge Indian schools, 135-136
Land policy, as applied to Indians, 127-128; Everett Dick writes on, 14; operation of on plains, 64-65; use of in corporate farming, 156-158
Law, application of to Indians, 128-129
Lawyers, on frontier, 74
Leavenworth, Henry, at Ft. Atkinson, 188; reports on expeditions of, 182
Lee, J. M., report by, 199-200
Lee, Robert E., source materials on, 193
Lincoln, Nebraska, arms marshals, 112; crime in, 108; record of marshals in, 116; treatment of vagrants in, 111
Lincoln County War, source materials on, 193
Little Big Horn, Battle of, source materials on, 182
Logan, Benjamin, as Kentucky pioneer, 23
Los Angeles, treatment of Chinese in, 89
Lure of the Land, writing of by Dick, 14
Lux, Charles, use of Mexican grants by, 162, as large land holder, 163-164, 166
Lyman, I. L., as marshal, 113

Magee, William and John, as frontier revivalists, 27
Magill, Edward H., urges Indian reform, 140

Maps, as historical sources, 180
Marshall, General George, aids Medical Cadet Corps, 17
Marshals, actions against, 114-115; duties of, 103-106; equipment of, 111-112; evolution of office of, 115-116; in mining camps, 79; legends of, 101-102; opinion of, 113-114; origins of office of, 102; sources for study of, 197; treatment of gamblers by, 107-109; treatment of vagrants by, 109-111; uniforms worn by, 116-117; use of guns by, 112-113
Masonic Order, on mining frontier, 76
Masters, Edgar Lee, quoted, 104-105
Masterson, Ed, as Dodge City marshal, 112
Mattes, Merrill J., essay by, 45-62; sketch of, 45
Maxwell, William, as frontier editor, 35
McDowell, Irvin, heads trial court, 198
McKendree, Timothy, as frontier revivalist, 28
McKinney, John, as frontier teacher, 37
McReady, James, as frontier revivalist, 27
Medical Cadet Corps, creation of, 15-16; operation of, 16-19
Medicine, sources for study of on frontier, 188-189
Meeker, Ezra, on Oregon trail, 50
Mencken, Henry L., quoted, 87
Methodists, on early frontiers, 27-28, 75
Mexican-Americans, in gold rush, 192; sources for study of, 184; treatment of in mining camps, 78, 88, 90, 91, 92, 93
Mexican land grants, use of by Kern County Land Company, 158-160, 162-163; use of in California, 155-156

Mexican War, Texas Rangers in, 90-91
Migration, as frontier trait, 79-80; continuity in on frontier, 21-26; on mining frontier, 64; on overland trails, 55-59
Military posts, sources on history of, 185-189, 199-200
Military Reservation Division, records of, 199-200
Miller and Lux Company, breakup of holdings, of, 155-156; receives government benefits, 148-149
Miller, Henry, as large land holder, 163-164, 166; uses Mexican land grants, 162
Millington, Ada, keeps diary on overland trail, 59
Mining, absence of stages in, 81; destruction of environment by, 67-68; hardships of, 67; immigrants in, 77-78; importance of transportation to, 71-72; labor troubles in, 193-194; land claims in, 65; life in mining camps, 72-77; misuse of Chinese in, 89-90; nativism, in, 78-79; nature of rushes, 63-64; operations of safety valve in, 80-81; techniques of, 69-70; urban settlement by, 66-67
Missions, sources on California, 192
Mississippi Valley Historical Association, Everett Dick in, 15
Missouri, schools in, 189; settlement of, 25; sources for study of warfare in, 183-184
Modoc Indian War, sources for history of, 182
Montana, Everett Dick in, 5-6; mining rushes to, 64, 67; overland trails to, 50, 60
Moreland, Jesse, as frontier revivalist, 28
Morgan, Marshal, killed on duty, 113

Index

Morgan, Thomas J., as Commissioner of Indian Affairs, 131; opposes Catholic Indian schools, 138; proposes Indian school system, 125-137; quoted on Indian policy, 133; urges assimilation, 134; urges breakup of tribal organization, 127; urges missions to Indians, 140
Mormons, on overland trails, 60; sources for study of, 194; treatment of on frontier, 96-97
Mormon Trail, defined, 47-48
Mt. Whitney Farms, receives government benefits, 149
Murieta, Joaquin, as Mexican-American hero, 92
Music, on mining frontier, 77

Nader Task Force, reports on large-scale farming, 150, 169
National Archives, source materials in, 176-200
National Commission on the Causes and Prevention of Violence, report of, 97
National Farm Institute, speeches before, 153
National Farmers Organization, attacks large-scale farming, 155
National League for the Protection of American Institutions, opposes Catholic Indian schools, 139
Navaho Indians, reports of expeditions to, 180
Nebraska, records of Indians in, 190
Nebraska Centennial Project, contributions of, 46-47, 55, 56-57
Nebraska City, on overland trails, 47
Nebraska, University of, Everett Dick student at, 6-7; John D. Hicks teaches at, 3
Negroes, in mining camps, 78; on overland trails, 51; records on in Texas, 195-196; subjected to frontier violence, 88, 96-97; treatment of in gold rush, 92
Nelson, Gaylord, opposes corporate farming, 154
Nesmith, J. W., death of, 41
Nevada, photographs of, 180
Newhall Land and Farming Company, farming operations of, 154, 167; receives government benefits, 149; use of Mexican land grants by, 155
New Mexico, photographs of Indians in, 181; records for study of, 189, 192, 193, 198; source materials on Indians in, 180, 183, 190-191
Newspapers, as frontier institutions, 35-37; invent stories of frontier violence, 98; on mining frontier, 73
New York Times, quoted, 150, 152
Nixon, Richard M., nominates Secretary of Agriculture, 152
Norris, Samuel, as large land holder, 163
North Dakota, corporate farming in, 154. See also Dakota Territory
Northern Pacific Railroad, building of, 186
Northwest Ordinance, educational provisions in, 37

Oak Park Academy, Everett Dick teaches at, 7
Occidental Petroleum Company, seeks to acquire Kern County Land Company, 168
Oklahoma, records on opening of, 195; rush of 1889 in, 98
Omaha, treatment of vagrants in, 110
Optimism, as trait on mining frontier, 83-84
Oregon, land holdings in, 167;

origins of population of, 41; sources for study of, 192
Oregon Trail, deaths on, 57-58; described, 47-48; effect of on emigrants, 56-57; food on, 34-35; motives for following, 55-56; nature of travel on, 53-55; need for research on, 45-46; number of travelers on, 49-50; sources for study of, 52-53; treatment of minorities on, 28; women on, 58-61
O'Sullivan, Timothy H., as frontier photographer, 180-181
Oswego Academy, Everett Dick in, 5
Ozawkie, Kansas, Everett Dick in, 4

Painter, Charles C., urges Indian assimilation, 131
Paiute Indians, placed on reservation, 199-200
Pancoast, Henry S., defends Indian legal rights, 128
Patrons of Husbandry, as social institution, 76
Paxson, Frederic L., as Everett Dick's teacher, 6-8
Peck, John Mason, as religious influence, 28; quoted on frontier violence, 26, 29
Peniston, Francis, as frontier editor, 36
Perkins, Elisha D., as pioneer, 30; quoted, 34-35
Perkins, William, quoted, 92, 93
Peruvians, mistreatment of in gold rush, 92
Philadelphia, as center for Indian reform, 121-122
Photography, as source for frontier history, 181; by early exploring expeditions, 180; use of by historians, 200
Pillow, Gideon, sources for study of, 198

Pioneering, techniques of, 29-32
Plattsmouth, as source of overland trails, 47
Police, evolution of from marshals, 115-116
Pollock, Tom, as Denver marshal, 112
Ponca Indians, removal of, 121
Porter, Lavinia, keeps journal on overland trail, 59
Portland, Oregon, law enforcement in, 114; use of marshal in, 116
Prairie schooners, use of an overland trails, 53
Presbyterians, on early frontiers, 38, 75
Prostitution, as frontier problem, 106-107
Provost Marshal General's Office, importance of records preserved by, 197
Prucha, Francis Paul, S.J., essay by, 120-145; sketch of, 120
Puritan Work Ethic, applied by Indian reformers, 129-130, 136

Quartermaster Department, importance of records preserved by, 198-199
Quartermaster General, as source for records on exploration, 178; use of records preserved by, 186-188

Railroads, effects of on plains frontier, 71-72
Ranching, relation of to mining frontier, 81
Reading, Pearson B., ranch of acquired, 163
Reconstruction, records of troops active in, 195, 196; sources for study of, 198; violence during, 91, 97
Red Cloud, Chief, sources for study of, 190
Red River War, reports on, 182

Religion, effect of on education, 38-39; effect of on overland emigrants, 56; influence of on frontier continuity, 26-29; influences of on Indian policy, 122-141; on plains frontier, 75
Rhoads, James B., essay by, 175-203; sketch of, 175
Rice, David, on Kentucky frontier, 27
Riley, Bennett, reports on gold rush, 192
Roads, reports on feasibility of, 179-180
Robb, John S., as frontier editor, 36
Rock Springs, Wyoming, sources for study of nativism in, 193; treatment of Chinese in, 89-90
Rosenheim, A., as Portland marshal, 114
Russell, William, as pioneer, 24
Russell, William Henry, as pioneer, 24

S. A. Camp Company, receives government benefits, 150; sells citrus properties, 168-169
Safety valve, discussed as frontier effect, 80-81
St. Joseph, overland trails start at, 47
St. Louis, adopts uniforms for marshals, 111; crime in, 108-109; defines duties of marshals, 104; gamblers in, 107
Salyer Land Company, receives government benefits, 148-149
Sanford, George B., sources for study of, 183
San Francisco, treatment of Chinese in, 89; use of marshals in, 104
San Francisco Chronicle, condemns large-scale farming, 166
San Juan Rancho, as part of Kern County Land Company, 163
Sargent, Aaron A., sponsors Desert Land Act, 164-165
Schools, as frontier institutions, 37-39; as means of Indian assimilation, 134-138; as propagators of "Americanism," 132-133; church influence in founding of on frontier, 39; established by Catholics for Indians, 138-141; in frontier communities, 74-75; on military installations, 189
Schurz, Carl, quoted on assimilation, 133-134
Scott, Harvey W., quoted, 41
Scott, Winfield, in Mexican War, 91
Seattle, use of marshals by, 104
Seventh-day Adventist Church, Everett Dick's services to, 5, 14-19
Seventh-day Adventist Medical Cadet Corps, see Medical Cadet Corps
Simpson, James H., reports on expedition under, 180
Sioux uprising, reports on, 182
Slavs, treatment of in mining camps, 77
Smalley, Hannah F., as Everett Dick's mother, 4
Smiley, Albert K., as Indian reformer, 122
Smith, Duane, quoted, 84
Sod-House Frontier, The, contributions of appraised, 63-64, 84; writing of, 11-12
Sod houses, building of, 68
South Dakota, sources for study of Indian affairs in, 191; vagrancy statute of, 110. See also Dakota Territory
South Lake Farms, receives government benefits, 149
Stagecoaching, on mining frontier, 71
Steamboats, disorders on, 105-106; use of in Yellowstone Expedition of 1819, 178

Stevenson, Adlai E., III, attacks large-scale farming, 154
Stiles, D. E., report of on Oklahoma, 195
Stoudenmire, Dallas, as El Paso marshal, 112
Stout, Elihu, as frontier editor, 35-36
Stratification, on mining frontier, 82
Sublette Brothers, as pioneers, 23-24
Surgeon General's Office, importance of records preserved by, 188-189
Swamp Lands Act, abuse of, 156

Tales of the Frontier, writing of, 14
Taylor, General Maxwell, aids Medical Cadet Corps, 18
Taylor, Zachary, in Mexican War, 91
Tejon Ranch Company, development of, 161-162; formation of, 158-161; receives government benefits, 148-149; sold to Los Angeles capitalists, 161; uses Mexican land grants, 155
Tenancy, increase of, 147
Tenneco, acquires Kern County Land Company, 168
Tevis, Lloyd, attack on, 166; conveys land to Los Angeles concern, 167; forms Kern County Land Company, 162-165
Texas, law enforcement in, 115; records of army in, 195-196; sources for study of, 184-185, 189, 193; treatment of Mexican-Americans in, 90-91
Texas Rangers, use of violence by, 91
Thayer, James B., on Indian legal rights, 128-129
Theaters, on mining frontier, 77
Thompson, Ben, as frontier criminal, 87

Thompson, Jacob, land policy of, 156-157
Timber Culture Act, purpose of, 157
Timber and Stone Act, purpose of, 157
Topographical Engineers, sources on exploration kept by, 179-180
Towns, growth of on Great Plains, 71-72; on mining frontier, 66-67; on overland trails, 47; violence in, 97
Transportation, importance of to mining, 71
Turner, Frederick J., frontier theory of, 84; influences John D. Hicks, 6; quoted, 14
Tyson, Philip, report of expedition under, 179-180

Union College, Everett Dick student at, 5-6; Dick teaches at, 18-20; Medical Cadet Corps at, 15-17; writes history of, 14; teacher at, 8-11
Union College Academy, Everett Dick at, 4-5
Union Pacific Railroad, building of, 186
Urban frontier, mining camp as example of, 84
Utah, large-scale farming in, 154; sources for study of, 182-183, 194; sources for study of Indians in, 190

Vagrants, as criminals, 109-111
Vancouver Barracks, sources for study of, 188
Victoria, Chief, sources on campaigns of, 183
Vigilantes, in mining camps, 78-79; reasons for rise of, 96; in 1930s, 169; sources for study of, 193
Violence, on frontier, 86-100; use

Index

of against gamblers, 106-107
Vista del Llano, receives government benefits, 149

Wade, Richard, quoted, 97
Wagon trains, on overland trails, 53-54
War Department, sources for history of, 181-182
Water, need of by Great Plains farmers, 69-70. See also irrigation
Watkins, T. H., quoted, 84
Wells Fargo Express, investment in, 162
Welsh, Herbert, as Indian reformer, 122-124
Western History Association, Everett Dick as founder of, 15
Weston, Missouri, on overland trails, 47
Wheeler, George M., leads exploring expeditions, 181
Wheeler, Opal, marries Everett Dick, 6
Whipple, A. W., reports of explorations of, 179
Whitley, William, as Kentucky pioneer, 23
Wiley, Allen, as frontier revivalist, 28
Williams John S., attacks large-scale farms, 147-148, 152; quoted, 149
Williams, Joseph, as frontier minister, 28
Wisconsin, University of, Everett Dick student at, 6-8; teaches at, 13-14
Women, hardships of on Great Plains, 68; on mining frontier, 69; on Oregon Trail, 58-60
Women's National Indian Association, formation of, 121-123
Wounded Knee, Battle of, sources for study of, 191
Wyoming, military operations in, 186; sources for study of, 190, 199; treatment of Chinese in, 89-90, 193

Yellowstone Expedition of 1819, sources for study of, 178
Young, Brigham, sources for study of, 194